D0049207

Canadian Copyright Law

Canadian Copyright Law

4th Edition

Lesley Ellen Harris

WILEY

Cover image: Inspired by RetroCircle; © iStockphoto.com/Webtoaster777
Cover design: Wiley

This book is printed on acid-free paper. ∞

Copyright © 2014 by Lesley Ellen Harris. All rights reserved.

Published by John Wiley & Sons, Inc., Hoboken, New Jersey.
Published simultaneously in Canada.

No part of this publication may be reproduced, stored in a retrieval system, or transmitted in any form or by any means, electronic, mechanical, photocopying, recording,
scanning, or otherwise, except as permitted under Section 107 or 108 of the 1976
United States Copyright Act, without either the prior written permission of the
Publisher, or authorization through payment of the appropriate per-copy fee to the
Copyright Clearance Center, 222 Rosewood Drive, Danvers, MA 01923, (978)
750-8400, fax (978) 646-8600, or on the web at www.copyright.com. Requests to
the Publisher for permission should be addressed to the Permissions Department,
John Wiley & Sons, Inc., 111 River Street, Hoboken, NJ 07030, (201) 748-6011,
fax (201) 748-6008, or online at www.wiley.com/go/permissions.

Limit of Liability/Disclaimer of Warranty: While the publisher and author have used
their best efforts in preparing this book, they make no representations or warranties
with the respect to the accuracy or completeness of the contents of this book and
specifically disclaim any implied warranties of merchantability or fitness for a particular purpose. No warranty may be created or extended by sales representatives or written sales materials. The advice and strategies contained herein may not be suitable
for your situation. You should consult with a professional where appropriate. Neither
the publisher nor the author shall be liable for damages arising herefrom.

For general information about our other products and services, please contact our
Customer Care Department within the United States at (800) 762-2974, outside the
United States at (317) 572-3993 or fax (317) 572-4002.

Wiley publishes in a variety of print and electronic formats and by print-on-demand.
Some material included with standard print versions of this book may not be
included in e-books or in print-on-demand. If this book refers to media such as a
CD or DVD that is not included in the version you purchased, you may download
this material at http://booksupport.wiley.com. For more information about Wiley
products, visit www.wiley.com.

ISBN 978-1-118-07851-8 (cloth); ISBN 978-1-118-08356-7 (ebk);
ISBN 978-1-118-08355-0 (ebk)

Printed in the United States of America

10 9 8 7 6 5 4 3 2 1

To my children, Bennett and Ari, who are the newer generation of copyright creators and consumers.

CONTENTS

A Note on the Text

I wrote this book for the lay reader. It is in no way a treatise on Canadian copyright law or a survey of case law, but a simplified description of a complex area of the law. The examples I have chosen in the text are merely examples. Each particular case must be examined on its own facts. My intention is to provide you with information that you can then apply to your own situations and facts at hand—not to offer legal advice. If you face a legal issue, seek professional advice.

The book can be read from cover to cover or used, as required, for reference purposes. You might wish to first read the entire book before using it as a reference, since the nature of copyright is such that understanding one area of copyright law is often necessary to understanding other areas of the law.

I have quoted cases or specifically referred to them only to illustrate a point that reference to a particular case makes clearer. The consolidated Canadian Copyright Act is at http://laws-lois.justice.gc.ca/eng/acts/C-42. You should take caution when reading the Copyright Act without being familiar with legal jargon and without access to the court cases that interpret the Act.

You might find certain sections of the book oversimplified—others overly complex. I have tried to find a balance between explaining the law simply, yet providing enough detail for you to understand its intricacies.

I have avoided technical terms or legal jargon as much as possible. Words such as *work, creation, copyright-protected works, copyright materials* or *other subject-matter* refer to something protected by copyright law. *Creators* create copyright-protected works, and the word *creator* is used interchangeably with the word *author*. *Creator* and *user* are two words often used when talking about items protected by copyright law. The creator is the person who creates the work. The user is the person who uses copyright materials; he or she is also called a consumer of copyright material.

Copyright is not an area of law that can be seen in black and white. Terms such as *arguably, probably, likely, most likely,* and *it depends on the circumstances* are necessary to address the many grey areas of copyright law. When you come across these words, take extra caution in applying the law to your particular circumstance.

The book is comprehensive in that it covers, or at least mentions, most provisions in the Canadian Copyright Act. However, I have omitted a small number of provisions because they apply in a miniscule number of cases and/or are too complex or specific for a general book on copyright law.

I have predominantly dealt only with copyright law, while ever-so-briefly touching upon other areas of intellectual property law. I may refer to, but I do not specifically deal with related legal issues such as personality rights, privacy, contract, libel and slander, passing off, tax, and bankruptcy. All of these areas may be of some interest to those who create, own, or use copyright materials, and most of these topics could be books themselves.

The law I describe in this text is the law as it stands at the time of writing: June 1, 2013. Legislative changes and court cases interpreting the law may change some of the law as described. Technological developments may also impact upon some of the information set out in this book. Current copyright information and information on how to manage copyright issues is at www.copyrightlaws.com.

PREFACE

It is hard to believe that 22 years have passed since the first edition of this book was published. At the time of approaching my publisher in 1990, I had written a few articles on copyright and given some talks on copyright to various groups, and was continually being asked by the public what more they could read on Canadian copyright law. Back in 1990, there was not much content on Canadian copyright law, especially for nonlawyers; hence I proposed a book on the topic. The first edition of this book received a warm welcome upon its publication as has every subsequent edition. I am delighted to be providing you with the fourth edition of this book.

When this book was initially published in 1991, I had not heard of the Internet. In 1995, when the second edition of this book was being written, I had my very first e-mail account on the Ottawa's free-net, officially known as the National Capital Freenet. I had never surfed the web though I was familiar with the Internet as it then existed, consisting of Archie and Veronica and Gopher. And so by 2001 and the third edition of this book, I had claimed real estate on the Internet @ www.copyrightlaws.com, and I had a virtual office. Almost all my correspondence with clients and students went online. I no longer carried business cards but merely handed out my URL and told people to click on my website photo to access me via e-mail. I cancelled my telephone line and began using only a cellular phone.

At the time of this book (the fourth edition!), now available in print and, for the first time, also as an e-book, social media have exploded.

We have yet again new ways of communicating with friends, family, and colleagues, and sharing copyright-protected content, with LinkedIn since 2002, Facebook since 2004, and Twitter since 2006. Every day we read about social media such as Pinterest (launched 2011) and how it may infringe copyright; new copyright infringement cases settled out of court or decided by a court; proposed and enacted copyright statute amendments in countries around the world; as well as proposed and new trade agreements and international treaties that deal with copyright issues.

So how has Canadian copyright law fared during the explosion of the Digital Age? You will soon be able to answer this question for yourself. In preparing this book, I have examined new legislation, recent court cases, and the content we use and the way we use it. I have added many examples throughout the book that relate to social and digital media, and have updated contact information including website, blog, and e-mail addresses.

Over the years, I have heard from many of my readers with comments on the book and their questions about copyright law. One of the most rewarding parts for me of writing a book is to engage with my readers. I encourage you to ask your questions at Copyright Questions & Answers (www.copyrightlaws.com/copyright-qs-as/copyright-questions-answers/), to visit my blog (www.copyrightlaws.com), and to follow my copyright tips on Twitter @Copyrightlaws.

ACKNOWLEDGEMENTS

I would like to thank the numerous people who generously gave their time and shared their expertise and knowledge in reviewing sections and chapters in the book and responding to my e-mails; your suggestions and knowledge are much appreciated. They include Bruce Couchman, Elizabeth Kelly, Aidan O'Neill, Craig Parks, and Susan Progoff, as well as people from copyright collectives, organizations, associations, and government agencies listed in this book. And thanks to my husband for his various input.

A Cancun vacation, a kid's broken leg, and serendipity led me to Wiley publishers; thank you to Ellen Roseman for pointing me in that direction. I would like to thank John Wiley & Sons for publishing this book and working with me, specifically Lauren Freestone, Karen Milner, Brian Neill, and Lucas Wilk.

And thank you to the readers of earlier editions and those who frequent my blog on copyright law; you keep me thinking about copyright law and encourage me to be creative in discovering and building new ways to share what copyright law means.

INTRODUCTION

If Glenn Gould were alive today, he would be celebrating his 80th birthday, posting to his blog, releasing another podcast and figuring out how to license downloads of his recordings.

—Kate Taylor, "The meaning of Glenn Gould,"
The Globe and Mail, September 22, 2012

Copyright affects everyone. Anyone who has ever written a letter or e-mail message, made a sketch, or taken a photograph (even with a smartphone) is a creator of copyright material. And anyone who has ever photocopied an article, digitized an image, or downloaded a document from the Internet is a user or consumer of copyright material (assuming of course that these materials are protected by copyright).

Copyright law, however, is very complicated, and my purpose in writing this book is to demystify it and set out its fundamental principles in everyday language. This book is written for those who create copyright materials, use copyright materials, acquire the rights to content, and share and disseminate content. Its audience is the private individual as well as those who work in institutions and organizations across a broad range of fields including culture, entertainment, education, information, and computer software, whether for-profit or non-profit organizations, and whether the use of content is for commercial, noncommercial, or personal purposes. Many of us share the same experience in that the Internet and digital content and digital distribution have made copyright everyone's business.

Intellectual property, and especially copyright, is a growth industry. It is also an often misunderstood area of the law. One of the basic problems in understanding copyright is that we cannot see it. Perhaps that is why people who would not dare steal a towel from a hotel room would, without a second thought, photocopy a book or reproduce a computer program or image found online.

Copyright law has been struggling with technology ever since the invention of the Gutenberg printing press. With each new technology—like photocopiers and VCRs and the Internet—it becomes easier for consumers to reproduce copyright-protected works (often more quickly, less expensively, and at higher or perfect quality). At the same time, creators and owners find it more difficult to control unauthorized reproduction. Technology and business models are constantly being reexamined and are evolving to deal with the use of digital content.

In writing this book, I have come to recognize that Canadian copyright law is even more complex than I had realized before! I have done my best to simplify the law and to set out generalizations and the most important information for practical purposes. I have included some, but not all, transitional provisions, and I wish I could have provided examples to go with all of the explanations; space, however, was limited. In some cases, I have mentioned the policy behind certain provisions and the thinking of legislators as a way to explain parts of the law that seem mysterious, but I have not been consistent in doing so. My main goal is to put my mind inside of yours and to explain things so that you may comprehend them and to provide you with sufficient information for you to be able to apply the law to your specific situations. I hope that I have made your task of applying copyright law to your specific situations a bit easier.

CHAPTER 1

UNDERSTANDING INTELLECTUAL PROPERTY

A great literary work can be completely, completely unpredictable. Which can sometimes make them very hard to read, but it gives them a great originality.

—Yann Martel

WHAT *IS* COPYRIGHT?

Literally, copyright means the "right to copy." The Canadian Copyright Act grants copyright owners the sole and exclusive right to reproduce, perform, or publish a work. These rights give copyright holders control over the use of their creations, and an ability to benefit, monetarily and otherwise, from the exploitation of their works. In addition, moral rights (which are also in the Copyright Act) protect the reputation of creators. The rights are subject to specific limitations as set out in various provisions in the Copyright Act.

Copyright law is one area of a larger body of law called "intellectual property," or IP. The word *intellectual* is used to distinguish it from "physical" property. Intellectual property law refers to and protects the intangible or intellectual nature of an object, whereas physical property law refers to and protects the tangible or physical aspect of an object.

As an illustration, there is both an intellectual and physical property component to a book or refrigerator. The physical component of the book or refrigerator is the object itself, the book that you can hold in your hand or the refrigerator whose door you can open and close. The intellectual component of the book is the words that appear on the page and the expression of any ideas contained in those words. The intellectual component of the refrigerator is the material that led to its creation, such as sketches containing its design or plans for its motor, computer software incorporated into the refrigerator, and even the name of the refrigerator.

The physical and intellectual components of any creations are separate. By owning the physical or intellectual property in a creation, you do not necessarily own the other sort of property in it. In other words, purchasing or owning a print book does not mean that you own the copyright in that book. You are limited in what you can do with that book, and you cannot make any uses of the book that only the copyright owner may make.

There are traditionally five areas of intellectual property in Canada:

1. Patents
2. Trade-marks
3. Industrial designs
4. Copyright
5. Confidential information and trade secrets

Since 1993, an additional area of IP has been recognized in a Canadian statute for integrated circuit topography protection. Protection for databases that are not protected by copyright also exists in some countries. Database protection is further discussed in Chapter 6, "What Is Protected by Copyright?"

By examining the various types of IP, you will gain a better understanding of how copyright fits into this body of law. You will also realize, as we go through various examples under each area of IP, that each type of IP protects a different kind of creation or a different aspect of a creation, and that each type provides its own special set of rules of protection.

Note that the term *intellectual property* is sometimes interpreted in a narrow sense to apply to copyright and other subject-matter, and the term *industrial property* is used to refer to patents, trade-marks, industrial designs, confidential information, and trade secrets, as well as integrated circuit topography protection.

OVERVIEW OF INTELLECTUAL PROPERTY

"Can I patent my book?" or "Can I copyright my idea for a new mousetrap?" These are examples of questions a copyright lawyer is frequently asked. Such questions demonstrate a general knowledge of IP, in that patents or copyright protect inventions or creations, but they also show a lack of comprehension of the distinction between the various areas of IP. This section of the book explains the different kinds of IP and examines whether something you have created, or someone else's creation that you may want to use, is protected by one of the areas of IP, and if so, under which type of intellectual property. This section also briefly describes the nature of protection provided by each area of IP.

PATENT LAW

A patent is a document issued by the government that describes an invention. According to the Patent Act, the patent legally protects an inventor, or patent owner, and allows him or her to prevent others from making, using, and selling that invention within Canada for 20 years after an application for a patent is filed.

EXAMPLES OF THINGS PROTECTED BY PATENTS
- Articles such as a washing machine.
- Compositions such as a chemical composition used in a lubricant for that washing machine.
- Apparatus; for example, the machine used for making the washing machine.
- Processes; for example, the method used to make the washing machine.
- Any improvement on any of the above. Ninety percent of patents in Canada are for improvements to existing patented inventions.[1]

A patent is granted only for the physical embodiment of an idea, or for a process that produces something saleable or tangible. New medicines, communications systems, energy sources, and electric can openers are all patentable. However, you cannot patent a scientific principle, an abstract theorem, an idea, a method of doing business, a computer program, a medical treatment, or any inventions having illicit or immoral purposes.

In order for an article, composition, apparatus, or process to be patentable, it must meet all of the following criteria:

- It must be new (i.e., the same such invention must not already exist).
- It must be useful (i.e., functional and operative).
- It must be "unobvious" (to someone skilled in that area).

Preparing and prosecuting a patent application is a complex, tedious task and is usually done by a registered patent agent. It can take approximately three years from the date of application to obtain a patent.

If you obtain a patent, you may then sue anyone who makes the patented product or uses the patented process without your permission. However, there are certain situations where "compulsory licences" exist and you must let others use your patented invention, provided they make royalty payments to you.

The law does not require a patented object to be marked as "patented" or an awaited patent as "patent pending," though doing so may remind others of your rights, or pending rights. It is illegal to mark an article as patented where a patent has not yet been granted.

If you plan on securing patent protection, you should be careful not to disclose your invention before filing an application with the Patent Office because it may preclude you from obtaining a valid patent. If you must disclose your invention, for example, to evaluate potential commercial interest, you should only do so on a confidential basis and require the party to whom you are disclosing it to sign a confidentiality agreement that states that he or she will not disclose your invention to anyone else. You will not be able to obtain a valid patent if you disclose your invention more than one year prior to filing a patent application in Canada. In many countries, such disclosure results in an absolute bar to obtaining a valid patent.

If you are granted a patent in Canada, that protection is good throughout Canada. To get patent protection in other countries, you must apply separately in each country, or apply through the treaty called the Patent Cooperation Treaty (PCT). This treaty provides a standardized international filing procedure for many of our principal trading partners including the United States, Japan, and most European countries. Just as a Canadian patent is not automatically valid in other countries, a foreign patent has no effect in Canada unless a separate Canadian patent has been obtained.

The patent system is not always being fully utilized in certain industries where rapid changes occur, due to the relatively long period of time it takes to obtain a patent (normally three years), and the high cost to obtain and maintain a patent. Some owners of patentable inventions have found adequate alternative protection in other areas of the law such as trade secrets or through contractual arrangements.

TRADE-MARK LAW

A trade-mark is a word, symbol, picture, logo, design or shaping of goods, or a combination of these elements, used to distinguish the goods or services of one person or organization from those of another in the marketplace. A trade-mark allows its owner exclusive use of that mark to be identified with certain goods or services.

Examples of trade-marks are the word "Coca-Cola," the Coca-Cola logo, and the distinctive shape of the Coke bottle.

The following marks are not registrable under the Canadian Trade-marks Act (the examples below are not in the Act):

- Names and surnames of living persons even if they are the applicants' own names or surnames (for example, *Lesley Ellen Harris*), unless the name has become distinctive and has acquired a secondary meaning to the public.

- Words that are descriptive of the goods or services associated with the trade-mark (for example, *caffeine* for coffee or *ink set* for pens).
- Words that clearly describe the place of origin of wares or services (for example, *Vancouver* for shoes or *Nepal* for backpacks).
- Words that describe the goods or services in any language (for example, *vin*, *vino*, or *wine* for wine).
- Coats of arms of the Royal Family, badges and crests of the Royal Canadian Mounted Police (RCMP), and the Canadian Armed Forces, the Red Cross, and national symbols.
- Any mark that is obviously immoral or offensive.
- Deceptively misdescriptive marks.

Certification marks can also be trade-marks if the certification mark is used to distinguish goods or services that meet a defined standard. An example of a certification mark is the "cotton mark" on clothing used to indicate the presence of cotton.

Sound marks may also be registered as a trade-mark.[2] An example of a sound mark is the roaring lion sound associated with Metro-Goldwyn-Mayer (MGM) Corporation movies.

A trade name, that is, a business name of a corporation, partnership, or individual is not necessarily a trade-mark, but may be registered under the Trade-marks Act if it is used as a trade-mark.

A trade-mark may be protected in two manners. It may be protected through use (common law protection); that is, by using the mark in connection with a service or product. This protection is perpetual so long as use of the mark is not abandoned. Also, common law protection is only in the geographic area in Canada in which a reputation for the mark has been acquired through use. Alternatively, the mark may be protected by registering it under the Trade-marks Act. Registration provides *prima facie* evidence or ownership of the mark and provides stronger protection than that provided by the mere usage of a mark. Registration entitles the registered owner to exclusive use of the mark throughout Canada even in geographic areas where use of the mark has not occurred. At the time of writing this book, registration normally takes 12 to 18 months if no major difficulties are encountered. Registered protection lasts for 15 years, renewable indefinitely for 15-year periods.

It is not mandatory to use the symbol ® for registered trade-marks, or for common law marks, to identify trade-marks. Likewise, it is not obligatory to complement a trade-mark with an asterisk followed by a footnote that describes the trade-mark as such and the owner of it. Identifying trade-marks does, however, inform others that the mark is a trade-mark, and can provide information of the origin of the mark. Trade-mark notices can also help to identify the source of the wares/services associated with the mark and inform a consumer as to who is responsible for their character and quality.

If you have a registered trade-mark, you have the exclusive right to use that mark throughout Canada in respect of such wares or services. If anyone else sells, distributes, or advertises wares or services in association with your mark or a similar confusing one, you may enforce your rights against that person.

Your Canadian trade-mark registration is good throughout Canada, and separate registration must be obtained, if necessary, in other countries. Similarly, foreign trade-marks are not protected in Canada unless they have been registered here, though some may be protectable in Canada through use in Canada, or by massive spillover advertising, acquired reputation, and goodwill in Canada.

INDUSTRIAL DESIGN

An industrial design is any original shape, pattern, or ornamentation applied to a useful article of manufacture. The functional or utilitarian features of that article are not protected by industrial design, but may be protected by a patent. It is the "visually appealing" part of the design, and not the article to which it is applied that is protected as an industrial design.

The shapes of a table, a telephone, or a decoration on a plate are examples of industrial designs.

Registration of a design is mandatory under the federal Industrial Design Act within 12 months of the publication of the design in Canada. Registration generally takes 9 or 10 months to secure. Protection lasts for 10 years, beginning on the date of registration of the design. However, five years before the expiry date of the registration of the design, you must pay a maintenance fee, or your protection will expire.

It is not mandatory to mark a product to indicate that it is registered as a design, but marking will give you certain benefits both regarding remedies in an infringement lawsuit and notice to the public that the design is registered and you are its owner. The marking should consist of a capital "D" inside a circle, or abbreviated name, of the design's owner, on the article, its label, or packaging. Older designs may carry the prior marking procedures, a mark consisting of the name of the design owner, the letters "Rd." and/or "Enr." and the year of registration.

The owner of the design has the right to make, use, rent, or sell a product incorporating the design. The owner may sell or license some or all of those rights.

Protection in foreign countries must be separately obtained in each country.

The relationship between creations protected by copyright and those protected by industrial design is further discussed in Chapter 6, "What Is Protected by Copyright?"

COPYRIGHT LAW

Copyright law protects a diverse list of creations including interoffice memorandums, books, computer software, weblogs, photographs, sculptures, and films. Print/analogue and digital works are protected by copyright law.

According to the Canadian Copyright Act, copyright protection is automatic in Canada, upon the creation of a work once the work is in some sort of tangible form such as on a hard drive, written on paper, or recorded. Copyright protection lasts for 50 years after the creator's death. The protection gives creators exclusive use of their works, and protects the reputation of the creator by protecting his or her "moral rights." Once a creator is automatically protected in Canada, the creator is protected in 166 countries around the world. The Act also protects the rights of performers, makers of sound recordings, and broadcasters, referred to as "other subject-matter" or neighbouring rights.

INTEGRATED CIRCUIT TOPOGRAPHY PROTECTION

Canada has had IP protection for the topography of integrated circuits through the Integrated Circuit Topography Act (ICTA) since the Act came into force on May 1, 1993, a relatively new IP protection. These integrated circuits, referred to as "microchips," are tiny electronic devices found in everything from common appliances such as DVD players and washing machines to robots. Since the traditional areas of IP do not provide adequate protection for microchips, at least 20 countries have recognized this newest kind of intellectual property by establishing protection in a separate statute.

The ICTA protects the original design of a registered topography on its own or when embodied in a product such as a washing machine. A topography is considered original if it is developed through the application of intellectual effort and is not the mere reproduction of a substantial part or whole of another topography.

Some integrated circuit products may be entitled to protection under other areas of IP. For example, random access memory (RAM) and read only memory (ROM) devices, which may be used to store sets of instructions for electronic processors, may be entitled to microchip protection for the topographies embodied in such circuits, and the sets of instructions they store may be subject to copyright protection as literary works, and may be entitled to patent protection as industrial methods.

Owners of registered topographies may prevent others from the following activities with respect to a protected topography or any substantial part of the topography: reproducing it; manufacturing a product incorporating it; and, importing or commercially exploiting it or a product or industrial article incorporating it (commercially exploiting could be, for example, sale, lease, offering or exhibiting for sale or lease or other commercial distribution).

A topography must be registered in order to be protected. The application for registration must be filed within two years of the first commercial exploitation of the topography. Registered integrated circuit topographies are protected for up to 10 years from the date of filing the application for registration. The term expires on December 31 on the tenth year after the year of the first commercial exploitation, or the year of the filing date, whichever happens first.

The rights of an owner of a topography are limited by the following three exceptions. After the first authorized sale of a product embodying a registered microchip, the registered owner has no right to control the product's use, rental, resale, or redistribution (unless expressly reserved through a contractual arrangement). Also, a protected topography may be freely copied for the sole purpose of analysis or evaluation, or for the sole purpose of research or teaching with respect to topographies. Further, the topography may be taken apart to design a new and original one. This new topography must meet the originality requirements in the statute if it is exploited commercially without the authorization of the original owner of the rights.

It is not obligatory to identify products embodying registered microchips. However, failure to do so may be a valid defence in an infringement lawsuit if a defendant can prove that he or she had no knowledge of the registration of the topography. The voluntary notice may include the registered title, or similar wording, used to identify the topography in the registration application.

Protection under the federal statute protecting microchips is extended to nationals of other countries on a reciprocal basis. Canada has reciprocal agreements with the United States, Switzerland, Japan, and Australia.

CONFIDENTIAL INFORMATION AND TRADE SECRETS

Ideas, per se, are not recognized as protectable subject-matter of patents, trade-marks, industrial designs, topography protection, or copyright. The closest thing to protecting an idea is through an agreement or contract that treats that idea as confidential information or as a trade secret.

Thus what is unique to the intellectual property area of confidential information and trade secrets is that it protects concepts, ideas, and factual information. For example, an idea for computer software, or a television show, or machinery to build cars may be considered confidential information. Further, a customer list or knowledge of a recipe, say, for a certain soda pop, obtained through employment at a soft drink company, may be considered trade secrets.

Unlike the other areas of IP, confidential information and trade secrets are not governed by a statute (except in the province of Quebec, where trade secrets fall under the Civil Code), but are based upon common law.[3]

Generally, a duty to maintain confidential information or trade secrets arises from a certain relationship. The relationship puts you under a legal obligation not to divulge the information to others. That relationship can be established because of the association of people, as in an employer-employee situation, or due to the nature of the information conveyed, as in a discussion of an idea. In order to be protected, the information conveyed must not be common knowledge, and it must be communicated in such a way, whether implicit or explicit, to instill an obligation of confidence.

One of the best ways to protect confidential information or trade secrets is through written contractual arrangements. Such a contract should describe in sufficient detail the type of information, the length of protection—if it is a limited one—geographical limitations on divulging the information, and any allowable uses of the information. The more specific and limited the terms and conditions in the contract, the more likely a court of law would uphold such an agreement.

In certain extreme circumstances, one may disclose confidential information; for instance, when it is in the public interest. Otherwise, such information may only be used within the limits of an agreement.

If no agreement exists, you may disclose confidential information where no competitive edge can be gained from the use of the information, and the information will not be used in a way that will detrimentally affect the originator of the information. A court may be requested to grant an order to stop the continuing use of information, or may order monetary compensation to be paid by a person who unlawfully uses confidential information.

OVERLAP OF INTELLECTUAL PROPERTY PROTECTION

In some circumstances, you will find that a particular creation, or aspects of it, qualifies for more than one type of intellectual property protection. Where more than one type of protection is possible, you should consider the nature of protection(s) that most appropriately fits your needs. For instance, consider such things as the use to be made of the creation and which type of protection(s) would cover that use, the various durations of protection, rights attached to protected works, and the costs and procedures required for protection.

Further Information and Registration Forms

With the exception of confidential information, each of the above areas of IP has an office within the Canadian Intellectual Property Office (CIPO). CIPO provides general information on the various areas of IP, access to the patents, trade-marks, copyrights and industrial designs databases, IP registration forms, and more.

> The Canadian Intellectual Property Office (CIPO)
> Place du Portage I
> 50 Victoria Street, Room C-114
> Gatineau, Quebec K1A 0C9
> Tel.: 866.997.1936 (toll-free from anywhere in Canada and the United States)
> Fax: 819.953.2476 (for general enquiries only and not official correspondence)

E-mail: cipo.contact@ic.gc.ca
Web: www.cipo.ic.gc.ca

SUMMARY

At the beginning of the section on the areas of IP, two questions were asked: "Can I patent my book?" and "Can I copyright my idea?" You should now be able to answer these questions. To help you, the six areas of IP are set out in the following table.

The Six Areas of Intellectual Property

	Patents	Trade-Marks	Industrial Designs	Copyright	Integrated Circuit Topography	Confidential Information
Types of Protectable Works	Article, composition, apparatus, process, improvement	Word, symbol, picture, sound	Shape, pattern, design applied to a useful article	Literary, dramatic, musical, artistic works	"microchips"	Idea, concept, factual information
Lamp Example	Remote control for lamp	Name of lamp	Design on lamp shade	Instruction guide	Microchip in the lamp	Idea for an improved lamp
Basis of Protection	Federal statute	Federal statute and common law (unregistered marks)	Federal statute	Federal statute	Federal statute	Common law
Foreign Protection	Must apply in each country or through the treaty	Must apply in each country	Must apply in each country	International protection	On a reciprocal basis	Depends on agreement
Term of Protection	20 years	If registered 15 years + 15 year renewable periods; if unregistered, perpetual protection	10 years (but must pay a maintenance fee after 5 years)	Life + 50 years	Up to 10 years	Depends on agreement
Registration	Necessary	Not necessary	Necessary	Not necessary	Necessary	n/a
Markings Required?	No	No	Yes	No	No	n/a

CHAPTER 2

COPYRIGHT LAW IN CANADA

I just do what I do. I like to make music.

—Neil Young

HISTORY OF CANADIAN COPYRIGHT LAW

In Canada, copyright law falls under federal jurisdiction. The copyright law, then, does not vary from province to province but is consistent throughout the country. This is because the Parliament of Canada was given exclusive jurisdiction to deal with the matter of "copyrights" under subsection 91(23) of the Constitution Act of 1867.

The current Canadian copyright legislation is found in one statute called the Copyright Act.[1] This piece of legislation, based on the United Kingdom Copyright Act, 1911, was introduced in 1921 and came into force on January 1, 1924. Since that time, it has remained the governing copyright legislation in Canada, along with its schedules, annexes, and rules, and including various amendments made to it.

The Canadian Copyright Act, consolidated with amendments made to it since its enactment in 1924, related information, and related regulations are at http://laws.justice.gc.ca/en/C-42/index.html.

Before the 1924 Act came into force, the governing legislation consisted of various pre-Confederation provincial legislation, post-Confederation federal statutes, British statutes, and the Berne

Convention (an international convention on the protection of copyright-protected works, which is discussed in Chapter 5).

Since 1924, there have been a number of amendments made to the Copyright Act, and in 1988 the Act was substantially modified. The bill introduced in the House of Commons that resulted in the 1988 amendments was numbered "Bill C-60" and was at the time known as "Phase I" of the amendments in the then copyright revision process. Nine issues were dealt with in these amendments:

1. The protection of choreographic works.
2. The protection of computer programs.
3. The right to exhibit an artistic work at a public exhibition.
4. The clarification between industrial design and copyright protection.
5. The abolition of the compulsory licence for the making of sound recordings.
6. The collective administration of copyright.
7. The role of the Copyright Board.
8. The enhancement of rights to protect the reputation of a creator.
9. Fines for the infringement of copyright.

Since 1988, the 1924 Act has been amended a number of times. It was amended in order to comply with the Canada–United States Free Trade Agreement and the North American Free Trade Agreement (NAFTA). The definition of *musical works* was amended by Bill C-88. Certain administrative provisions were amended by the Intellectual Property Improvement Act. On January 1, 1996, amendments to the Copyright Act became effective to comply with aspects of Canada's obligations for the Trade-Related Intellectual Property Rights (TRIPs) of the General Agreement on Tariffs and Trade (GATT).

A further major reform to the Canadian Copyright Act took place in 1997 with the enactment of Bill C-32, also known as Phase II of the then copyright revision process. These revisions include the following:

- New rights for performers and producers, including royalty payments when their sound recordings are broadcast or performed in public.
- A levy on blank audio recording media to be collected and paid to performers, producers, and authors for private copying of their works (at the same time such copying was made legal).
- Exceptions for nonprofit educational institutions, libraries, archives, and museums to use copyright materials in specific ways without payment or authorization.
- An exception to allow broadcasters to make a temporary copy of an event or performance to be broadcast at a later time.
- Enhanced protection for exclusive distributors of books in Canada.
- Guaranteed minimum awards for copyright infringement (called statutory damages).
- An extension of rental rights to composers, lyricists, and performers of musical works.
- A change in the perpetual copyright protection in unpublished works to a term of life of the author plus 50 years.
- A change in the term of copyright in photographs to life of the author plus 50 years.

A recent major reform to the Canadian Copyright Act took place on June 29, 2012, with the Royal Assent of Bill C-11, the Copyright Modernization Act (CMA). Most of these provisions became effective November 7, 2012.[2] These revisions include the following.

In relation to provisions benefiting creators and owners of copyright materials, the CMA:

- Provides new rights (making available and distribution) as set out in the digital World Intellectual Property Organization (WIPO) treaties.
- Extends the duration of protection in sound recordings.
- Makes photographers the first owner of copyright in their photographs even in the case of commissioned photographs.

- Prohibits the removal or tampering of digital rights management ("DRM") on content.
- Prohibits the removal or tampering of copyright information on works (also called rights management information).

In relation to provisions benefiting consumers of copyright materials, the CMA:

- Permits certain education-related uses of content including allowing teachers to use content in lessons conducted over the Internet.
- Allows libraries, archives, and museums to digitize and copy material in an alternative format if there is danger of the original format becoming obsolete, and to provide interlibrary loans in a digital form.
- Permits Canadians with perceptual disabilities to adapt legally acquired material.
- Allows an individual to use protected materials when creating a new work such as a mash-up and to post the new work online on a site like YouTube.
- Permits time-shifting of a recording of communication signals or programs for private purposes.
- Permits reproduction of works for private purposes (e.g., individuals can copy music they legally own onto a computer, iPod, or MP3 player).
- Amends the existing statutory damages so that there is a distinction between commercial and noncommercial infringement.
- Expands fair dealing to include education, parody, and satire.

Other provisions in the CMA include:

- A new secondary infringement action that covers peer-to-peer file sites that provide a system that they know or should know is designed primarily to infringe copyright.

- Clarification that Internet service providers ("ISPs") and search engines are exempt from liability when they are strictly intermediaries in communication, caching, and hosting activities. The bill obligates ISPs to notify subscribers who are allegedly infringing copyright.

In addition, the CMA requires review of the Canadian Copyright Act every five years "to ensure it remains responsive to a changing environment."

As is evident and notwithstanding some major revisions, the Canadian Copyright Act remains a statute originally enacted in 1924, subject to various amendments. The basic structure and many of the provisions in the statute remain the same as in 1924, which is remarkable considering the law was enacted in an era before photocopiers, computers, DVDs, DVRs, and the Internet, as well as Google, Facebook, and Twitter. The wording in the Act and amendments is intended, for the most part, to be technology neutral. As an example of technology neutral wording in the 1924 Act, prior to the amendments made in 1988, that Act, which obviously did not deal with computer software, was interpreted by the courts to protect computer software. The 1988 amendments legislated this court decision.

This book deals with the Canadian copyright law as it exists at the time of writing. It does not consistently point out whether provisions were originally found in the 1924 Act, or have since been added, except for information purposes or when the date of a provision or an amendment has relevance on its comprehension and its practical effect. That being said, the provisions added through the CMA are all brand-new at the time of writing this book and have yet to be interpreted by court cases. What does this mean to you as a creator, owner, or consumer of copyright materials? The provisions or wording in the Copyright Act may be interpreted by the courts of law, which will guide us in interpreting the Act. For example, the meaning of *education* under fair dealing may be shaped by court cases. The shaping of the law by court cases must always be taken into account when understanding Canadian copyright law.

GOVERNMENT RESPONSIBILITY FOR COPYRIGHT IN CANADA

There are two departments within the federal government that are primarily responsible for copyright matters in Canada. Industry Canada (www.ic.gc.ca) is responsible for the administration of the copyright registration system under the provisions of the Copyright Act. To be specific, the Copyright Office, directed by the Registrar of Copyrights, is responsible for registering copyrights in Canada. The Copyright Office is part of the Canadian Intellectual Property Office (CIPO) (www.cipo .ic.gc.ca) that comes under the jurisdiction of Industry Canada.

Functions of the Copyright Office include registering copyrights, maintaining the Register of Copyrights, and registering assignments and licences.

Industry Canada and Canadian Heritage (www.pch.gc.ca) are jointly responsible for developing policy for the revision of the Copyright Act.

In addition, an independent tribunal, the Copyright Board of Canada (www.cb-cda.gc.ca), among other things, sets royalties in certain circumstances for the use of copyright-protected materials. The Board describes its own mandate as:

> The Board is an economic regulatory body empowered to establish, either mandatorily or at the request of an interested party, the royalties to be paid for the use of copyrighted works, when the administration of such copyright is entrusted to a collective-administration society. The Board also has the right to supervise agreements between users and licensing bodies and issues licences when the copyright owner cannot be located.[3]

The Canadian government does not have a role vis-à-vis enforcing the rights provided in the Copyright Act. The Act sets out private rights for citizens to enjoy. As such, it is not the responsibility of the government to monitor the use of copyright materials or to ensure that such uses are within the parameters of the law. Although individuals must generally enforce their own rights, there are certain cases where "criminal remedies" as set out in the Act are appropriate to deal with an infringement of copyright and the Crown may institute an action.

These criminal remedies are further discussed in Chapter 13, "What Are the Remedies for the Infringement of Copyright?"

THE CONCEPT OF COPYRIGHT LAW

There are two very important concepts in Canadian copyright law that must be appreciated for a full understanding of the law, and consequently, much of the information provided in this book. These concepts relate to property rights in a creation, and to copyright protection and how it relates to ideas.

Property Rights in a Work Protected by Copyright

In physical objects that embody a copyright work, such as books, CDs, or DVDs, there are two types of property rights. First, there is a right in the physical property, the object itself. Second, there is a right in the intangible property. Copyright protects this intangible right. Thus, if you own a print book, you may read it, display it on your coffee table, and even lend it to a friend. However, you may not do anything that only the copyright owner has the exclusive right to do. For example, by virtue of owning the physical book, you may not reproduce, translate, or digitize it (that is, without permission of the copyright owner).

Print Books versus E-Books

The concept of copyright protecting the intangible aspect of a work must also be examined with respect to a work that only exists in a digital form, such as an electronic book or e-book. By "purchasing" (more accurately described as "licensing") an e-book, you have certain rights in that e-book, but similar to a print book, you do not have unlimited rights. For example, you may read the e-book but you cannot reproduce the book (other than perhaps a technical reproduction that allows you to access the book on your e-book reader). Also, you cannot translate or modify the e-book without permission of the copyright owner.

Copyright Protection and Ideas

It cannot be overemphasized that ideas are not protected by copyright law. What copyright law protects is the expression of these ideas. This is based on the notion that ideas are not owned by anyone. This basic copyright principle applies no matter how novel or great an idea.

What this concept implies is that anyone can follow an idea set out in a book or an instructional video, or create a work based on the same idea, without infringing copyright. It also means that there can be copyright in two works expressing the same idea since it is the original expression of the idea that is protected by copyright. For example, two people may independently make sketches of the same tree, each sketch being protected by copyright and neither of them infringing the copyright in the other one.

Unlike the Canadian Copyright Act, the American Copyright Act is very explicit in stating items to which copyright protection does not extend. Section 102 of the U.S. Copyright Act states the following: "In no case does copyright protection for an original work of authorship extend to any idea, procedure, process, system, method of operation, concept, principle, or discovery, regardless of the form in which it is described, explained, illustrated, or embodied in such work." Although this definition has no binding impact on Canadian law, it illustrates the notion concerning the lack of copyright protection in ideas and the like.

SUMMARY

Current Canadian copyright legislation is found in a federal statute called the Copyright Act, which came into force in 1924 and has been subject to numerous amendments. Revision of the Act is an ongoing process.

In general, individuals are responsible for enforcing their rights under the Copyright Act, while the government is responsible for the administration and revision of the Act.

Canadian copyright law protects the intangible aspect of a work. The law does not protect ideas, but protects the expression of ideas.

CHAPTER 3

IS YOUR CREATION ELIGIBLE FOR COPYRIGHT PROTECTION?

The best fame is a writer's fame: it's enough to get a table at a good restaurant, but not enough that you get interrupted when you eat.
— Fran Lebowitz, in *Observer*, May 30, 1993,
"Sayings of the Week"

CRITERIA FOR COPYRIGHT PROTECTION

The first part of this chapter discusses the three criteria for the protection of traditional copyright materials known as "works." The second part focuses on the protection of nontraditional material, often referred to as "other subject-matter" or "neighbouring rights," including performers' performances, sound recordings, and broadcasts. This "other subject-matter" of copyright has more limited protection than "works."

Copyright protection exists as soon as a creation is created or comes into existence. However, in order for a creation to be eligible for this protection, the creation must be a "work" within the meaning of the Copyright Act.

WORKS

A "work" within the meaning of the copyright law will be protected by copyright upon its creation provided three criteria are met. These criteria and basic requirements for copyright protection relate to:

1. Originality
2. Fixation
3. Nationality of creator and place of publication

This chapter explains these three criteria. In doing so, the chapter also answers, in a broad sense, the question of who can obtain copyright protection in Canada. This latter question is revisited from a number of points of view in later chapters, for instance, when discussing who can register a work, and who can sue for infringement of copyright.

Specific types of works protected by copyright are discussed in Chapter 6, "What Is Protected by Copyright?"

Originality

In order for a work to be protected by copyright, it must be original in the copyright sense of the word. The Copyright Act emphasizes this prerequisite for protection by stating that "copyright shall subsist in Canada for the term hereinafter mentioned, in every *original* literary, dramatic, musical and artistic work." The definition section defines "every original literary, dramatic, musical and artistic work" to include "every original production in the literary, scientific or artistic domain, whatever may be the mode or form of its expression." Thus, if a work is original and otherwise qualifies for copyright protection, then it will be protected by copyright.

What Does Originality *Mean?*
Although the term *original* is used in the Copyright Act, this term is not defined in the Act. In order to fully understand the meaning of originality, one must first return to the basic copyright principle that protection extends to the expression of an idea and not to the idea itself. Thus,

original in the copyright sense must also relate to the expression of an idea and the effort exerted to express that idea, and not to the originality of the idea, the thought itself, or the novelty of the words used.

Second, one must examine the standard of originality in the copyright law. The lay perception is that the criterion of originality means that a creation must be completely novel (as is required in patent law) and also possess some aesthetic, artistic, or literary quality. This is not true. In fact, the standard of originality is very low, at least in relation to our preconceptions.

The term *original* in the copyright sense means that a work originates from an author and is not copied from another work. Creativity is not mandatory, and the work need not be novel or unique. The expression of the idea must be an exercise of skill and judgment that necessarily involves intellectual effort. This is something more than a purely mechanical exercise. For example, the skill and judgment involved in simply changing the font of a work to produce "another" work would be considered too trivial to be original for copyright purposes. Skill means using one's knowledge, developed aptitude, or practiced ability. Judgment means using one's capacity for discernment or ability to form an opinion or evaluation by comparing different possible options in making the work.[1]

Whether a creation is original in the copyright sense is always a factual question and one of degree that ultimately a court must decide. The court will apply the circumstances and facts of a particular case to the definition of originality as set out above.

With these guidelines in mind, the type of materials that may be protected by copyright include print and e-books, songs, paintings, tables, compilations (including websites and blogs), directories, translations, adaptations, and dictionaries, as well as a new arrangement of a work in which copyright protection has expired. Chapter 6 specifically discusses the categories and kinds of works protected by copyright.

The low threshold of originality means that anyone can create a similar (or even identical work) provided he or she does so independently. As a result, in theory, two identical works may exist, each one being separately protected by copyright, as long as each of them was created independently of the other one. For example, two books on sailing written at the same time, published at the same time, and intended for the same audience may each be original in the copyright sense of the word. Each would enjoy separate copyright protection, provided each book's author wrote it independently of, and without access to, the other. This example also points out that a work may be original where common knowledge has been drawn upon. Further, a work may be original even if an author received suggestions for parts of it.

Fixation

You now know that in order for a work to be protected by copyright, it must be original. In order for an original work to be protected by copyright, it must also meet the criterion of "fixation." (The relatively newer sections of the Copyright Act that deal with "other subject-matter" do, however, provide limited protection for subject-matter that has not been fixed.)

Fixation is not defined in the Copyright Act. In fact, the concept of fixation is not something explicitly discussed in the Act as a general criterion for copyright protection (except in the case of dramatic works, as discussed later). It is a criterion that has, for the most part, developed through court cases.

The court cases in which the concept of fixation has arisen have determined that copyright subsists only in works that are "expressed . . . in some material form, capable of identification and having a more or less permanent endurance."[2] This criterion reinforces the principle that copyright protects the "form" in which an idea is expressed and not the ideas contained within that form.

In addition to being necessary for copyright protection of works in Canada, fixation may have important practical functions. For example, fixation may provide proof of the existence of a work and perhaps the identity of its author. It may provide a means of preserving and maintaining a historical record, and it may provide some valuable insight into the author of the work and the author's creative process.

Dramatic Works

Dramatic works are the one type of work defined in the Copyright Act as dependent upon fixation. The Copyright Act defines a dramatic work to include "any piece for recitation, choreographic work or mime, the scenic arrangement or acting form of which is fixed in writing or otherwise. . . ." It is interesting to note that the definition was included in the Act prior to the court case making the concept of fixation a necessary criterion for the copyright protection of all works.

What we learn from the definition is that fixation of dramatic works is not limited to writing. According to the provision in the Act, and the inclusion of the word "otherwise," there are other possible methods of fixation. So, it was most likely acknowledged even when the Act was drafted in 1921 that there is no single precise method of transcribing dramatic works. The wording of the Act implies that an audio or audiovisual recording of a dramatic work may qualify as the method of fixation. Also, the wording of the legislation indicates that fixation is required only of the "scenic arrangement or acting form" and therefore not of every specific detail. What need be captured in any fixation of a dramatic work are the movements and general characteristics of the dramatic work in question.

Musical Works

The meaning of musical works is discussed in Chapter 6, "What Is Protected by Copyright?" However, it is important to understand that in this section, musical work refers to a song and not to a recording of a song.

Until the 1993 amendments to the Copyright Act, there was some debate as to what would be considered fixation of a musical work: whether the musical work must be notated in some manner or whether a recording of that musical work would by itself be sufficient to meet the requirement of fixation. The debate was due to the definition then in the Copyright Act that defined a musical work to mean "any combination of melody and harmony, or either of them, printed, reduced to writing or otherwise graphically produced or reproduced." Musical notation obviously fit within this definition. However, since the definition limited the methods of fixation to being printed, reduced to writing, or otherwise graphically produced or reproduced, it was more than arguable that a recording of the musical work would not constitute fixation of it.

The current Copyright Act defines a *musical work* to mean "any work of music or musical composition, with or without words, and includes any compilation thereof." Thus, the requirement to have the melody and/or harmony printed, reduced to writing, or otherwise graphically produced or reproduced no longer exists. It is now clear that any sort of fixation of a musical work such as musical notation, audio or audio-video recording, or other means by which the music is expressed in material form capable of identification and having a more or less permanent endurance, is sufficient to meet the criterion of fixation.

Examples of "Fixed" Works

A simple illustration of a fixed work is a book manuscript, in handwriting, on paper. This work would likely be considered fixed if it was in draft form or point form and probably even if the handwriting is illegible. The final form of the manuscript as well as its published editions would probably all be considered fixed. A typed version of the manuscript, or one on a computer hard drive or portable storage device, or printed on a computer's printer, would in all likelihood, also be considered fixed for purposes of the Copyright Act. Also, an e-book, or audio recording of the manuscript, would be considered fixed for copyright purposes.

The manuscript example set out above is fairly straightforward. There are a number of other situations that are not as obvious. In order to examine other situations of fixed works, one must return to the definition of fixation as developed by case law, which is that a work "must be expressed to some extent at least in some material form, capable of identification and having a more or less permanent endurance." From this definition, one can see that fixation is not necessarily restricted to something put down in writing. For example, a computer program embedded on a DVD may qualify as fixation of a copyright work.[3] Further, fixation of a choreographic work may be through sketches, by special dance notation (Laba notation or Benesh notation) or computer notation, or by a simple recording of the work on video or film. Another example is that a work may be fixed simultaneously with its communication to the public, for instance, in the case of a broadcasted work. For example, a football game is generally not a work but if the game is recorded at the time of a TV broadcast of it, the recording is protected as a cinematographic work.

Examples Where There Is No Fixation

Now that we have examined examples of fixed works, let us look at examples where a work may not be considered fixed for copyright purposes. One such example may be lectures, speeches, addresses, and sermons that have not been written down or recorded in some manner prior to their presentation (however, there is some thought that this may be an exception to the fixation requirements; this is discussed in Chapter 6). The same may be true of an improvised comedy skit, a jam session, or an improvised tune. An image or text on a computer screen (that has not automatically or intentionally been saved) may not be considered fixed. A work transmitted by broadcast or cable without being recorded prior to, or simultaneously with, its transmission may not be considered fixed.

Nationality and Place of Publication

In order for a work to be protected by copyright, it must meet the criteria of originality and fixation. It must also meet certain conditions concerning the nationality of the author and the place of first publication of the work. In summary, everyone legally and permanently (though it need not be indefinitely) living in Canada enjoys automatic copyright protection. The details are set out below. These details are fairly specific and should you need to apply them to your situation, it is best to consult the exact wording in the Copyright Act rather than rely on the summary below.

In order to be eligible for copyright protection, the author of any published or unpublished work, including a cinematograph, must, at the date of the making of the work, be a citizen or resident (including a landed immigrant or refugee claimant) of Canada or another treaty country. A treaty country includes any Berne Convention (Berne) country, any country adhering to the Universal Copyright Convention (UCC), any country member of the World Trade Organization (WTO),[4] and any country member of the WIPO Copyright Treaty (WCT).[5] To further understand the eligibility requirements and how the international system of copyright works, see Chapter 5, "Canada and International Copyright Law."

References in the Act to "British subject" and "Her Majesty's Realms and Territories," specifically that British subjects and residents within Her Majesty's Realms and Territories were eligible authors, were removed in 1997. However, these previously eligible authors are protected for any copyright or moral rights that subsisted in Canada before September 1, 1997.

The Canadian government can extend copyright protection to other countries where that country provides similar protection to Canadians. This is true even where the remedies for enforcing rights or restrictions on the importation of works differ from Canadian law.

There are two ways in which a cinematograph may be eligible for copyright protection. One, if the maker of the cinematograph is, at the date of the making of it, a corporation with its headquarters in a treaty country. Second, if the maker is a natural person, and is, at the time of making the cinematograph, a citizen or resident of a treaty country. For a cinematograph, its maker is the individual or company who makes the necessary arrangements to make the cinematograph. Note that the concept of "maker" is relatively new to the Canadian Copyright Act, and it is possible that courts of law may interpret it in an unexpected manner; however, the intent of the maker qualifying (as opposed to the author) was to have an additional way for a cinematograph to be eligible for copyright protection without relying on the status of who is the author of a cinematograph.

You are also entitled to automatic copyright protection if your work was first published in a treaty country. The first publication must be in a quantity as to satisfy the reasonable demands of the public. Satisfying this demand will depend on the nature of the work and is something that is not specifically defined. If a work is initially not published in a treaty country but a second publication in a treaty country occurs within 30 days (or a longer period as fixed by order-in-council), that would be sufficient to have automatic copyright protection in Canada.

Although corporations are not specifically mentioned as being protected "persons," they are recognized as being protected by copyright in certain circumstances, and it is most likely that corporations incorporated in any of the eligible countries would be protected in Canada.

Protection of these persons is according to the Canadian Copyright Act when copyright protection is claimed in Canada.

OTHER SUBJECT-MATTER: SOUND RECORDINGS, PERFORMANCES, AND BROADCASTS

As mentioned earlier, the copyright protection afforded other subject-matter is generally narrower than for works. For example, the owners of sound recordings (the "makers") and the performers whose performances are embodied on those recordings may not prohibit the broadcast of their creations but may claim, through copyright collectives, "equitable remuneration" for such airplay.

Sound recordings may be protected in three manners. First, a sound recording may be protected if its maker is a citizen or permanent resident of Canada or a Rome Convention (Rome), Berne, WTO, or WIPO Performances and Phonographs Treaty (WPPT) country at the time the record was first fixed. Second, a sound recording may be protected if its maker is a corporation and the corporation's headquarters are in Canada, or a Rome, Berne, WPPT, or WTO country when the record was first fixed. If neither of these conditions is met, the sound recording may be protected if it was first published in a Rome, Berne,

WPPT, or WTO country in a quantity sufficient to meet reasonable public demand. Also see below for performers' performances fixed on sound recordings.

Performers are eligible for protection of their performances for different rights depending on how they are eligible for protection in Canada. Since January 1, 1996, a performer has rights in his or her live performances in Canada or another WTO country. Note that the performance itself need not take place after January 1, 1996. However, the retroactive protection against pre-1996 bootleg audio recordings, which goes back 50 years, is not absolute and is subject to certain limitations. As of September 1997, performances that occur in Canada or another Rome country, or that are simultaneously broadcast from Canada or from another Rome country by a broadcaster headquartered there, are protected.

Protected performances fixed on sound recordings are those where the maker of the record is headquartered in Canada or another Rome country, or first publication takes place there. Protection also extends to performer's performances that take place in a WPPT[6] country, and where the performer's performance is fixed in a sound recording whose producer was a citizen or permanent resident of a WPPT country at the time of making the sound recording. Protection further extends to a corporation that had its headquarters in a WPPT country, or where the first publication of the sound recording that satisfies the reasonable demands of the public was in a WPPT country, or the performer's performance was transmitted at the time of performance by a signal broadcast from a WPPT country by a broadcaster headquartered in that country. First publication of a sound recording happens in a WPPT country (despite an earlier publication elsewhere) where there are 30 days or less between the publication in that country and the earlier publication.

To be entitled to the blank audio recording media levy, the performer must be a citizen or a resident of Canada. For further information on this levy to compensate private copying of sound recordings, see Chapter 9, "Rights Protected by Copyright," and Chapter 14, "Legally Using Content."

Broadcasters headquartered in Canada or a Rome or WTO country have a copyright in signals broadcast from that country.

The Minister of Industry may expand the category of protected performances, sound recordings, and broadcasts to other NAFTA countries, or to other countries, on a reciprocal basis.

SUMMARY

In order for a "work" to be protected in Canada by Canadian copyright law, it must be original in the sense that it was not copied from another work, it must be fixed in some material form with a more or less permanent endurance, and the copyright holder must be a citizen or resident of Canada or another treaty county, and/or any published work must be first published in a treaty country. "Other subject-matter"—performers' performances, sound recordings, and broadcasts—must meet their own specific requirements in order to be eligible for protection in Canada.

CHAPTER 4

ARE FORMALITIES REQUIRED TO OBTAIN COPYRIGHT PROTECTION?

Before anything else, preparation is the key to success.
—Alexander Graham Bell

AUTOMATIC PROTECTION

Copyright protection is automatic in Canada. Under the Canadian Copyright Act, there are no formalities requisite to obtaining copyright protection. The protection exists upon the creation of a work or sound recording, or when a performance or broadcast signal occurs. There is no requirement, for example, to register a work or other subject-matter, mark it with the copyright symbol, or deposit it with a deposit registry for copyright purposes. Also, adding phrases like "All Rights Reserved" does not entitle you to any further protection than you would have had without the inclusion of such a phrase. You have copyright protection in your work or sound recording upon the creation of it, or when a performance or broadcast signal occurs, without doing any of these things, once the criteria for protection (discussed in Chapter 3) have been met.

Although copyright protection in Canada is not dependent upon any formalities, registering, marking, and depositing a work or other subject-matter may help you enforce your rights. Because such "formalities" are optional under Canadian law, you must decide whether

35

you want to register, mark, or deposit your creation, and if so, the best method to use. Options include the Canadian government voluntary registration system, the American government registration and deposit mechanisms—which is open to Canadians—and nongovernmental organizations where you can register and deposit a work or other subject-matter. This chapter discusses advantages and procedures for voluntarily marking, registering, and depositing materials protected by copyright.

Marking Your Creations

The Copyright Symbol

The copyright symbol, ©, is used universally to identify a copyright-protected work and to indicate its copyright owner. This universally recognized symbol appears in one of the international copyright conventions, the Universal Copyright Convention. Note that the symbol and requirement of marking a work do not appear in the leading copyright treaty, the Berne Treaty; in fact, automatic protection of a work is one of the underlying premises of the Berne Treaty. Some people believe that if a work does not bear a copyright symbol, especially a work such as an article or image found online, then that work is not protected by copyright law—that is not true!

Using the © symbol is not mandatory under Canadian copyright law nor is any other marking of a creation in order for it to be protected under Canadian copyright law. However, there are advantages to marking a work and using the © symbol.

First, the copyright symbol is a reminder to the world at large that copyright exists in a work. As such, it provides evidence in a court action that the alleged violator should have known that copyright existed in the work. Second, it may help people who want to use the work to locate the copyright owner and obtain permission to use it. Third, marking is beneficial if a court case is pursued in the United States since the American Copyright Act precludes an alleged violator from submitting that he or she did not know that copyright existed in a work where a proper copyright notice has been placed on the work.

There are three elements to a copyright notice. First, the "c in a circle"—©—or the abbreviation "Copr." Or the word "Copyright" should be presented. Second, the name of the copyright owner (not necessarily the author) should be included in the notice. Third, the year of first publication should be set out. These elements need not necessarily appear in this sequence.

One form of marking a work is the following:

© Year of First Publication Name of Copyright Owner
or
© 2014 Lesley Ellen Harris

This notice should be clearly placed in a manner and location best suited to alert the user of the work in question to the fact that copyright subsists in the work. This can vary depending on the type of work involved. For a website or blog, a suitable location for the copyright notice may be on the home page, or on a page that appears by clicking through to a specified copyright or legal notices page, or both. For instance, you may include a simple copyright notice on your home page and perhaps on other pages of your website or blog, with a click through to a more detailed copyright and legal notices page.

As a general rule, place the notice in a manner and location that gives reasonable notice of the claim of copyright, so that it appears in a conspicuous position on a work that will not be missed by a casual observer.

The year to include in a copyright notice should be the year of first publication, or the year in which substantial revisions to a work occurred. For constantly evolving websites, blogs, and other online spaces, the year in the notice may be updated whenever more than trivial revisions or additions are made to the site. While earlier years can remain as part of the notice, the date of the latest substantial revisions must be included. If only one year is to appear in the notice, it should be the oldest year—the year associated with the oldest elements in the work. It is best to err on the side of omitting newer years as opposed to omitting older years. Alternatively, you could include a range of years (e.g., 1999–2014), starting from the date of the oldest elements in the work and ending with the date of the newest elements in the work.

Copyright Warning/Information

In addition to a copyright symbol, some copyright owners include a "copyright warning" or additional copyright-related information on any copyright-protected works. The warning/information may be as simple as:

For requests to use this copyright-protected work in any manner, e-mail xxx@xxx.ca or call xxx.xxx.xxxx.

More comprehensive copyright warning/information may refer to concepts like fair dealing, and may mention whether permission is required for nonprofit and noncommercial uses of the work. Most print publications, images, videos, and online spaces have some form of copyright warning/information. This information is helpful in determining what uses are permitted without contacting the copyright owner.

Notice on Online Work

In prescribed circumstances it is not an infringement of copyright for a nonprofit educational institution to reproduce, broadcast, and perform in public, for educational or training purposes any copyright-protected content that is available through the Internet. If you do *not* want your online content used for such purposes, you must place a clearly visible notice, and not just the copyright symbol, prohibiting that use. This must be posted at the Internet site where the content is posted or on the content itself.

The Sound Recording Symbol

Often you will see the symbol ℗ on a sound recording. Again, this is not mandatory for protection in Canada. The ℗ is used like the ©, but only with respect to sound recordings. The advantages of marking a work with ℗ are similar to those for marking a work with ©. The form of the notice for a sound recording is the following:

℗ Name of Copyright Owner Year of First Publication

The notice should be placed on the label attached to the recording, or on the cover or container accompanying the recording, or both.

REGISTRATION WITH THE CANADIAN GOVERNMENT

Is It Necessary?

The Canadian government provides a registration system for works and other subject-matter protected by copyright. The Copyright Office is part of the Canadian Intellectual Property Office (CIPO), which falls under the jurisdiction of the federal government department, Industry Canada. Since copyright is automatic in Canada, registration with the Copyright Office does not confer copyright protection, nor does it guarantee the existence of it. In other words, a work or other subject-matter need not be registered to be protected by copyright.

There are certain advantages to voluntarily registering a copyright work or other subject-matter with the Canadian government. The Copyright Act sets out some of these advantages. According to the Act, a certificate of registration creates the following two presumptions:

1. That copyright subsists in a work or other subject-matter.
2. That the person registered, that is, the name appearing on the certificate of registration, is the owner of the copyright in that work or other subject-matter.

These presumptions are helpful in a court action since a copyright owner of a registered work or other subject-matter need not prove that copyright subsists, and that the person registered is the owner. The copyright owner need only provide evidence to these points if the alleged infringer argues otherwise; that is, that copyright does not subsist in the work or other subject-matter, and that the person registered is not the owner of the copyright.

Further, registration may be advantageous in a court action since it creates a presumption that the alleged infringer knew of the existence of copyright in the work in question. Thus, it is up to the alleged infringer to show that he or she was unaware that the work was subject to copyright protection. It would be difficult for someone to defend the existence of copyright and to argue that he or she was unaware that a work was subject to copyright protection if the work was registered with the Canadian Copyright Office. This is because the alleged infringer could have checked the Register of Copyrights for copyright information on the work, for example, the owner of the copyright in the work. However, since mere registration does not give copyright protection, an alleged infringer could argue, notwithstanding registration, that the work lacked copyright protection.

Registration may, in some circumstances, entitle a copyright owner to certain remedies other than merely stopping the infringer from continuing the illegal acts. Where a work is not registered with the Canadian Copyright Office, a copyright owner may only get a court order to prevent further infringements of copyright. However, where the work or other subject-matter is registered, the copyright owner may be entitled to stop further infringements as well as be eligible for a range of other remedies including monetary compensation. Remedies are further discussed in Chapter 13, "What Are the Remedies for the Infringement of Copyright?"

In addition to registering a copyright work, the Canadian registration system allows for the registration of any assignment or "grant of interest" by licence in a copyright, or in a part of the copyright. If you become a subsequent owner of copyright, you should consider registering this interest. Doing so will give you priority over a similar grant of interest if that other interest has not been registered. In other words, if A and B are both granted an interest in a copyright-protected work and only B registers this interest, B may have priority over A with respect to his or her rights in the work.

Despite the advantages of registering copyright with the Canadian government, many copyright owners choose not to register, or at least not immediately upon the commencement of copyright protection (i.e., when a work is created and first put in a fixed form). This is for two reasons. First, registration can be made at any time prior to the commencement of a lawsuit. Note, however, that lack of registration at the time of an infringement of copyright may limit a copyright owner's recourse to a court order to stop the infringing act from continuing, as opposed to other recourse such as being monetarily compensated. Also, since registering helps establish the date of creation of that work, it may be advantageous to register it immediately upon creation. An earlier date of creation may be necessary if others claim that they created the work before you and that your work or sound recording is a copy of their work or sound recording.

The second reason that some copyright owners do not register their works with the Canadian Copyright Office is that they use alternative registration/deposit methods to establish proof of ownership of copyright and date of creation. See the later section "Registration or Deposit Other Than with the Canadian Government."

There are certain issues relating to the Canadian government registration system of which you should be aware. One concern is that registering a work does not provide authenticity with respect to that registration. An applicant is asked to provide limited information on the Application for Registration of a Copyright, and this information is not validated by the Copyright Office or supported by a deposit of the protected material. Since the Copyright Office does not examine applications, there may be more than one work registered under the same title. Also, there is no publication that lists all registered copyrights in Canada, and there is no publication that notifies the public on an ongoing basis of new works or other subject-matter registered by the Copyright Office. However, the Copyright Office does keep records of all registered copyrights in its register. Searching these registers is discussed in Chapter 14, "Legally Using Content."

LEGAL DEPOSIT AT LIBRARY AND ARCHIVES CANADA

The deposit requirements with Library and Archives Canada are not related to copyright applications and registration and not related to the deposit of copyright material with the Copyright Office (a process that does not exist). The Library and Archives of Canada Act (2004) is a federal statute that mandates and legally empowers legal deposit. This legal deposit is not related to copyright. Its purpose is that "the documentary heritage of Canada be preserved for the benefit of present and future generations."[1]

Legal deposit requires all publishers in Canada in relation to all publications in all mediums, to send them one or two copies (depending on print run) of all books, serials (journals, periodicals, newsletters), spoken word sound recordings, video recordings, electronic publications in physical formats such as CD/DVD-ROMs, and microforms. One copy is required for musical sound recordings, CDs, and multimedia kits. On January 1, 2007, legal deposit was extended to maps and online publications. Online publications include books (monographs), serials (journals, periodicals, newsletters, and magazines), and annual reports, and research and working papers made available to the public.

Further information on legal deposit may be obtained by contacting:

Legal Deposit
Library and Archives Canada
395 Wellington Street
Ottawa, Ontario K1A 0N4
Telephone: 819.997.9565
Toll free: 1.866.578.7777
Fax: 819.953.8508
E-mail: legal.deposit@lac-bac.gc.ca
Web: www.collectionscanada.gc.ca/legal-deposit/index-e.html

International Standard Numbers

International Standard Numbers are unique codes that are used by publishers, libraries, and suppliers to identify certain published works including monographs, serials, and music. There are three different types of these numbers. These numbers are not related to and should not be confused with copyright. The ISBN (International Standard Book Number) is assigned to books, pamphlets, educational kits, microforms, CD-ROMs, and other digital and electronic publications. The ISSN (International Standard Serial Numbers) is assigned to serial publications. The ISMN (International Standard Music Numbers) is assigned to printed music publications.

Further information on ISBN and ISMN may be obtained by contacting:

Canadian ISBN Agency
Library and Archives Canada
395 Wellington Street
Ottawa, Ontario K1A 0N4
Telephone: 819.994.6872
Toll free: 1.866.578.7777
Fax: 819.997.7517
E-mail: isbn@lac-bac.gc.ca
Web: http://www.collectionscanada.gc.ca/isn/041011-1010-e.html

Further information on ISSN may be obtained by contacting:

ISSN Canada
Library and Archives Canada
395 Wellington Street
Ottawa, Ontario K1A 0N4
Telephone: 819.994.6895
Toll free: 1.866.578.7777
Fax: 819.997.6209
E-mail: issn@lac-bac.gc.ca
Web: http://www.collectionscanada.gc.ca/isn/041011-2000-e.html

How to Register Copyright with the Canadian Government, Canadian Intellectual Property Office (CIPO)

The current fees are:

$50.00 CDN   Filing an application for registration for a work or other subject-matter, online via the CIPO website. Filing an application by fax or mail is $65.00 CDN.

$65.00 CDN   Filing a request for the registration of an assignment, licence, and so on.

$65.00 CDN   Processing a request for accelerated action on the above services.

Fees may change. Current CIPO tariff of fees for copyrights is at www .cipo.ic.gc.ca/eic/site/cipoInternet-Internetopic.nsf/eng/wr00091 .html.

Registration is valid for the full term of copyright protection, and no additional registration fees are required during this term.

Who Can Register?

Any author, owner, assignee of copyright, or person who has an interest in the copyright granted by a licence can register copyright material in the name of the owner. A creator or copyright owner can register by himself, or have a lawyer or other representative do so on his behalf. If registration is pursued after an author's death, it can be registered by the author's heirs or legal representatives.

In Whose Name?

Registration establishes the owner and not necessarily the author of copyright in a work.[2] The person whose name is registered is presumed, in the absence of any contrary evidence, to be the owner of the copyright in the work or other subject-matter. The name of both the copyright owner and the author of the copyright material must be included on the registration application. The name of the author will help establish the duration of copyright protection. The name of the author is also important with respect to moral rights that, as you will soon see in Chapter 7, attach to an author of a work protected by copyright notwithstanding that the author is not the owner of copyright in that work.

If the author uses a pseudonym it may be set out in the application, but the full legal name of the author must also be indicated. Otherwise, it will be impossible to determine the term of copyright. The same is true in an employer/employee situation. The employer may register in his name as owner of the copyright, but the employee's name must be indicated as the author.

Procedure

CIPO provides two forms to be completed for copyright registration, to be accompanied with the required fee. Note that there are two different forms for registration. The Application for Registration of a Copyright in a Work (see Appendix III) could be used for a book or computer software or photograph, all of which fall under one of the following categories of works: literary, musical, artistic or dramatic work. The Application for Registration of a Copyright in a Performer's Performance, Sound Recording, or Communication Signal (see Appendix IV) is for registering other subject-matter such as a performer's performance, sound recording, or communication signal. Works and other subject-matter are fully described in Chapter 6, "What Is Protected by Copyright?"

Applications are available online for filing online or for printing and submitting by fax or mail. The following forms are available online:

- Application for Registration
- Application for Registration in Other Subject-Matter
- Filing a Grant of Interest
- Request for Certificate of Correction
- General Correspondence
- Order Copyright Documents

The latter four items are only for online submission.

For online submissions of applications or other forms, you must register to access a secure area of the Industry Canada website. Register at https://strategis.ic.gc.ca/app/scr/registration-inscription/home.html?lang=eng.

To obtain copyright forms and information about the registration process, contact:

Canadian Intellectual Property Office
Client Service Centre
Place du Portage I
50 Victoria Street, Room C-229
Gatineau, Quebec K1A 0C9
Telephone: 866.997.1936 (toll free from anywhere in Canada and the
   United States)
Telephone: 819.934.0544 (international calls only)
Fax: 819.953.2476 (for general enquiries only and not official
   correspondence)
E-mail: cipo.contact@ic.gc.ca
Web: www.cipo.ic.gc.ca/eic/site/cipointernet-internetopic.nsf/eng/
   h_wr00021.html#copyrights

What Information Is Required on the Registration Application?

Basically, the registration application is a declaration that the applicant is the author of the work, owner of the copyright in the work or subject-matter, an assignee of the copyright, or a licensee of copyright in the work or subject-matter[3] and that the work has or has not been published (if published, date and place when it was first published by the issue of copies to the public must also be specified), and that registration is requested.

The forms are straightforward and require the following information:

- Title of work is mandatory for a literary, artistic, musical, or dramatic work, but is optional for other subject-matter. Subtitles, alternative titles, and descriptive matter are not to be included as part of the title. Each application must refer to one work or other subject-matter only.

- Category of work or type of other subject-matter.
- Publication information (if published, date and place of publication), date of fixation, performance, or broadcast for other subject-matter depending on the type.
- Name and address of author (address is optional). Not required for other subject-matter.
- Name and address of copyright owner (telephone, fax, and e-mail address is optional).
- Declaration that the applicant is the author, owner, assignee, or licensee of copyright in the work or other subject-matter.
- Agent for applicant (if applicable).

Larger Bodies of Works

Larger bodies of works such as encyclopedias, newspapers, reviews, magazines, or other periodical works, or work published in a series of books or parts, may be registered as one work. Also, a book of poems, or a book of photographs of sculptures (for example), may be registered under one title.

Multimedia and Digital Works

Multimedia works including a website or blog are registrable as a single work since they are considered a "compilation." The registration application for this work should indicate the predominant category (i.e., literary, dramatic, artistic, musical) that describes the work.

Do Not Deposit Copies

The registration application specifically states, "Please do not send copies of your work." Copies of the work or other subject-matter should not be sent to the Copyright Office with your application for registration or at any other time. The Copyright Office in Canada does not have any depository system or facilities to store these items. Any copy of a work sent to the Copyright Office will be sent back to the applicant, without any examination of the work or verification of its relation to the application with which it was sent. See subsequent section in this chapter on Registration or Deposit other than with the Canadian Government.

THE ROLE OF THE COPYRIGHT OFFICE AND THE REGISTRAR OF COPYRIGHTS

The Copyright Office does a cursory examination of the application. It will not undertake an extensive examination of the application. The Registrar of Copyrights will not examine the veracity of the applicant's declaration and takes no responsibility for the veracity of the entries made in the Register. The responsibility of the Copyright Office is to make sure the information required under the Copyright Act is provided before registration.

The Copyright Office keeps records, called the Register of Copyrights, in which "names or titles of works and other subject-matter and the names and addresses of authors, owners and of any agents for the applicant, and such other particulars as may be prescribed" are entered. Once the copyright is registered, a certificate will be issued to the registrant. This certificate of registration is evidence that copyright subsists and that the person registered is the copyright owner.

The Register is kept at the Copyright Office and is open to inspection by the public. Any person may make copies of or take extracts from the Register. Also, you can do an online search in CIPO's Canadian Copyrights Database. Chapter 14, "Legally Using Content," provides information on searching the records of the Copyright Office.

All registration applications must be done in writing or online. Correspondence with the Copyright Office may only be by an applicant or his or her agent.

The Copyright Office will not provide any advice on matters concerning the interpretation of the Copyright Act, fair dealing, or any other question of law.

If the Copyright Office makes a clerical error while preparing a registration document, it may fix this error without obtaining further authority. A corrected certificate of registration is issued bearing the same registration number.

The Copyright Office's power to amend a registration document is limited. It has no authority to alter a registration after a registration certificate has been issued. For example, it cannot make a correction to the title or type of work unless ordered to do so by the court. The Registrar of Copyrights or any "interested person" may apply to the Federal Court for such an order. The procedure of obtaining a court order is outlined in the Federal Court Rules.

Unpublished Works

If an unpublished work is registered, it need not be re-registered once it is published since proof of ownership and creation has been established by the first registration.

Do You Need to Register Different Drafts or Versions of the Same Work?

You do not need to register different drafts or versions of the same material. Generally, you should register the final draft or version—the one that you will be circulating or distributing. Once you register copyright material and you prepare a subsequent draft or version of it, consider registering the new version if it is substantially different from the earlier registered version. For example, register each edition of a book.

How Long Does Registration Take?

At the time of writing, the standard service for an online filing is five days and seven days for paper filing. The Canadian Copyright Office commits to deliver service on request for accelerated action within three days.

Registration takes effect when the application is accepted by the Copyright Office, whether at the time of filing or after any required amendments are made by the applicant. The sort of amendments discussed here refer to information needed to complete an application or to correct spelling mistakes.

What If You Have a Change of Address?

A change of address need not be registered with the Copyright Office. If notified, the Copyright Office will note the change in the database for the convenience of searchers, but not in the Copyright Register.

What Is the Most Misunderstood Issue Relating to Copyright Registration in Canada?

Informal feedback from CIPO's Client Service Centre indicates that some Canadians may not understand the role and scope of the Copyright Office. According to the Copyright Act and Copyright Regulations, the Copyright Office's role is only to receive and process applications for voluntary registration of copyright. The Office does not verify copyright ownership or examine any works, nor offer advice on copyright subject-matter, scope of protection, or infringement. The Office advises the public to seek a legal professional knowledgeable in the area of intellectual property in those latter areas.

The Canadian Copyright Office has helpful FAQs on copyright registration at http://www.cipo.ic.gc.ca/eic/site/cipointernet-internetopic .nsf/eng/h_wr02281.html#faq. These questions relate to before filing an application; filing the application; and, after filing the application.

REGISTRATION OR DEPOSIT OTHER THAN WITH THE CANADIAN GOVERNMENT

Due to the voluntary nature of the Canadian copyright registration system and the fact that no deposit is required, some copyright owners use other methods of "registering" or "depositing" their materials either as the sole method of registration or in conjunction with the Canadian government registration system. Using an alternative method is no sub-stitute for registration under the Canadian Copyright Act, though in practice it may provide some proof in a courtroom. However, a copyright owner would not be entitled to the advantages in the Copyright Act that benefit creators and copyright owners who register with the Copyright office. Thus, a copyright owner not registered with the Canadian gov-ernment would have to prove in a court proceeding that copyright existed in a work and that he or she is the owner of that copyright. On the other hand, using an alternative method in conjunction with the Canadian government registration system may provide additional proof to that obtained from merely using the Canadian registration system.

All registration/deposit systems have the same underlying purpose: to provide evidence that you are the copyright owner in a specific work and the date of creation of the work. Different creators' and copyright owners' associations and lawyers recommend different methods of reg-istering and/or depositing a copyright-protected work, depending upon the intended exploitation of a work, the possible violation of copyright by others, and the value of the work. Another factor in choosing one or more methods is the cost involved with each method. In deciding whether to register a work, keep in mind that you need not do so at the time of creation, but the earliest date possible at which you can prove the creation of your work will be advantageous in court proceedings. Needless to say, if registration and deposit are not undertaken imme-diately upon creation of the work, you are not barred from doing so at a later date. However, also keep in mind that lack of registration at the time of a violation of copyright may limit your recourse to a court order to stop the violating act from continuing, as opposed to other recourse such as monetary compensation.

MAILING A COPY TO YOURSELF

This method of copyright "registration/deposit" is sometimes referred to as "poor man's copyright."[4] It is one of the least complicated, least time-consuming, and least expensive ways to "register/deposit" a work or other subject-matter.

This method is straightforward. Put your manuscript, photographs of sculptures, lead sheet, or any other reproduction of your work in an envelope and mail it to yourself by registered mail. When you receive the envelope/package, put the registered mail slip and envelope/package in your files or safety deposit box or give it to your lawyer. DO NOT OPEN IT under any circumstances, unless and until you are before a court of law. Once opened before a judge, the envelope and its contents will act as evidence in establishing a date of creation and ownership of copyright, in that protected material.

Alternatively, you can mail the envelope/package to a friend or directly to your lawyer, who may, if necessary, later be called as a witness regarding the envelope/package.

REGISTERING WITH THE U.S. COPYRIGHT OFFICE

Once you have copyright protection in Canada, you automatically have protection in the United States. It is not mandatory to register in the United States to have protection there.

There are, however, important benefits for Canadians as well as American citizens to register in the United States. One benefit is the U.S. Copyright Office's requirement of depositing copies of the work when you file a copyright registration application. This deposit can provide further proof of copyright ownership beyond that obtained from voluntary registration with the Canadian Copyright Office, where no such deposit is necessary or possible. Note that the American law also requires deposit of foreign (e.g., Canadian) works if they are published in the United States through the distribution of copies that are imported or are part of an American edition.

There are additional advantages of registering in the United States. For example, if a copyright infringement suit is initiated in an American court, American registration provides certain advantages in court proceedings. These additional advantages are especially important for copyright holders who exploit their works in the United States and are further explored in Chapter 15: "An Overview of American Copyright Law." Registration may be made at any time during the duration of copyright protection.

The recommended method for filing a copyright registration with the U.S. Copyright Office is through its Electronic Copyright Office, referred to as eCO. Through eCO you can register basic claims for literary works, visual arts works, performing arts works including motion pictures, sound recordings, and single issues of serials. eCO is at https://eco.copyright.gov/eService_enu/start.swe?SWECmd=Start&SWEHo=eco.copyright.gov.

Alternatively, you may register with a paper form, Form CON (continuation sheet for applications), which is available upon request at www.copyright.gov/forms/formrequest.html. The fee for a basic registration for filing a paper form is $65.00 US, and for registration online through eCO is $35.00 US. A detailed list of fees for copyright registration, recordation, and other services is at www.copyright.gov/docs/fees.html.

There are several advantages of filing a registration online; including a lower registration fee of $35.00 US. Also, you will receive e-mail acknowledgement that your application has been received (whereas the other filing methods do not provide a confirmation of receipt). The registration processing time is significantly quicker. As of September 2012, processing time is two and a half months for online filings and six and a half months for Form CO and paper forms. You can see the current average processing times at www.copyright.gov/help/faq/faq-what.html#certificate. In addition, you can track the status of your online registration application online. You can pay online for your application by secure payment by debit or credit card, electronic check, or through a Copyright Office deposit account. Registration is open 24/7 except for Sundays from midnight to 6 AM EST (for maintenance.)

Unlike in Canada, whether you file a copyright application in paper form or electronically, you must deposit one or two copies of the work with your application. The U.S. Copyright Office will review your application and deposit, and that the work is copyrightable subject matter, the work is correctly described on your application, and the application is otherwise correctly filled in. The Copyright Office will register the work even if it has reasonable doubt that the work is not copyrightable as this is a matter for the courts, and in this case the Copyright Office will notify the claimant that the copyright claim and application may not be valid. For unpublished works, one complete copy of the work must be deposited; for published works, two complete copies must be deposited. Certain categories of deposits of registrable works can be directly uploaded into eCO as electronic files. The U.S. Copyright Office has various circulars on deposit requirements at www .copyright.gov/circs/.

Note that the U.S. Copyright Office has several different forms depending on the work being registered. Some of these forms include Form TX for a literary work; Form VA for visual arts; Form PA for performing arts; and Form SR for sound recordings. Select the correct form for your work. You can see the various forms at www.copyright .gov/forms/.

If you live in Canada, one of the advantages of registering with the U.S. Copyright Office is that you will have to deposit a copy of your work with it.

In the United States, you can preregister a copyright work. This is different from a copyright registration application, and you still need to register your work once it is published. The U.S. Copyright Office cautions that preregistration is not useful for the majority of works, and it is intended for those works that may be infringed prior to their release and also for unfinished works. Only unpublished works that exist in some form that are being created for commercial distribution may be preregistered. This includes motion pictures, musical works, sound recordings, computer programs, books, or advertising photographs.

Copyright Office
Library of Congress
101 Independence Avenue SE
Washington, DC 20559–6600

Telephone: 202.707.5959 or 1.877.476.0778 (toll free)

E-mail: Submit your question through an online form at www
.copyright.gov/help/general-form.html

Web: www.copyright.gov

REGISTERING WITH A NONGOVERNMENTAL ORGANIZATION

There are "specialized" registration and deposit places. This book refers to them as "specialized" since they generally only deal with specific types of materials. Certain creators' organizations and/or unions have set up these specialized systems to deal with the type of materials that they represent. Contact your own professional organizations to see what is available to you. The systems are generally open to organization/union members, as well as to nonmembers. These specialized systems may provide evidence of ownership and proof of creation on a particular date, but they do not confer any copyright protection or give you the benefits of registering with the Canadian or U.S. Copyright Offices.

One caution in depositing your materials with any of these specialized depositories is that there are no specific formalities or regulations that govern them. You will want to ensure that any depository you use is legitimate and can guarantee that your work will be kept in safe storage for the necessary period of time. A second caution relates to the time period that the depository will keep your protected materials. When you register with the Canadian or U.S. Copyright Offices, that registration is good for the full term of copyright. When you deposit your material with one of these nongovernmental depositories, the deposit may be valid for a limited number of years, subject to a renewal (at an additional fee). The depository may, without notifying you, dispose and destroy your material within a certain time period following the expiration of the time of deposit. It is your responsibility to renew the registration. Lastly, these specialized agencies do not verify any registrations or deposits of your materials.

An example of a nongovernmental registration service is through the Writers Guild of Canada (WGC) Registration Service at www.wgc.ca/script_reg/index.html. For a fee, anyone may register with the WGC literary material including film scripts, treatments, synopses and outlines, and written works for television, radio, home video and interactive media, as well as book manuscripts, poetry, short stories, stage plays, and periodical articles. The WGC will store the material for five years, and the term may be renewed upon payment of the then-current registration fee. If not renewed within a specified time period, the material will be destroyed. The WGC registration information states that "it does not verify the originality or authenticity of the material, make comparisons of registration deposits nor provide any assurances that the registered material enjoys copyright protection."

SUMMARY

Copyright is automatic in Canada upon creation of a work or sound recording, or when a performance or broadcast signal occurs, provided certain criteria have been met. Notwithstanding automatic protection, one may mark a copyright-protected work with ©, name of copyright holder, and year of first publication, and deposit and register copyright material in the Canadian Copyright Office (and elsewhere such as with the U.S. Copyright Office and through nongovernmental depositories).

CHAPTER 5

CANADA AND INTERNATIONAL COPYRIGHT LAW

"If all the Scrabble tiles ever produced were placed end to end they would reach the equivalent of eight times around the earth."

—"Scrabble: 60 Facts for Its 60th Birthday"
(published in *The Telegraph*, December 15, 2008)

RELEVANCY OF INTERNATIONAL COPYRIGHT LAW TO CANADIANS

When you photocopy an article in Canada that has been written by a U.S. author, an international copyright issue arises. When Canadians post and distribute content online, and access and use online content, an international copyright issue often arises: Internet-based content by its very nature of being accessible around the world involves international copyright law. This chapter discusses the relevancy of international copyright law to Canadians. Specific aspects relating to international copyright issues are also in other chapters, including Chapter 15, "An Overview of American Copyright Law."

THE CONCEPT OF INTERNATIONAL COPYRIGHT PROTECTION

International copyright protection does not, per se, exist. There is no one international copyright law. Each country has its own copyright laws. However, you can have protection in other countries under that country's copyright law through the copyright relations countries share with each other.

INTERNATIONAL COPYRIGHT CONVENTIONS

There are two principal international copyright conventions (or treaties), the Berne Convention for the Protection of Literary and Artistic Works ("Berne Convention") and the Universal Copyright Convention ("UCC"). Canada is signatory to both of them. These conventions do not by themselves provide copyright protection. Their purpose is to provide minimum standards that member countries include in their domestic copyright legislation. This establishes a minimum level of copyright protection in national copyright statutes around the world. Countries may provide greater copyright protection than the minimums set out in the Berne Convention and the UCC. Based on the principle of national treatment, the Berne Convention and the UCC ensure that authors are protected in countries other than their own.

National Treatment

In copyright treaties, national treatment means that each country signatory to the treaty must give citizens or permanent residents of other signatory countries at least the same copyright protection that it gives its own nationals. For example, a Canadian author is entitled to the same copyright protection in Australia as any Australian citizen, by virtue of both countries being members of the Berne Convention. Likewise, an Australian author is entitled to copyright protection in Canada in the same manner as any Canadian author. This protection includes duration of copyright, rights of the author, as well as remedies available for the infringement of these rights.

National treatment is the general rule. One exception to national treatment is "the rule of the shorter term." The Berne Convention provides a minimum term of copyright protection for most types of works of 50 years after the death of the author, known as life-plus-50. If countries grant a longer term than life-plus-50, they have the choice of granting that longer term to works from all treaty partners or only to works from those treaty partners that grant the longer term. For example, both the United States and the European Union countries have a life-plus-70 duration whereas Canada (and many other countries) has a life-plus-50 duration. The United States grants national treatment to all of its treaty partners. Therefore, Canadian works are protected for life-plus-70 years in the United States (even though Canadian works are only protected for life-plus-50 in Canada). However, the European Union countries use the rule of the shorter term. Therefore, Canadian works are protected for life-plus-50 years in European Union countries. Chapter 8, "The Duration of Copyright," discusses the various terms for copyright protection in Canada.

THE BERNE CONVENTION

The Berne Convention is the older of the two copyright conventions, and also the primary or leading copyright treaty. The Berne Convention was concluded in 1886 and has been revised a number of times, most recently in 1971, often to reflect technological changes. Effective June 26, 1998, Canada became a member of the most recent version, Paris (1971), of the Berne Convention. The Canadian Copyright Act meets the minimum levels of protection required in the Paris (1971) level of the Berne Convention. Canada protects creators from Berne Convention member countries that belong to any level of the Convention. As of September 1, 2013, there are 167 member countries to the Berne Convention.

A copy of the Berne Convention, information on the treaty, and a list of member countries are at www.wipo.int/treaties/en/ip/berne/.

Notwithstanding Canada's membership in the Berne Convention, the Convention has no legal effect in Canada. It is, however, sometimes referred to by Canadian courts to interpret the Canadian Copyright Act.

The Berne Convention is administered by the World Intellectual Property Organization (WIPO or OMPI in French.) See www.wipo .int. WIPO is a specialized agency of the United Nations' system of organizations with headquarters in Geneva, Switzerland. Its function is to promote the protection of intellectual property internationally through cooperation among its member states and other international organizations, and to administer treaties on intellectual property, including copyright. WIPO encourages the establishment of new international treaties and the updating of national legislation, provides technical assistance to developing countries, and collects and disseminates information. Among WIPO's current goals relating to copyright is "to fulfill its mandate more effectively in response to a rapidly evolving external environment, and to the urgent challenges for intellectual property in the 21st Century."

Automatic Protection in Berne Convention Countries: National Treatment

The Berne Convention is based on the principle of national treatment. Each member country must protect works of non-nationals in the same manner as they protect copyright in the works of nationals of their own country.

Once copyright is secured in one's own country, provided that it is a Berne Convention country, protection is automatic in all other countries that are also signatories to the Convention. There are no prerequisite formalities to the protection like registering a work or marking it with the copyright symbol ©. In fact, Berne Convention countries are not allowed to require any formalities. Article 5(1) of Berne states: "The enjoyment and the exercise of these rights shall not be subject to any formality." Thus, protection of a work must be automatic upon the creation of a work. The degree of protection and available remedies for the infringement of copyright are governed solely by the laws of the country where the protection is claimed.

Minimum Standards

The Berne Convention sets minimum standards of protection that member countries are required to include in their domestic law; some of these provisions are optional. These minimum standards relate to the categories of works protected, the rights protected, and the duration of the protection. For example, member countries must provide copyright protection for most types of works for at least 50 years after an author's death.[1] Countries may provide a longer duration of protection and the United States and European Union countries now provide protection for 70 years after an author's death for many copyright-protected works.

In addition to the economic rights of reproduction, performance in public and others, Berne member countries must grant moral rights to authors of works. Authors must have "the right to claim authorship of the work and to object to any distortion, mutilation or other modification of, or other derogatory action . . . which would be prejudicial to his honor or reputation." Moral rights in Canada go beyond these minimum Berne requirements; these rights are discussed in Chapter 9, "Rights Protected by Copyright."

Berne provides allowance for free uses or exceptions from the right of reproduction in certain special circumstances as long as the reproduction does not conflict with the normal exploitation of the work and does not unreasonably prejudice the legitimate interests of the author. It is up to each country to interpret these requirements and in implementing provisions for special interest groups such as libraries, archives, museums, and educational institutions, each Berne member country has taken a unique position.[2] Such provisions in Canada's Copyright Act are discussed in Chapter 10, "Limitations on Rights."

Membership in the Berne Convention

Certain countries could not join the Berne Convention because their domestic laws did not conform to Berne Convention minimum standards, or because they had fundamentally different legal systems. For example, prior to March 1, 1989, the United States could not join the Berne Convention because its domestic law contained formalities prerequisite to copyright protection (e.g., registering a work and marking it with the copyright symbol). In order to have more formal legal relationships between Berne and non-Berne countries, another copyright convention, the Universal Copyright Convention (UCC), was initiated.

As of March 1, 1989, the United States is a member of the Berne Convention (in addition to the UCC). Berne member countries may now claim protection in the United States through the Berne Convention and need not comply with the UCC formalities as discussed below.

Canadians claiming and enforcing copyright protection in non-Berne countries may be entitled to do so under the UCC if that country is a UCC member. However, when both countries are Berne members, the provisions of Berne Convention apply. Since most UCC members now belong to the Berne Convention, the relevance of the UCC has diminished.

THE UNIVERSAL COPYRIGHT CONVENTION

The Universal Copyright Convention was concluded in 1952 and was revised in 1971. Canada is a member at the 1952 level. A copy of the UCC and UCC members is at http://portal.unesco.org/en/ev.php-URL_ID=15381&URL_DO=DO_TOPIC&URL_SECTION=201.html.

Minimum Standards

Similar to the Berne Convention, the UCC sets minimum standards of protection that member countries are required to include in their domestic law. These minimum standards relate to the categories of works protected, scope of protection, and duration of the protection. For example, member countries must provide copyright protection for at least 25 years after an author's death; and signatory (or member) countries must provide "adequate and effective protection" to copyright holders including the exclusive right of reproduction by any means, translation, broadcasting, and public performance. Moral rights are not provided for in the UCC.

No Automatic Protection

Unlike the Berne Convention, copyright protection is not automatic in UCC countries upon protection in one's own country. Authors from UCC countries are only protected on a national treatment basis in other UCC countries if they comply with certain conditions. One of the principal conditions is use of a copyright notice. The UCC requires that, from first publication, all copies of a work published with the authority of the author or other copyright proprietor bear the symbol ©, accompanied by the name of the copyright proprietor, and the year of first publication, placed in such manner and location as to give reasonable notice of claim of copyright.

© Year of First Publication Name of Copyright Owner
or
© 2014 Lesley Ellen Harris

If an owner includes this copyright notice, then he or she is considered to have complied with other formalities such as "deposit, registration, notice, notarial certificates, payment of fees or manufacture or publication in that Contracting State." However, an owner must also check the formalities in the copyright act in the country where he claims protection because contracting states are still free to require further formalities or conditions for the acquisition and enjoyment of copyright within those countries.

THE ROME CONVENTION

Concluded in 1961, The International Convention for the Protection of Performers, Producers of Phonograms and Broadcasting Organizations (Rome Convention) protects the rights of performers, producers of sound recordings, and broadcasters. Effective June 4, 1998, Canada became a member of the Rome Convention. The Rome Convention sets out minimum standards for member countries to include in their domestic legislation including a remuneration right for performers and producers of sound recordings when their recordings are either performed in public or broadcast in countries that have joined the Rome Convention to the extent to which the other Rome Convention country provides that right.

A copy of the Rome Convention and a list of member countries is at www.wipo.int/treaties/en/ip/rome/.

WIPO INTERNET TREATIES

On December 20, 1996, negotiators from 160 countries reached agreement on two "new" treaties, the WIPO Copyright Treaty (WCT) and the WIPO Performances and Phonograms Treaty (WPPT). These treaties deal with copyright needs in the digital era and changing international copyright norms in light of new technologies. The treaties came into force in 2002. At the time of writing this book, Canada has not ratified these treaties.[3] As relatively new treaties, the country members to them are continuously increasing. As of September 1, 2013, there were 90 member countries to the WCT; and 91 member countries to the WPPT. Member countries enjoy national treatment in all member countries.

A copy of the WCT and a list of member countries is at www.wipo.int/treaties/en/ip/wct/.

A copy of the WPPT and a list of member countries is at www.wipo.int/treaties/en/ip/wppt/.

Building upon the minimum requirements in Berne, the WCT mentions two additional works to be protected by copyright: computer programs and databases "which by reason of the selection or arrangement of their contents constitute intellectual creations." The WCT provides for the author's right of distribution, rental of certain types of works, and communication to the public. The WPPT sets out digital rights (reproduction, distribution, rental, and making available) for actors, singers, musicians, and other performers; and producers of phonograms. Both the WCT and WPPT require member countries to guard against the removal of rights management information (i.e., data that identifies works of their authors for rights management purposes); and to circumvent technological measures (e.g., bypass encryption.)

INTERNATIONAL TRADE AGREEMENTS AND COPYRIGHT LAW

Trade agreements are separate from copyright conventions and are not intended to replace conventions like Berne or the UCC. In fact, trade agreements sometimes require that countries provide as a minimum the protection required by the copyright treaties. The purpose of intellectual property in trade agreements is to strengthen intellectual property rights and encourage foreign investment by combating piracy, enhance standards for the protection of copyright around the world, and strengthen the enforcement of rights both internally and at the borders. Similar to copyright treaties, trade agreements do not directly provide copyright protection in Canada. Rather, the agreements obligate member countries like Canada to include certain minimum copyright provisions in its domestic copyright legislation.

International trade agreements that have provisions for intellectual property including copyright which Canada has signed include:

- The Canada–United States Free Trade Agreement (FTA)
- The North American Free Trade Agreement (NAFTA)
- The agreement on Trade Related Aspects of Intellectual Property Rights (TRIPs), which is part of the Uruguay Round of the General Agreement on Tariffs and Trade (GATT)

Countries that signed the GATT are members of the World Trade Organization (WTO).

Information on trade agreements signed by Canada and negotiations in progress is at http://www.international.gc.ca/trade-agreements-accords-commerciaux/agr-acc/fta-ale.aspx?lang=eng.

Changes made to the Canadian Copyright Act by virtue of trade agreements such as the FTA, NAFTA, or TRIPs are discussed, where appropriate, throughout this book.

MEMBER COUNTRIES OF THE BERNE CONVENTION, UCC, AND WTO

Certain provisions in the Canadian Copyright Act refer to and apply to a "treaty country," which means a Berne, UCC, WCT,[4] or WTO member country.[5]

USING CONTENT FROM ANOTHER COUNTRY

When you are physically in Canada and you use copyright-protected content from another country, you apply Canadian copyright law to that use. For example, if you are reproducing a portion of an article from a U.S. author or publication, you may be able to claim the defence of fair dealing to that reproduction (and not the U.S. defence of fair use.) As a further example, if you are modifying a play in Canada by a U.S. dramatist, then moral rights as they exist in Canada apply to that modification (even though the same dramatist would not be entitled to moral rights in the United States and even if the dramatist no longer owns copyright in the play). Additionally, if you are publishing an Italian photographer's photograph in a print newsletter in Canada, you apply the duration of copyright protection in Canada (life-plus-50) rather than the Italian duration (life-plus-70), to determine if the copyright protection is still in effect in Canada.

Foreigners who are initially protected by copyright in their own country, a country that is a member of Berne, WCT, the UCC, or the WTO, are protected and entitled to most of the rights and remedies set out in the Canadian Copyright Act when their works are used in Canada.

The use of content while physically in Canada means that you apply Canadian copyright law to that use. However, any online use of content may entail a more complex analysis as to where that content is being used for legal purposes (see below.)

CANADIAN CONTENT OUTSIDE OF CANADA

When Canadians distribute their content outside of Canada including distributing it online, their rights are governed by the copyright laws of the country where the works are used.

If you enjoy copyright protection in Canada, you automatically have protection in all Berne Convention countries and, as of January 1, 1996, in all WTO countries. You may claim protection in a WTO country for a work still protected by copyright as of January 1, 1996, notwithstanding when that work was created or published. In order to secure protection in UCC countries, you must mark the work from the time of first publication with ©, the year of first publication, and the name of the author or owner of the copyright.

If the country in which you claim protection belongs either to Berne, the UCC, or the WTO, then you can claim protection in that country by virtue of one of these memberships. That country need not be a member of Berne and the UCC and the WTO. Therefore, if you claim protection in a country that is both a member of Berne and/or the WTO and the UCC, and you have not complied with the UCC copyright notice requirement from the time of first publication, you can claim protection under Berne or the WTO, which do not have the notice requirement. Almost all UCC members are also members of Berne, and by the terms of the conventions Berne governs relations between members of both conventions.

If you are claiming protection in a country that is not a member of either of the copyright conventions or the WTO, you may still be able to obtain protection under specific provisions of that country's national laws. If this situation applies to you, consult a copyright expert before first publication or dissemination of your work, in order to ensure that you comply with any requirements prerequisite to copyright protection that depend on the facts existing at the time of first publication.

If you are distributing and marketing your work outside of Canada, be aware that copyright laws vary greatly from country to country and different rights and remedies may apply to you outside of Canada. In some cases, these rights and remedies will be greater than, and sometimes less than, your rights and remedies in Canada. A copyright lawyer can help determine your rights and remedies in the foreign country where you claim protection and infringement, and in the case of infringement, whether you should proceed with enforcing those rights in Canada or in the country involved.

WHERE DO INTERNET USES TAKE PLACE?

With the Internet, it is often difficult to establish where a work is used. Is it used (in the copyright sense) where the work is uploaded onto a website, blog, or Facebook page, or where it is downloaded, and/or perhaps in other countries along the way? This is a much-debated issue among legal scholars, practitioners, and in courts in Canada and around the world. In each situation, a lawyer would have to look at the facts and undertake a jurisdictional analysis. Some practical considerations include where the content owner and the alleged infringed are located, costs of proceeding outside of Canada, and the likelihood of enforcing judgments in countries outside of Canada.

SUMMARY

There is no such thing as international copyright law. However, Canadians have automatic copyright protection in Berne and WTO countries, and have protection in UCC countries if the copyright notice has been properly used. Protection is according to the domestic laws of the country where the work is being used. Sound recording producers may also be protected in Rome countries.

Those outside of Canada who are initially protected in their own countries and whose countries are members of Berne, WTO, UCC, and Rome enjoy copyright protection when their protected material is used in Canada, and are entitled to the rights and remedies in the Canadian Copyright Act.

CHAPTER 6

WHAT IS PROTECTED BY COPYRIGHT?

Should not the Society of Indexers be known as Indexers, Society of, The?
—Keith Waterhouse (1929–2009), *Bookends* (1990)

THE MEANING OF *WORKS* AND *OTHER SUBJECT-MATTER*

You may have already noticed that this book uses the term *work* when referring to material or content protected by copyright. The term *work* is the word used in the Canadian Copyright Act, the Berne Convention, and the copyright legislation of many other countries to describe literary, artistic, musical, and dramatic creations protected by copyright. In addition, the Canadian Copyright Act protects "other subject-matter" which includes sound recordings, performances, and broadcasts (collectively referred to as neighbouring rights). Works and other subject-matter are both protected under the Canadian Copyright Act but enjoy somewhat different protection and are distinguished in the Act. Some refer to works as traditional copyright material and to other subject-matter or neighbouring rights as nontraditional copyright material. This book often uses the words *materials* or *content* to cover both works and other subject-matter.

Ideas

One important point to remember is that copyright protects the expression of an idea and not the idea itself. Thus, the material that is protected by copyright law is the expression of an idea, creation, or thought. For example, a book on how to build a kayak is protected by copyright, but anyone can use the ideas in the instructions to build a kayak or write their own book on building kayaks (of course, without copying the other book).

Facts

Similar to ideas, facts or factual information (for example, historical details) are not subject to copyright protection. Note, however, that other areas of the law may protect facts and restrict the use of information; for example, if facts are obtained on a confidential basis. Here again, facts must be distinguished from the expression of those facts. If original, and expressed in some material form, there may be copyright protection in the expression of facts. For example, there may be copyright protection in a book setting out the history of the film industry in Canada. However, there is no copyright protection in the facts concerning the film industry in Canada that are set out in the book; there is merely copyright protection of the expression of those facts.

Real-Life Events

Similar to facts and information, real-life events are not protected by copyright. However, if you are producing a docudrama, for example, and there is an article or book about the real-life event, obtaining permission from the author of the article or book would ensure that the author does not later make a claim of copyright infringement against you. Also, the author may have valuable research materials you can use. In addition, producers of projects based on real-life events often obtain releases or rights to the stories from involved people to protect themselves against other legal claims based on defamation, invasion of privacy, and the right of publicity. Further, having exclusive rights to a story from the people involved can give the producer an advantage over others basing a project on the same people or facts.

WORKS PROTECTED BY COPYRIGHT

Copyright law was originally concerned with the protection of printed material, but has, over the years, been expanded, either explicitly or by interpretation, to extend to a large variety of works and what we now commonly refer to as content. Most creations and content, whether an interoffice memorandum, a sculpture, film, computer software, digital image, or online periodical, qualify and fall within one of the main categories of works specifically mentioned in the Copyright Act. These works are protected by copyright provided they meet the necessary criteria for copyright protection, such as originality and fixation, discussed in Chapter 3. As one court case has put it, "there remains the rough practical test that what is worth copying is *prima facie* worth protecting."[1]

A work (or content) is eligible for copyright protection notwithstanding the mode or form of that work. The creation could be in draft or final form, or it could be a sketch for a larger work such as a painting or the painting itself, or even a poem written on a napkin. The Act protects a work prepared for commercial or noncommercial purposes. It protects published and unpublished creations, and creations produced by amateurs, children, or professionals. It protects print and analogue works as well as digital content. It protects works in any language, even nonhuman languages. It protects humorous, common, or crude works. It may even protect indecent, obscene, or immoral works though the rewards upon suing for infringement of copyright in such works may be somewhat limited.

General Rule

The Copyright Act sets out specific categories of protected works under which the wide variety of creations fall. The Copyright Act states that copyright subsists "in every original literary, dramatic, musical and artistic work." It further states that "every original literary, dramatic, musical and artistic work includes every original production in the literary, scientific or artistic domain, whatever may be the mode or form of its expression, such as compilations, books, pamphlets and other writings, lectures, dramatic or dramatico-musical works, translations, illustrations, sketches and plastic works relative to geography, topography, architecture or science." Note that the creations set out at the end of this definition are merely examples to illustrate the meanings of the words. Protection is by no means limited to these creations.

The categories of protected material are helpful in terms of providing some order to the large number of items protected by copyright. As well, they are relevant when determining duration and ownership of copyright, and the rights attaching to material protected by copyright. If a creation fits within one of the categories of material protected by copyright, and that creation meets the general criteria necessary for copyright protection set out in Chapter 3—originality, fixation, nationality, and place of first publication—then the creation will be protected by copyright. The *four* broad categories of *works* protected by copyright (and the manner in which this chapter is organized) are:

1. Literary works
2. Dramatic works
3. Musical works
4. Artistic works

In addition, there are three broad categories of "other subject-matter" (neighbouring rights) protected by copyright:

1. Sound recordings
2. Performer's performances
3. Communication signals

This chapter is organized in the order of works and other subject-matter listed above.

Courts have interpreted the Copyright Act in specific cases to protect new types of works not specifically mentioned in it. In some cases, these "new" types of works are a result of new technology or new ways to use content and as such could not have been contemplated by the drafters of the original statute in the early 1920s. This was the case with respect to computer software. The Copyright Act was interpreted to extend to computer software without any specific mention of computer software in the legislation. Throughout this book, there are references to digital content that may be interpreted to be protected under the Canadian Copyright Act. A 2006 Supreme Court of Canada case[2] points out that the current Copyright Act was first introduced in 1921 and "It was promulgated a year after the Westinghouse Electric and Manufacturing Company released the first domestic radio sets, and many decades before the technological revolution that produced, among other innovations, online databases."

The remainder of this chapter will look at specific examples of works under each of the categories, followed by a discussion of what is protected as "other subject-matter." Other subject-matter is the term the Copyright Act uses when referring to neighbouring rights. In this book the terms *other subject-matter* and *neighbouring rights* are used interchangeably. The works listed below are merely examples of protected works. It would be impossible to include an exhaustive list of works protected by copyright. If your work is similar to one of the examples given, it is likely that it is a work protected by copyright.

For the sake of clarity, different or additional headings from those used in the legislation are used in this chapter. Also, when going through the list of protected works under specific headings, you may notice that some works fall into more than one category. For example, a book could be a book of short stories and be protected as a literary work. Further, these books could be collections and therefore also be protected as collective works or could be works of joint authorship and be protected as such.

You may also note that some works incorporate other works and that some works enjoy more than one "layer" of copyright protection (in other words, has two copyrights in the one work). For example, a magazine may enjoy separate copyright from the articles in it, or a choreographic work may enjoy distinct copyright from the set of musical works that are a part of it. Finally, a film may enjoy separate copyright from the underlying screenplay. This is also true for all of the underlying copyright-protected works in a multimedia work like a DVD or a website.

When looking for the protection of a certain work, look under the category that most logically or prominently applies to that work.

LITERARY WORKS

The Copyright Act defines a "literary work" to include tables, computer programs, and compilations of literary works. These are merely examples of creations protected as literary works and do not, by any means, represent the full scope of works protected as literary works. In fact, this definition would be deceiving if you followed it as setting out the only types of literary works protected by copyright. Much to the contrary, the types of works protected by copyright as literary works are quite extensive, as you will see below.

The term *literary* with respect to literary works should not be taken in its literal sense. For one thing, the work need not necessarily be "written" in the ordinary sense of the word to be protected as a literary work. Also the work need not possess particular literary merit to be protected.

Generally, a literary work exists if the author has used skill and ingenuity to arrange his or her thoughts. A court case protecting exam papers as literary works succinctly sets the meaning of literary with respect to literary works:

> . . . it seems to be plain that it is not confined to "literary work" in the sense in which that phrase is applied, for instance, to Meredith's novels and the writings of Robert Louis Stevenson. In speaking of such writings as literary works, one thinks of the quality, the style, and the literary finish which they exhibit. Under the Act of 1842, which protected "books," many things which had no pretensions to literary style acquired copyright; for example, a list of registered bills of sale, a list of foxhounds and hunting days, and trade catalogues; and I see no ground for coming to the conclusion that the

present Act was intended to curtail the rights of authors. In my view the words "literary work" cover work which is expressed in print or writing, irrespective of the question whether the quality or style is high.[3]

With this sort of description of literary works, a legal contract would constitute a literary work, as would a head note or summary of a court case, or correspondence written on the inside of tree bark. Most items that afford information, instruction, or pleasure in the form of literary enjoyment would also qualify as literary works. For example, poems, short stories, magazines, newsletters, instruction manuals, exam papers, game rules, and advertising material may also be literary works, even if they are only in a digital form. Specific examples are set out below.

Books

As already suggested, a book need not have any "literary" merit to be protected as a literary work. An instruction manual for your dishwasher is protected as much as a book of poems by e.e. cummings; a book explaining Einstein's theory has protection equal to a book by Margaret Atwood.

Under the Copyright Act, the term *book* may have a different meaning than the traditional sense of the word. For instance the Act defines a "book" to include every volume, part or division of a volume, pamphlet, sheet of letter-press, sheet of music, map, chart, or plan separately published. These are only illustrations of what may constitute a book for purposes of the copyright law, but it does suggest some examples that may not usually occur to us.

Although most people would define a book as a literary work, that is not necessarily true under the copyright law. If the book contains poems or tables, then it would be protected as a literary work. However, certain books may also be protected under other categories of protection. For instance, a book of photographs could be protected as an artistic work or as a compilation of artistic works.

Letters

All letters, whether business or personal, are protected by copyright. This includes e-mail.

Other Text

All "written" documents, whether prepared for internal or external purposes, whether in draft or final form, whether in print or in digital form, are protected by copyright. In fact, each draft of a document may be separately protected by copyright. This includes papers, dissertations, and other school assignments prepared by students as part of course and degree work. Whether a new draft is protected by copyright depends on the circumstances in each particular case and whether that draft meets the criteria for copyright protection of a work as set out in Chapter 3. Protected text also includes manuscripts, court records, judicial decisions, law reports, statutes, and government records and reports. If you are reproducing federal legislation, statutes, regulations, court decisions, and tribunal decisions, see the Reproduction of Federal Law Order discussed in Chapter 14.

Titles, Names, Slogans, Words

As a general rule, copyright does not protect words, slogans, titles, short phrases, pseudonyms, names of people, goods, services, business associations, domain names, and the like. In some cases, trade-mark or other forms of protection may be available.

The Copyright Act makes specific mention of the copyright protection of titles. This is in relation to the definition of a work. The Act defines a "work" as including the title of it when such title is original and distinctive. Thus, even though titles are not protected independently from a work, a title may be protected as part of a work.

There may be an exception to the general rule of titles not being protected by copyright. A judge in one court case said, "This Hour Has Sixty Minutes is a title which could not be considered as original and distinctive, whereas This Hour Has Seven Days is a title which probably could be considered as original and distinctive, because normally no one expects to hear that an hour is composed of seven days."[4]

Although the Act is not as specific with respect to slogans, short phrases, and the like, as it is with titles, one may be able to argue that the same type of protection may apply. Also see discussion under "Social Media" and whether tweets are protected by copyright.

Lectures, Addresses, Speeches, Sermons

A lecture is protected as a literary work. In general, a lecture must be fixed in some form in order to be protected. For example, if you give a lecture on "Irony in David Cronenberg Films," and the lecture is not written down or otherwise "fixed," then you have no copyright in that lecture, despite it being a type of work protected by copyright law.[5] A recorded webinar containing a lecture would be fixed and protected by copyright.

A lecture may be an address, speech, or sermon, or other similar work such as a lesson or a pleading.

News

Like ideas and facts, news has, per se, no copyright protection. However, once the news is put in some material form, copyright protection may subsist in that particular expression of the news. For example, a news article in a print newspaper, or a news article on a newspaper's website, is protected by copyright since the article is a form or expression of that news.

Editions

Editions per se are not protected by copyright; that is, the way in which a work is typographically arranged (format, type fonts, and layout) is not protected by the law. Thus, anyone can photographically copy or reset an edition of Shakespeare's *King Lear* (which is no longer protected by copyright), and thereby benefit from the work and expense of the original publisher.

Copying an edition, however, should be done with caution. This is because even though an edition is not, as a whole, protected by copyright, certain elements of the edition may be protected by the law. For instance, art work on the cover, the table of contents, the foreword, editorial comment(s), and marginal notes may all be protected by copyright, if they meet the criteria for copyright protection. These protected portions are all "new" or added elements to an original work, and it is only these portions that are protected, not the entire edition. If you copy an entire edition of a work that contains such new or added elements you may be infringing copyright in these elements. Also, if you reproduce an "edition" that is an adaptation of a work in the public domain, that adaptation may have copyright protection even though the protection in the original work has expired.

Translations

Translations are protected by copyright. Any translated work is considered a "new" work and is separately protected from the original work. If you are translating a work, you must obtain permission to do so from the copyright owner in the original work, because the translation is considered a "derivative" work.

As such, there may be two copyrights at play: a copyright in the original work as well as in its translation. Thus, if you translate a play from French to English, the original French version is protected by copyright, and the translated English version is separately protected by copyright as a translation. A third party performing the translated version of the play must obtain permission from both the copyright owner of the original work and the copyright owner of the translated play.

Even if copyright has expired in a work that has been translated, there may be copyright protection in that translation. Thus, if you translate a play by Henrik Ibsen into Hebrew, even though copyright has expired in the original work, there may be copyright protection in the Hebrew version of the work.

An automated translation or the scanning of a document to create a digital format of it would not be protected by copyright because the resulting translation would not be original (no skill or judgment involved).[6]

Computer Programs

Computer programs are protected by copyright law. The Copyright Act defines a computer program as "a set of instructions or statements, expressed, fixed, embodied or stored in any manner that is to be used directly or indirectly in a computer in order to bring about a specific result." This definition was added to the Act in 1988. Types of programs protected by copyright may include an operating system, word processing program, online discussion list software, a computer or video game, or an accounting program.

With respect to a computer program, what is protected is the computer program itself and not the language used to write that program (since languages are not protected by copyright). Also, the idea of the program is not protected. Anyone can reach the same end result by creating his or her own program, as long as the other program was not copied in doing so. Since copyright cannot protect the idea of a program, trade secrets or confidential information may be other areas of the law to examine when dealing with the protection of computer software.

Note that material displayed on a computer screen is not protected by copyright (for example, as a literary work) unless and until the material is saved or fixed in some material form, for example, on a hard drive or USB drive.

CD-ROMS, DVDs, and Online Software

Computer programs are protected notwithstanding the physical object or type of physical object (or lack of physical object) on which the program is stored. A computer program is protected by the law, whether downloadable from a CD-ROM, a DVD, and/or online.

Public Domain Software or Shareware

Those of you familiar with computers and computer software have probably come across the terms *public domain software* and *shareware*. Public domain software is protected by copyright, but can be copied without obtaining permission from, or making a payment to, the copyright owner. The copyright owner of public domain software has decided to waive his or her rights in the software and is allowing the public to freely use it.

Shareware software is copyright protected but with an unusual distribution twist. Instead of asking users to pay for the software before they use it, shareware authors urge users to try it and to voluntarily pay a modest amount directly to the copyright holder if the user continues to use that software beyond a trial period.

Tables

Tables are protected by copyright as long as they are original (as defined in Chapter 3) and there is an exercise of skill and judgment involved in the making of the table. For instance, a table of statistics may be protected by copyright.

Games

A game, as a specific item, is not explicitly protected by copyright. However, various elements of the game may be protected by the law. For instance, the instruction manual may be protected as a literary work, and the game board (in a board game) may be protected as an artistic work. If it is an electronic game such as a computer or video game, there may be additional underlying copyright-protected works such as the game's computer software, music, images, video, and text.

DRAMATIC WORKS

Dramatic works form a second category of works listed in the Copyright Act. The term *dramatic work* is defined in the Act as including "any piece for recitation, choreographic work or mime, the scenic arrangement or acting form of which is fixed in writing or otherwise," and any cinematograph work and any compilation of dramatic works. It is evident from this definition that the term *dramatic works* encompasses a number of forms of expression including verbal and nonverbal, purely physical, and musical elements.

Basically, a dramatic work entails the representation of a dramatic element. Many things that may appear to be a literary work—mainly because they are written down—may be a dramatic work (or may be considered both a literary and dramatic work). In order for a work to be considered a dramatic work, there must be some dramatic action. These dramatic elements need to be "fixed" in some form in which the dramatic elements are recognized. Every precise element need not be in that fixation.

A dramatic work may be protected whether the work extends to amateurs or professionals, and may be protected wherever the performance takes place, be it a park, theatre, synagogue, or church.

Note that some dramatic works may lend themselves more to protection through the law of confidentiality as opposed to copyright since often what is being protected are ideas. This may be true with respect to an idea for a television series or electronic game.

Scripts for Radio, Television, Film, Electronic Games, and So Forth

Scripts and sketches for radio, television, film, DVDs, online sites, and other media may be protected as dramatic works. The script need not be an exact portrayal of the actual performance or dramatic event.

In one case, a court held that a sketch for a television show was a dramatic work even though the script was departed from on a daily basis. The criteria set in the case for the protection of the sketch was that the sketch need only be "fixed in writing sufficiently to say it was a dramatic composition capable of being published or performed and in which the dramatic element was present."[7]

Plays

The element of a play that is eligible for copyright protection is some sort of fixed description of the play. A script or any other descriptive material that captures the dramatic element of the play would probably be eligible for copyright protection.

For a work to be eligible for copyright protection, the end result need not necessarily be a play, as the common usage of that word connotes. In general, "any piece for recitation" may be protected by copyright if the general criteria necessary for protection are met.

Note that the different elements in the play may also have copyright protection by themselves. For example, any choreography, musical works, or sets used in the dramatic work may enjoy copyright protection on their own.

Radio Programs

Impromptu radio programs, talk shows, and the like are not automatically protected by copyright, since the general criterion of fixation may not always be met. If, however, these shows were previously recorded or simultaneously recorded when broadcast, that recording would constitute a fixation of the work. The criterion of fixation would also be met where there is some sort of script, or similar material, which captures the dramatic element of the radio program. For example, a radio sketch set out on paper may be protected. The same is true of a radio commentary that is read from a printed sheet of paper.

Operas, Musicals, and Comedies

Operas, comedies, musical dramas, plays, and the like may be protected by copyright as dramatic works as long as the criteria for such protection have been met; that is, a dramatic element is captured in a fixed form.

AUDIOVISUAL MATERIALS

The Copyright Act does not use the term *audiovisual material*; however, it does protect audiovisual materials as "cinematographs." Cinematographs are protected as dramatic works. For purposes of the Copyright Act, there are two different ways in which audiovisual material is protected. This is dependent upon the nature of the work; that is, whether the work possesses an "original character." The distinction between the two kinds of audiovisual works or cinematographs is relevant with respect to other areas of copyright protection, such as ownership of the work and duration of protection.

For purposes of this book and ease of comprehension, the terminology "scripted" and "nonscripted" audiovisual works or cinematographs will be used. These words have no legal significance and may not, in fact, be 100 percent accurate.

"Scripted" Audiovisual Materials Such as Films and Television Programs

Scripted works, for purposes of this book, are audiovisual works that possess an "original character." This "original character" is derived from the arrangement or acting form or the combination of incidents represented. Audiovisual works with "original character" may be films or videos that follow a script, are overseen by a director, and are subject to an edit.

"Nonscripted" Audiovisual Materials Such as Improvised Works, Home Videos, and News Coverage

"Nonscripted" audiovisual works are those without "original character" and include improvised works, a film of a news item, a film of a dog walking around a yard, and home videos (for example, ones made on your smartphone). "Nonscripted" works have no scripts, are not subject to much editing, and there is no control over any "dramatic" event in them. As mentioned above, it is possible that some so-called improvised works qualify as having an "original character" and would therefore fall under the above category of works arbitrarily called scripted works.

Expression by a Process Analogous to Cinematography

Whether the audiovisual work is scripted or nonscripted, in order for it to be protected by copyright, it must have been "expressed by any process analogous to cinematography." This criterion is broad and allows for different types of technologies that are arguably analogous to cinematography. It does not require that the work be made on film (with a negative) or on magnetic tape.

Soundtracks

The soundtrack of a film is protected as a film or cinematograph where it accompanies the film or cinematograph. Otherwise, the soundtrack is protected as a sound recording (see "Other Subject-Matter.")

CHOREOGRAPHIC WORKS

Choreographic works are protected by copyright. They are protected under the category of dramatic works, but are dealt with separately here because they are subject to different criteria for protection from other dramatic works.

The Copyright Act defines a *choreographic work* as including any work of choreography, whether or not it has a story line. This definition was added to the Copyright Act in 1988. Prior to this definition, choreographic works required, because they fell within the category of dramatic works, a plot or at least a sequence of action, to be protected by copyright. Many choreographic works do not, however, possess a plot or sequence and are simply visually aesthetic patterns. For instance, pantomimes, or certain works of performance, and some modern dance, jazz and abstract ballet, do not necessarily possess a plot.

The protection of a choreographic work extends to the choreographer's arrangement and selection of steps into a choreographic work and not to individual steps within that work. Because of the nature of a choreographic work, it must be notated, sketched, recorded on film or video, and so forth, to be eligible for copyright protection. Otherwise, there is no fixation of the work.

It is likely that a choreographic work would include figure skating. However, it is unlikely that a sporting event would be considered a choreographic work because it is not preconceived or fixed in any manner. Note, however, that a "playbook" for a sports team may be protected by copyright as a literary or artistic work.

MUSICAL WORKS

The Copyright Act defines a *musical work* to mean "any work of music or musical composition, with or without words, and includes any compilation thereof." A musical work, for copyright purposes, is a composition or song, but not a CD, DVD, or other object that embodies the composition. CDs, DVDs, and other sound recordings are separately defined in the law and are discussed below under specific headings.

As always, the general criteria of copyright-protected works must be met with respect to musical works. The criterion of originality is an interesting one. This is because many musical compositions have similar tone succession or slight variations in rhythm or harmony. Some originality or creative work in creating the song will help establish its originality. Whether a musical work is original is a determination to be made based upon the facts of each individual case. With respect to the criterion of fixation, a fixation of a musical work could be a musical notation or recording including a digital recording.

The type of musical works protected by the law is broad and includes beer commercials and opera and hip hop.

As stated in its definition, a musical work can be a musical composition with or without words. However, there is some confusion as to whether there are two copyrights where there are lyrics accompanying that music. If there are two copyrights, the music would be protected as a musical work, and the lyrics would be protected as a literary work. The legal quandary is not as relevant where the same person creates the tune and lyrics since a court case has held that where a single author has written a song, the song was subject to a single copyright.[8] However, this view has been criticized and, in practice, not always adhered to. These issues are important when permission is being sought to use a musical work.

Sheet Music

Musical scores are protected by copyright. This is true with respect to individual songs and compilations of songs.

If you write your own music, it is protected by copyright as soon as it is "fixed" in some permanent form, for example, on staff paper. If you write music on a computer, you should be aware that there is no copyright in what appears on your computer screen since what you see is ephemeral; a copy saved on your hard drive or disk drive, or a print-out of the music would satisfy the fixation requirement.

Sound Recordings

Sounds recordings are not a subcategory of musical works and are discussed below under Other Subject-Matter.

ARTISTIC WORKS

Artistic works constitute a further category of works provided for in the Copyright Act.

Just as a literary work does not need to have particular literary merit or standard to be protected by copyright, an "artistic work" is generally not judged by its artistic or aesthetic nature. The real test of an artistic work is whether the work is original; that is, an original expression from its creator and not copied from somewhere else.

The term *artistic work* is a generic term applying to works in a "visual medium." In fact, it has been suggested that a more appropriate name for this category of works may be "works of the visual arts and other artistic works" as this would more accurately define works that fall under this category.

The definition section of the Copyright Act sets out a number of examples of artistic works. These include paintings, drawings, maps, charts, plans, photographs, engravings, sculptures, works of artistic craftsmanship, architectural works, and compilations of artistic works. These and other artistic works are described below.

Logos may be protected by copyright if they meet the originality standards of skill and judgment.[9]

Paintings and Drawings

All paintings and drawings, whether on canvas or on a smartphone (once saved or fixed), are protected by copyright. Also a painting by a three-year-old is protected as is one by a well-known artist such as Robert Bateman. A painting used in the set for a play may also be protected by copyright.

Engravings

Engravings are protected by copyright. The term *engraving* is not specifically defined in the Act. However, the Act sets out certain examples of items that may be considered engravings including "etchings, lithographs, woodcuts, prints and other similar works, not being photographs." Since the definition is an illustrative one, other engravings may be protected if produced by a process analogous to the exemplary list of engravings included in the Act.

"Original prints" made in a numbered limited edition and signed individually, in accordance with the standards of the arts community, are each considered an artistic work under the Copyright Act. Unnumbered and unsigned prints are also considered to be artistic works. The legal rights attached to prints (as a type of engraving) are identical whether the print is a limited or unlimited edition, signed or unsigned, numbered or unnumbered. All prints that are protected as engravings have, in addition to the other rights of a copyright owner in other copyright-protected works, an exhibition right and an "absolute" right of integrity.[10]

Photographs

Photographs are protected by copyright. A photograph is defined in the Act to include "photo-lithograph and any work expressed by any process analogous to photography." Photographs made with a negative as well as instant or Polaroid photographs and digital photos (taken with a digital camera or smartphone or other electronic device) are equally protected by copyright. This is true for any photograph that is currently protected by copyright, notwithstanding when the photograph was taken and the fact that prior to January 1, 1994, only photographs with a negative were protected.

Sculptures

Sculptures are protected by the Copyright Act. The Act defines "work of sculpture" as including casts and models. According to this definition, a finished sculpture, and any and all casts, molds and models employed to create that sculpture are protected by copyright.

A Henry Moore sculpture or one you create in a pottery class may be protected by copyright.

Sketches and Illustrations

Sketches, illustrations, and the like are protected by copyright law. Sketches and illustrations used to create other copyright-protected works are separately protected by copyright from the work created with the aid of these sketches and illustrations. For example, sketches created for purposes of a painting are separately and equally created by copyright as the finished painting.

Geographical, Topographical, Architectural, and Scientific Plastic Works

Plastic works are protected by copyright. These works are defined in the Act as "any building or structure or any model of a building or structure."

Architectural Works

Architectural works are protected by copyright. These works are defined in the Act as "any building or structure or any model of a building or structure." Before 1988 and the legislative changes to the Copyright Act, in order for an architectural work to be protected by copyright, it required an "artistic character and design." Thus, it was necessary to judge the quality and merit of architectural works in order to determine their eligibility for copyright protection. Under the current law, these works need only meet the requirement of originality to which all works are subject.

Examples of protected architectural works may be a building, or a structure such as a tower, gate, bridge, or parking garage. The copyright protection in a building, structure, or model is separate from the copyright protection in the plans and sketches made with respect to that building, structure, or model.

Maps, Charts, and Plans

Maps, charts, and plans are protected by copyright. Copyright in plans is distinct from the copyright in a structure based on that plan.

Comic Strips

Comic strips are protected by copyright. The written part of the comic strip is protected as a literary work, and the drawings are protected as artistic works.

Cartoon Characters

Cartoon characters, such as Bart Simpson or Garfield (the cat), are not, by themselves, protected by copyright, but may have components that are subject to copyright protection. The different elements of fictional characters must be examined on their own. First, the name of a character is not protected by copyright as copyright does not protect names. Second, a physical portrayal of a character may attain some copyright protection. For instance, if the character is represented in a drawing in a comic strip, the drawing may be protected as an artistic work. Third, if a copyright-protected work contains a character as a substantial part of it, and includes highly distinctive characteristics of the character, the character may be subject to copyright protection (for example, if copied accurately and in detail, it might constitute an infringement of copyright).

In one court case, the illicit reproduction of the cartoon character Popeye the Sailor in the form of brooches, charms, and plastic dolls was held to infringe a substantial part of the original copyright work.[11]

In any legal suit dealing with the infringement of copyright-protected of a fictional character, a successful defence must show:

- A similarity in the expression of the idea of the character in the original and copied versions of the character.
- The character has significant importance to the original work.
- The character possesses original and distinctive characteristics.
- The character has a certain popularity, including one in the eyes of the infringer that entices a deliberate appropriation of the character.

Avatars and other digital characters may be protected by copyright, provided they meet the criteria of copyright protection.

INDUSTRIAL DESIGNS

We have already seen, in Chapter 1, that industrial design constitutes one of the five traditional areas of intellectual property. Until the 1988 legislative changes, there was much confusion concerning the relationship between the Copyright Act and the Industrial Design Act because of the overlapping protection provided by copyright and industrial design law. Under the current law, the Copyright Act carves out certain works, which, under certain circumstances, are no longer subject to copyright protection, but are protected under the Industrial Design Act (provided they meet the requirements including the registration ones in the Industrial Design Act).

In simplified terms, certain artistic works such as designs that are "applied to useful objects" that in turn are created in quantities of more than 50 units, or plates, engravings, or casts used to produce more than 50 units of such useful articles, are not protected by copyright but instead come within the realm of industrial design protection.

These artistic works that may be protected as industrial designs must fall into at least one of the following categories: shape, configuration, pattern, or ornament (which are appreciated solely by the eye). The design must not represent a purely utilitarian function or the method of construction of an article. The design itself will be protected by the law, but the functional part of the article to which the design is applied is not subject to protection. Examples of industrial designs are the pattern on wallpaper or the shape of a lampshade.

The exceptions to the general rule are set out in the Copyright Act. In the following circumstances, a design is protected by copyright even if it is applied to useful articles that are reproduced in quantities of more than 50 units:

- "A graphic or photographic representation that is applied to the face of an article." Examples: decoration on a calendar, a painting on a plate, posters.
- Items relating to "character" merchandising. Examples: representation of a real person (the prime minister), a fictitious being (Bart Simpson), event (the Olympic games), or place (the National Gallery), which is "applied to an article as a feature of shape, configuration, pattern or ornament" (i.e., a mug with a picture of Bart Simpson).
- A trade-mark or label used in conjunction with products reproduced in quantities of more than 50.
- "Material that has a woven or knitted pattern or that is suitable for piece goods or surface coverings or for making wearing apparel." Examples: printed wallpaper, woven draperies.
- Buildings that qualify as architectural works of art.
- "Articles that are sold as a set, unless more than 50 sets are made." Examples: golf clubs, set of dishes.

The Governor-in-Council has the authority to specify other types of works or articles that may come under this exception and be protected by copyright.

The law as set out above is complicated, and expert advice should be sought if you think your work may cross the line between industrial design and copyright protection.

FOLKLORE

Folklore includes traditions, customs, and stories preserved among a cultural group. Examples of folklore are oral stories, songs, dances, and dance steps. In some cases, folklore may fit within one of the categories protected by copyright. However, items classified as folklore do not always fit the criteria necessary for protection of copyright materials (for instance, they are not fixed) and, as such, are not protected by copyright. Since Canadian law does not deal specifically with the protection of "nonfixed" folklore, situations will remain where folklore is not protected by copyright law.

GOVERNMENT MATERIALS

Government materials, also called "Crown works," are protected by copyright. This includes the works of federal, provincial, and territorial governments. Generally, the works of municipal governments are not considered Crown works because municipal governments are not emanations of the Crown.

FURTHER PROTECTED WORKS

Works described under this subheading refer to, and include, many of the works mentioned earlier when they are adapted, compiled, or collected in a specific way or where more than one author is involved.

Arrangements and Adaptations

Arrangements and adaptations are relevant to all copyright-protected works. An arrangement or adaptation may attract copyright protection, provided it meets the general criteria for copyright protection including originality in the form of sufficient skill and judgment. One example might be an arrangement of a Vivaldi piece. Another might be a new adaptation, that is, the piano arrangement for the orchestral score of the opera *The Merry Wives of Windsor*.[12]

An arranged or adapted work has two layers of copyright protection. There is protection in the original work, and there is protection in the arranged or adapted version. Thus, if you use an arrangement or adaptation, you must clear copyright in both the original and the arranged or adapted version. And if you are adapting a work, and the original work is protected by copyright, you must obtain permission to adapt it from the owner of the original work.

Collective Works

A collective work is "any work written in distinct parts by different authors, or in which works or parts of works of different authors are incorporated." Examples of collective works are an encyclopedia, dictionary, year book or similar work, a newspaper, review, magazine, or similar periodical—whether in print or in a digital form. Collective works need not, however, be limited to literary works. A collective work may be a book of photographs or musical works. Also, a protected collective work need not be composed of works that are protected by copyright. There can be copyright in a collective work when elements, or all of the portions, making up the collective work are in the public domain. Further, there may be copyright in a collective work comprising previously published materials. For example, there may be copyright in a collection of *Best Canadian Short Stories of 2014* containing short stories by different authors that have previously been published in magazines and literary journals.

In order for a work to qualify as a collective work, there must be originality in the making of the work. In this sense, the originality relates to the skill and judgment exerted to make the collective work. For example, a mere joining of two individual works will probably not constitute a collective work. Whether there is sufficient skill and judgment in the making of a collective work is a question that must be examined based upon the circumstances in each individual case.

It is important to understand that two copyrights may exist where there is a collective work. First, there is copyright in the collective work itself, and, second, there is copyright in each individual work included in the collection, provided that copyright already exists in those individual works and the individual works are not in the public domain. For example, in the case of a newspaper, there is copyright in the newspaper as a whole. As well, there is copyright in each individual article in the newspaper.

Works of Joint Authorship

A work of joint authorship is sometimes confused with a collective work. However, the definitions of these two works as they appear in the Copyright Act help distinguish them.

The Copyright Act defines a work of joint authorship as a "work produced by the collaboration of two or more authors in which the contribution of one author is not distinct from the contribution of the other author or authors." Thus in order for a work to qualify as one of joint authorship, two conditions must be met:

1. The work must be created by two or more authors.
2. The contribution of each author must not be distinct from the contribution of any of the other authors.

The above definition of a work of joint authorship should help dissolve the confusion between a collective work and a work of joint authorship. Although in both cases works are created by more than one author, it is only in the case of a work of joint authorship that the contributions of each author are not separable and indistinguishable from that of the other author. In some cases, a collective work may also be a work of joint authorship, that is, where more than one person was responsible for gathering the individual works that comprise the collective work.

An example of a work of joint authorship is the song "Revolution," which was composed by John Lennon and Paul McCartney. This does not mean that all songs are works of joint authorship, especially if the words and music are credited separately. In each case, the law, as set out above, must be applied to the particular facts at hand.

Two of the factors that might be considered in determining whether a work is one of joint authorship are that each contribution must be substantial, though not necessarily equal, and that there must be "joint labour in carrying out a common design." Providing ideas or inspiration, or involvement in the expression of ideas is not enough, especially if such a contribution did not include any research, compilation, or writing necessary to create a work. In addition, the contributions need not be made simultaneously.

A court held, in a case involving the singer Sarah McLachlan, that whether the contribution of a coauthor is significant for a coauthorship depends on both quantitative and qualitative factors, including the relation of the contribution to the work as a whole. The Court decided that in order to be considered joint authors, each author must have contributed significant original expression to the work, intended that his or her contribution be merged with that of the other author into a unitary whole, and intended the other person to be a joint author of the work.[13]

One case has held that a person who merely suggests certain ideas without contributing anything to the literary or dramatic form of the work is not a joint author. However, where two people jointly write a book or screenplay, for example, and only one of them is actually putting the ideas, etc., on paper, both persons would most likely be considered joint authors.

A work that is created by more than one person using collaborative tools such as project management platforms, software, and/or created in an online space may be considered a joint work. This includes documents created by those in other cities, countries, and time zones.

Since there is only one work created when there are two or more authors of a work, there is only one copyright in a work of joint authorship. (However, if a collective work is also a work of joint authorship, there may be more than one copyright by nature of it being a collective work.)

Compilations

A compilation, in copyright parlance, is very close to the everyday meaning of the word. Basically, a compilation is the result of the gathering of materials from other sources. For example, an encyclopedia, dictionary, or DVD may qualify as a compilation. A compilation of reported judicial decisions was held by the Supreme Court of Canada to be an original work in which copyright subsists.[14] If the compilation is a compilation of works written by different authors, then the compilation is also a collective work.

For purposes of determining whether a compilation has copyright protection, it does not matter if the sources from which the data or information is gathered are protected by copyright, easily accessible, or in the public domain. However, if the sources are protected by copyright, the compiler must clear copyright in these works before including them in the compilation.

The Copyright Act defines a compilation as "a work resulting from the selection or arrangement of literary, dramatic, musical or artistic works or parts thereof, or a work resulting from the selection or arrangement of data." Whether a compilation is a compilation of literary, artistic, or other type of work is a matter of fact to be determined in each particular situation. It is difficult to predict how a court of law might determine the category of work in which to classify the compilation. For example, is a compilation containing five literary works, one musical work, and three artistic works a literary work compilation? It is possible that the test would be based on the duration of the works; that is, if there is a musical work seven minutes long and three readings of literary works each one minute long, the compilation could be classified as a combination of text and photographs or text and sounds and moving images. With text and photographs, the comparison could be the number of square inches or the number of bytes although, again, this is impossible to predict. It is most likely to be determined on a quantitative basis where a single large work, whether in duration or bytes or square inches, could outweigh more numerous works in a different category. The categorization of a compilation is important for such things as voluntary registration with the Canadian government, duration of copyright, and rights protected.

A compilation is protected by copyright if certain elements went into the making of it. Whether a work would be considered a compilation is a matter of fact, which must be decided based on the circumstances in each individual case. Some factors a court might take into account in making this factual determination would be the compiler's knowledge, experience, judgment, skill, evaluation of options, arrangement, and selection put into the making of the compilation.

Generally, there is only one copyright in a compilation; that is, the copyright in the compilation itself. However, if the materials that form the compilation enjoy copyright protection, they will continue to enjoy copyright and moral rights protection on their own. If there is a collection of compilations, that collection may qualify as a collective work.

Databases

Simply put, a database is an assembly or compilation of facts, data, content, or information in an organized format and whose individual components may be individually accessed. A database may be as simple as a collection of names and phone numbers, or as complex as a listing of every article ever written on astrology or a library catalogue.

In copyright parlance, a database could be considered a compilation, as it is a compilation of information. Thus, electronic and nonelectronic databases are protected by copyright. In order for a database to be protected by copyright, it has to meet the general criteria of compilations; for instance, there must be sufficient original skill and judgment put into the selection and arrangement of data.

Note that it is the database itself, the collection of data, and not the information contained in the database that is protected by copyright.

This is similar to the concept that an idea is not protected by copyright, only the expression of it. The components in a database are separate from the database, and if they are protected by copyright (for instance, they are eligible for protection or the duration of their protection has not expired), they continue to be protected as a separate copyright-protected work from the database. If these components are not protected by copyright, when compiled as a database, they do not by themselves acquire a separate copyright in them. However, whatever the copyright status of its underlying individual components, the database itself may have its own copyright protection.

Under Canadian copyright law, some databases, whether digital or not, are not protected by copyright. This is because these databases do not meet one of the general criterions for copyright protection—sufficient originality—which means that skill and judgment involved in the arranging and selecting of the content in the database is too low.

Blank Forms

Blank forms—that is, forms with grids or boxes into which information can be placed—may be protected by copyright. For copyright purposes, these forms may be classified as compilations (e.g., they could be compilations of literary or artistic works). As compilations, these forms must possess some literary information in the copyright meaning of this phrase. For instance, if the forms are more than mere copies of other forms, and skill and judgment are used in making them, they may be protected by copyright.

SOCIAL MEDIA

For purposes of this book, the term *social media* encompasses various terms such as *social networking* and *user-generated content* that relate to both content and the way in which we share and use content. In this section, we are specifically examining content created, published, and shared on social media sites and whether that content is protected by copyright. Such content includes text, images, music, and videos—content discussed under various headings in this chapter—and is protected whether in print, analog, or digital media. As social media continue to evolve, there will be many more circumstances where it is necessary to apply the current law to newer social media. Below are two types of social media that may be of interest.

Twitter

The popular social media site Twitter allows the use of messages up to 140 characters. These messages are called tweets. Whether a tweet is protected by copyright depends on the circumstances and whether that tweet meets the originality requirement discussed in Chapter 3.[15]

User-Generated Content (UGC)

User-generated content may be broadly described as content that an individual uploads to the Internet. UGC may include a comment on a blog or a blog itself; a book review or comment you post on Chapters. ca or Amazon; content uploaded on social networking sites, including Facebook, Flickr, YouTube, and LinkedIn; content uploaded to wikis such as Wikipedia; and content in virtual sites such as Second Life. This content may include any of the types of works protected by copyright as discussed in this chapter. In determining whether your UGC is protected by copyright, follow the same general guidelines set out in this chapter. (However, also be aware that when sharing your content, you may be providing implied consent to the content's further use and you may be subject to certain terms and conditions as set out on the Internet site where you post the content.)

OTHER SUBJECT-MATTER

Performers' performances, sound recordings, and communication (or broadcast) signals are nontraditional copyright materials referred to as "other subject-matter" in the Copyright Act. They are protected on a different basis than works, and issues like authorship and originality, which are discussed in various parts of this book, do not apply to these nontraditional copyright materials.

Performers' Performances

For purposes of copyright law, the term *performer's performance* refers to live performances such as a musician performing a song, a person reading a novel or poem, or an actor acting in a play. It also includes a performance of a work in the public domain or one that has not been recorded, an improvisation of a dramatic, musical, or literary work such as a jam session—and a recorded performance of an actor, author, singer, musician, and dancer on a variety of media including tape, CDs, DVDs, video and film, digital pad, smartphone, and compilations of these recordings.

Note that copyright protection in a performer's performance is different from and separate from the right of public performance, which is the right to perform a copyright-protected work as opposed to a right in the performance itself.

Sound Recordings

The Copyright Act defines a sound recording as "a recording, fixed in any material form, consisting of sounds, whether or not of a performance of a work" and it specifically excludes a soundtrack of a film where the soundtrack accompanies the film. Examples of sound recordings include a recording of a bird chirping, music, an acted-out drama, a recording of an oral history, audio books, a lecture, and recorded seminars. Even recordings of works that are in the public domain such as a Bach Prelude may be protected as a sound recording. Also included are compilations of sound recordings, for example, on a CD. The sound recording would be protected on any sort of media including vinyl, tape, CD, DAT (digital audio tape), on a computer or portable drive, online, or on any digital recording device.

An important and difficult concept to grasp is that three copyrights may exist when a sound recording is involved. First, there is copyright protection in the sound recording. Second, there may be copyright in any protected works embodied on the sound recording. Third, there may be a copyright in a performer's performance. These are important concepts to keep in mind when determining what rights attach to a work reproduced on a sound recording.

Music Videos

Different components of a music video may be protected in different manners. For instance, the soundtrack to a music video may be separately protected, arguably as a sound recording, though the category under which it would be protected is subject to debate. The visual aspect of the video may be protected in the same manner as other audiovisual works, discussed earlier.

Communication or Broadcast Signals

The Act defines a communication signal as "radio waves transmitted through space without any artificial guide, for reception by the public." Protected broadcasts include television broadcasts and pay-per-view broadcasts, but not satellite or cable retransmitted signals. A radio signal is also protected.

SUMMARY

Canadian copyright law protects, explicitly and implicitly, a broad variety of creations or "works" under the categories of literary, dramatic, musical, and artistic works. Adaptations, collective works, compilations, and works of joint authorship are also protected by copyright. In addition, copyright protects other subject-matter such as performers' performances, sound recordings, and broadcast signals. The classification of a work or other subject-matter protected by copyright is important with respect to duration of protection, ownership, and the rights of copyright owners.

CHAPTER 7

WHO OWNS COPYRIGHT?

Those who follow are always behind.

—A.Y. Jackson

OWNING COPYRIGHT

Recall from Chapter 2 that every creation has two property rights. There is a right in the physical property of the creation, and there is a separate and distinct right in its intangible property. The right in the physical ownership of a book is separate and distinct from copyright and, for instance, the right to adapt that book into a film. This chapter focuses on the second right—the intangible right—which you now know is copyright.

The ownership of copyright is important because it determines who has control over, and who is entitled to remuneration from, that protected material. The owner, who may or may not also be the author of a work, is the sole person with the exclusive right to say yes or no to a particular use of that work. He or she is the one who benefits from the exploitation of a copyright-protected work, and is the one to be contacted in order to obtain permission to use the work. Chapter 9 discusses the rights the Copyright Act provides to owners of copyright-protected works.

THE GENERAL RULE

The general rule of ownership is stated in the Copyright Act as the following: "Subject to this Act, the author of a work shall be the first owner of the copyright therein."

Who Is the Author of a Work Protected by Copyright?

According to the general rule of ownership of copyright-protected works, the author of a work is the work's first owner. This raises the question, who is the author of a work? There is no one definite definition of "author" in the Act. Court cases have helped interpret the meaning of author in the copyright sense.

According to these cases, the author is the person who creates the work, or the first person to express the idea in a tangible form; for example, the person who puts the work on paper or otherwise "fixes" it. A person who writes a book is its author; a person who draws a painting is its author; a person who composes a musical work is the author of the song, and a person who designs graphics for a web page is the author of those graphics. A stenographer, however, would not be considered an author, although a ghostwriter probably would be.

In determining the author of a work, remember the general copyright principle that copyright does not protect ideas but only the expressions of those ideas. It follows from this principle that the author is not the person who merely supplies ideas, but the person who expresses those ideas. However, if two people are jointly writing a screenplay, for example, and only one of them is actually putting the ideas in a tangible form (e.g., on paper), these persons would most likely be considered joint authors. However, someone who comments, edits, or suggests changes to a work would not likely be a coauthor of that work, unless the contributions were concrete enough to be a tangible part of the expressed idea. Also, where an author originally puts down an idea in a rough form and a second writer rewrites it, these authors would probably be considered coauthors of the finished work. The clearer situation is for coauthors or creators working together to clearly set out their intention (best in writing) to be coauthors to establish that joint authorship.

Some provisions in the Copyright Act are specific about the "author" of certain copyright-protected works. Where there is no such provision, the guidelines set out above must be applied to your particular case to determine the author of the work.

This book uses the terms *author* and *creator* interchangeably.

Although the author and owner of a copyright-protected work may be the same person, this is not necessarily the case. Different provisions in the Copyright Act distinctly speak of author and owner. For example, duration of copyright is based on the life of the author. Exploitation of copyright-protected works can only be by copyright owners. Moral rights only protect authors of copyright-protected works. The distinction between author and owner is referred to throughout this book.

There are no authors of other subject-matter, just owners, as is discussed later in this chapter.[1]

The Second and Subsequent Owners of Copyright in Works

Although the general rule is that the author is the first owner of copyright, the rule is qualified by the proviso "subject to the Act." The Act contemplates a number of specific circumstances where this general rule does not apply. The rule may not apply with regard to specific works and with regard to specific situations. Before assuming that the general rule of ownership applies in your particular case, check the discussion below in light of your specific circumstances.

Keep in mind that the owner of the copyright in a work can, and often does, change. This subject is further discussed in Chapter 11, "How Can Rights Be Exploited?"

SPECIFIC WORKS

Specific works that do not follow the general rule of ownership, or to which the general rule is difficult to apply, are discussed below.

Where your situation falls within one of the specific works, also check that one of the specific situations in the subsequent section does not override the principle set out with respect to the specific work.

Letters, E-Mail, and Other Correspondence

Normally, when you write a letter or e-mail, whether a personal or business letter or e-mail, you are the owner of copyright in that letter or e-mail. Even after a letter has been mailed, faxed, or e-mailed to someone, the author of the letter retains the ownership of copyright in it. Thus, only the author of the letter or e-mail has the right to reproduce it in a print or electronic book or in any other format.

The exception to this rule is business correspondence written as part of one's job. In that case, the employer will own the copyright in it.

Photographs

For any photographs taken November 7, 2012, and later, the photographer is the author of the photograph and the first owner of copyright in the photograph. This author may not be a corporate entity.

For photographs taken prior to November 7, 2012, the author of a photograph is the person or corporate entity who owns the initial negative or other plate at the time when that negative or other plate was made. If there is no negative or other plate, the author is the owner of the initial photograph at the time when that photograph was made. The author is the first owner of copyright in the photograph. Also, see the discussion below on portraits and on commissioned works.

Although the Act uses the terms *plates* and *negatives*, it is likely that modern equivalents of plates and negatives are captured by these older terms.

Portraits

Ownership of a portrait vests in the creator of that portrait. Also see section below, Commissioned Photographs and Portraits.

Audiovisual Works

Audiovisual works are subject to the general rule of ownership; however, it is not always straightforward who is the author and therefore first owner of copyright of an audiovisual work.

Scripted Works

The author or first owner of copyright in a scripted audiovisual work (or film) is not expressly identified in the Act. This is a matter of controversy.[2] Some argue that the author is the producer of the film (i.e., the one principally responsible for the arrangements undertaken for the making of the film), while others argue that a film's director, or even a screenwriter, is its author. It is further arguable that the producer is the owner and the author is the director (by himself or herself or along with other contributors to the film). There is no Canadian case law on this point. Unlike ownership of copyright, authorship is a matter of law and cannot be changed by contractual arrangements. Once one decides who is the author of an audiovisual work, then the general rule—author as first owner—is applied. Notwithstanding who owns the copyright in a film, the author of the film owns the moral rights in it and duration of protection is based on the author's life. Because the duration of a scripted audiovisual work is based on the life of the work's author, a corporation could not be the author of the work.

Although the author or first owner of copyright in a scripted audiovisual work is not specifically mentioned in the Act, the Act states that the maker of a cinematographic work is "the person by whom the arrangements necessary for the making of the work are undertaken." The maker is referred to in other parts of the legislation.

Although a film is a copyright work itself, the screenwriter, music composer, stage designer, and others continue to have copyright in the works they created for the film.

Nonscripted Works

Like scripted works, the author of a nonscripted work is not expressly identified for in the Act and is a matter of controversy. Where a production company hires and is the employer of a director and producer, the company is the first owner of copyright in the nonscripted work; however, this does not help determine who is the author of the work.

Nonscripted Works Made before January 1, 1994

For nonscripted works made prior to January 1, 1994, the author and first owner is the owner of the medium of fixation regardless of whether it is a negative or magnetic tape.

Musical Works

The law is unclear with respect to the ownership of musical works. This is because of the confusion over whether musical works are subject to two copyrights—one in the music as a musical work and a second one in the lyrics as a literary work. Where the same person creates the tune and lyrics, ownership in that song, as tune and lyrics, vest in that one person. Also, where two or more people together write a tune and lyrics and the contribution of each person is indistinguishable from that of the other person, then those two or more persons are joint authors of the song. However, the situation is not as straightforward where one author writes the lyrics and another person composes the tune. It is arguable that each contributor owns copyright in his or her contribution and that they jointly own copyright in the song as a whole.

In practice, most copyrights in musical works are assigned (that is, ownership is transferred) to a music publisher who then administers on behalf of the authors the rights in the musical works. Thus, the vast majority of copyright permissions can be cleared through the music publisher, without regard to authorship ambiguities. Where there is no music publisher, permission to use the song should be sought from both authors whether the contribution of each person is distinct or indistinguishable from that of the other person(s). The right of public performance in a musical work is almost always cleared through SOCAN, a copyright collective, which is discussed in detail in Chapter 14, "Legally Using Content."

Newspaper, Magazine, or Periodical Contributions

This subheading refers to any contributions to newspapers, magazines, or periodicals, including contributions by writers and photographers. Recall that copyright does not exist in news, facts, and information, but in the manner in which these things are conveyed. As such, the contributions referred to in this section are not news, facts, or information, but expressions in any format of the news items, facts, or information. For purposes of this discussion, newspaper, magazine, and periodical contributors will be divided into two categories: freelancers and staff persons.

Freelancers (Such as Authors, Photographers, and Illustrators)

As a general rule, freelancers are authors and first copyright owners of their individual contributions to newspapers, magazines, or periodicals, unless they have agreed otherwise. For purposes of clarity, it is prudent for a freelancer to have a written agreement with the publisher that explicitly states what uses may be made of the freelancer's contribution. For instance, may an article or image be published in both print and electronic format? (Licensing works is discussed in Chapter 11.)

A Supreme Court of Canada case underlines the need for freelancers to specifically address copyright and authorized uses in written agreements. In this case, a national newspaper included (without permission) two articles by a freelancer from its print edition in three electronic databases.[3] There were no written agreements addressing the copyright in the two articles. The court allowed the national paper to include the articles in a compendium of daily newspaper editions in a CD-ROM without obtaining permission from the freelancer. However, new collective works or electronic databases of various articles including those two articles did require permission from the copyright owner of the two articles.

Staff Persons

Staff persons are also authors of their contributions, but are in a different position from freelancers with respect to copyright ownership. Generally, staff persons or "employed" persons have no copyright in their distinct contributions to newspapers, magazines, or similar periodicals. In these cases, the employer of the staff person owns the copyright in that work, but this is a limited type of ownership: the author has the right to prohibit the work's publication outside of a newspaper, magazine, or similar periodical. These rules apply unless there is an agreement to the contrary.

Collective Works

If you recall, a *collective work* is "any work written in distinct parts by different authors, or in which works or parts of works of different authors are incorporated." Examples of collective works are a newspaper, an anthology, and an encyclopedia. Two or more separate copyrights may exist in a collective work. Copyright exists in the collective work itself and separately in each individual work that is part of that collection.

With respect to the collection as a whole, the person who selects or arranges the works that go into the collection is the author and first owner of the copyright in it. This means that the authors of the individual contributions are not joint owners of the copyright in the collection. There may be circumstances where there is more than one owner of copyright in a collective work. This may occur where more than one person was responsible for "collecting" the individual works that comprise the collection. In this case, these persons may be considered joint authors and co-owners of the collection.

With respect to the individual contributions that make up a collective work, the individual copyright holders of these contributions continue to hold copyright in them.

An example best illustrates the concept of ownership in collective works. Let's look at a collection of poems. In our example, prior to the collection being compiled, each poet has copyright in his or her poems (and none is in the public domain). When a collection is made of these poems, there are two different layers of copyright ownership. Each individual poet will continue to own copyright in his or her contribution; the compiler of the collection of poems will own copyright in the collection as a whole. The same principles apply in the case of a magazine. There is copyright in the entire magazine that may, for example, belong to the publisher, and there may also be copyright in each individual article in that magazine, belonging to the author of each article (provided the authors are freelance writers and are not employees of the publisher).

Compilations

A compilation is a selection or arrangement of parts or wholes of copyright-protected works or data, resulting in a new work such as a dictionary or database. The person responsible for making the compilation is the author and first copyright owner of that compilation. If copyright subsisted in any of the works from which the compilation was made, the copyright owners of those works would continue to hold copyright in them. The compiler must clear copyright in any copyright-protected underlying works.

A website illustrates the concept of ownership in a compilation. The person who operates the website—compiles the content on it—is the author and first copyright owner of that website. This is true whether this person creates all original content to post on the website, publishes pre-existing content of his or her own or by others, or posts content that is in the public domain. The website owner may need to obtain permission to use content on his or her website. If any of the content on the website enjoys copyright protection, the owners of that content will continue to own copyright separate from the ownership of copyright in the website as a whole.

Adaptations and Arrangements

Examples of adaptation or arrangement include turning a book into a screenplay, and scoring a musical work composed for violin or piano. The author and first copyright owner in these "new" works is the person who adapts the work, in the above examples, the screenwriter and person who creates the new musical score.

Note that permission must be sought from the copyright owner of the original work before adapting it. Also, use of an adaptation may require copyright permission from both the copyright owner of the original work and the copyright holder of the adaptation. Further, not every adaptation is a new copyright work; as explained in the previous chapter, the adaptation must involve a sufficient level of skill and judgment to qualify as a copyright-protected work.

Translations

The author and first copyright owner of a translation is the person who produces the translation.

Permission must be obtained from the copyright owner of the original work before a translation is begun. If a third person wants to use the translation, for example, for broadcast, permission must be obtained from both the copyright owner of the original work and the copyright holder of the translation.

Papers, Dissertations, and Other School Work

The author and first owner of any paper, dissertation, or other work prepared for school courses and degree programs is the author of the work; that is, the student preparing the paper, dissertation, and so forth. This is true unless the author has assigned the copyright to someone else.

SPECIFIC SITUATIONS

Commissioned Works

Commissioned works belong to the author and not to the commissioner of the works, unless the commissioner and author enter into an agreement stating otherwise. Then it is up to the parties to the agreement to decide on the appropriate terms and conditions of the commission.

Commissioned Photographs and Portraits

On or after November 7, 2012, if a photograph or portrait is commissioned, the photographer or creator of the portrait (e.g., painter) is still the owner of the copyright. However, if the photograph or portrait was commissioned by an individual for personal purposes and made for valuable consideration, that individual may use the photograph or portrait for private or noncommercial purposes, or permit its use, unless the individual and copyright owner have agreed otherwise. For example, a bride can make copies of her wedding photographs, or post commissioned wedding photographs on her family blog or on Facebook.

Before November 7, 2012, a special rule applies. For these works, the person ordering the work is deemed to be the first owner of the copyright if the following conditions were met:

- The person ordering the work offered valuable consideration, such as money or services.
- The work was created because of the order and was not created prior to the order being made.

This holds true provided there is no agreement between the commissioner and the creator stating that copyright subsists with the creator of the work.

Works Made in the Course of Employment

Many of the principles concerning ownership of specific works are reversed where these works are made in the course of employment.

Works made in the course of employment may include anything from letters to internal memoranda to computer software to film scripts to photographs. Some employees are employed for the purpose of creating copyright-protected works, such as scriptwriters, website designers, and photographers, where others incidentally create copyright-protected works while performing their regular tasks, for example, lawyers or policy analysts. The discussion here applies equally to all types of employment situations.

The general principle regarding works made in the course of employment is that copyright ownership in such works initially belongs to the employer. There are three criteria that must be met in order for a work to be owned by an employer:

1. The employee must be employed under a "contract of service."
2. The work must be created in the course of performing this contract.
3. There must not be any contract or provision in a contract (in writing or otherwise) that states that the employee owns the copyright.

The Copyright Act does not set out exactly what constitutes an employment relationship, and each situation must be determined according to the facts of that particular situation. These are some of the factors and questions a court may examine when determining whether there is an employment relationship:

- Did the employee conceive the work during employment?
- Did the employer give orders to create the specific work?
- Did the employer give orders on how the work was to be done?
- Was the work carried out under the supervision of the employer?

- Did the employer have control over the author's work?
- Was the work created as part of the ordinary duties of the creator?
- Was the work created in the course of the employment or employment contract?
- Was the work created during the normal hours of employment?
- Was the work created on the employer's premises?
- Was the work created for the business (as opposed to being created for personal use)?
- Is the work closely related to the type of business of the employer?
- Was the work created for the exclusive use of the business?

Where the majority of answers to the above questions are in the affirmative, then you are leaning towards an "employment" situation.

An example where copyright belongs to an employer is the case where a math teacher creates examination papers to be used with the teacher's students. On the other hand, if this same teacher writes a work of fiction during the weekends, he or she would own copyright in that fiction work. Another example where an employer would own the copyright is in photographs taken by a staff photographer; however, photographs taken by the same photographer while on vacation belong to the photographer.

Copyright conditions in any employment situation may be reversed by a contract. A contract granting copyright to employees for works made in the course of employment may be done individually for each work, or generally for all works made during the term of employment. All items in such an agreement are negotiable.

Because an employment situation always depends on the particular facts of the case, it is best to have a written agreement that sets out whether or not it is an employment situation, at least for purposes of ownership of copyright materials.

Note that even where employers own copyright in their employees' creations, the employees are still the authors of these creations. This is important with respect to the duration of copyright protection, and also with respect to moral rights.

Working in Other Countries

If you are working in other countries or are working in Canada for a foreign company, you may be subject to different cultures, laws. and contractual relationships concerning the ownership of copyright-protected works. Be sure to check your contracts and also read Chapter 5, "Canada and International Copyright Law," which sets out principles relating to international copyright. Chapter 15 contains specific information on how the United States deals with works created in the course of employment.

Works Created During an Apprenticeship

Works created during an apprenticeship are subject to the same rules as works created during the course of employment.

Independent Contractors

Independent contractors, including professionals and consultants, are the authors of, and generally own the copyright in, their works, unless they have agreed otherwise. Thus, lawyers or self-employed statisticians will own the copyright in any documents they prepare, even if on behalf of a client, unless they have agreed otherwise. Whether you are an employee or an independent contractor is a question of fact that can only be determined by examining your particular circumstances. In order to help determine whether you qualify as an independent contractor, go through the questions listed under the subheading "Works Made in the Course of Employment," as these are the questions a court would consider when determining the same.

Works Made for or Published by the Government

The Copyright Act states that where any work is, or has been, prepared or published by or under the direction or control of any government department, the copyright in that work belongs to the government. This is subject to any agreement to the contrary.

Government employees include those employed in federal or provincial government departments as well as Crown Corporations.

Even where the government owns copyright in works prepared by or under its direction or control, the creators of these works are their authors.

Works Made by Two or More Authors

There are two types of works that may be made by two or more authors. One type is a collective work, which is discussed above under specific works, and the second, discussed here, is a work of joint authorship.

A work of joint authorship is a work produced by the collaboration of two or more authors in which the contribution of one author is not distinct from the contribution of the other author or authors.

There is only one copyright in the case of works of joint authorship. Coauthors of "works of joint authorship" are co-owners of the work. They must jointly exercise their rights in the specific copyright-protected work. Neither author is an exclusive owner of the copyright in the work, and neither author can authorize the use of the work without the other author's approval. For example, neither co-writer of a screenplay can license the right to a producer to produce the screenplay without the permission of the other co-writer.

A work of joint authorship may also be a collective work if the joint authors produced the resulting work from other sources or works. In this situation, there will be two copyrights and two copyright owners—the joint authors will own the copyright in the collective work, and each individual author will own copyright in his or her individual contribution (provided copyright still exists in the contribution).

Corporations

Corporations may also be owners of copyright materials where an author has assigned copyright to them or in the case of employed, apprenticed, or commissioned creators. Corporations may also be able to use copyright materials through contractual arrangements (e.g., licences as discussed in Chapter 11) with the creator or copyright owner.

Works Generated by, and with the Aid of, Computer Software

The Copyright Act does not specifically address the situation of works generated with the aid of computers and computer programs. In general, if you create, control, and manipulate an image or other copyright material with the help of a computer or computer program (including an online-only program), you are the author of the new work (assuming that it is considered an original work for copyright purposes). Whether you own that creation depends on the factors discussed in this chapter set out for the determination of ownership of creations. By creating works with the help of a computer program, you will never acquire rights in that computer program. Also, keep in mind that you require permission to scan a copyright-protected work into a computer and to adapt or manipulate it.

Where a copyright work is generated by a computer in a circumstance where there is no human author, the author would probably be the person who made the necessary arrangements (i.e., controlled or manipulated the computer in order to create the copyright-protected work).

OTHER SUBJECT-MATTER

The above rules relating to who is the author and owner of a work do not apply to other subject-matter. Specific rules for other subject-matter are set out next.

Performer's Performances

The performer owns the copyright in his or her performance.

Sound Recordings

The "maker" of a sound recording owns the copyright in it. A "maker" is defined as "the person by whom the arrangements necessary for the first fixation of the sounds are undertaken," normally the record company that pays for the sound recording. For works not previously in a fixed form, such as a jam session, impromptu speech, interview, or oral history, the person who first fixes or arranges for the first fixation of the recording will be the owner of the sound recording.

Communication or Broadcast Signals

The broadcaster who broadcasts a signal owns the copyright in it. The Act defines a broadcaster as "a body that, in the course of operating a broadcasting undertaking, broadcasts a communication signal in accordance with the law of the country in which the broadcasting undertaking is carried on." It excludes a body whose primary activity regarding communication signals is their retransmission.

MORAL RIGHTS

This section will look at ownership of moral rights. You may wish to first read the full description of moral rights set out in Chapter 9, "Rights Protected by Copyright," then return to this portion, which discusses the ownership of these rights.

The purpose of moral rights is to protect the honour and reputation of an author. Since moral rights protect the author directly and are "personal" rights, they cannot be exercised except by authors or their heirs. Even after copyright has been assigned in a work, moral rights remain with the author. This is also true in employment situations. Even where an employer is, by virtue of employment, the owner of copyright in a work, the employee retains the moral rights in his or her creations. In short, moral rights cannot be assigned, but they can be waived (i.e., the author agrees not to exercise them); and they can be bequeathed to a beneficiary under the author's will. For further discussion on this topic, see waiving moral rights in Chapter 11, "How Can Rights Be Exploited?"

An example will illustrate the concept of ownership of moral rights. Mr. Smart purchases a painting of a lady and when doing so also expressly purchases the copyright in the painting. Because Mr. Smart owns the copyright in the painting, he can do anything with the painting that only the copyright owner may do. For example, he can reproduce the painting (e.g., photograph it or scan it into a computer) or exhibit it in public. However, notwithstanding that he owns copyright in the painting, he cannot do anything with that painting that might violate the author's moral rights (unless he has obtained a waiver of the moral rights). For example, Mr. Smart cannot put a moustache on the lady's face or use the painting in association with a service, cause, or institution in a manner that may be prejudicial to the honour or reputation of the artist.

Other Subject-Matter

A performer enjoys certain moral rights in his or her performance.

OWNERSHIP OF CONTENT IN SOCIAL MEDIA

Ownership of content in social media only warrants its own section due to its relative newness. The same rules discussed throughout this chapter apply to ownership of all content. For example, the author is the first owner of an article or a photograph whether it is in print or on a social media site such as Facebook. The author is the first person who fixes the work, for example, in print (then scans it), or saves it on his or her computer (in hard drive or RAM), or posts it (also considered a fixation) on a social media site. The use of content or posting content on social media does not change who is the author of the content under the Copyright Act (though a contract may assign the ownership of the work).

If the author is employed and the content is created for the purpose of social media as part of his or her employment duties (as further discussed above under "Works Made in the Course of Employment"), the employer is the first owner, and the author continues to hold moral rights in the content (unless the moral rights have been waived). If the content is created outside the scope of employment, then the content creator is both the author and first owner of the content.

SUMMARY

The general rule of ownership in copyright is that the author of a work is the first owner of the copyright therein. The author is the person who first fixes the work. There are a number of exceptions to this general rule that apply with respect to a number of specific works, and in a number of specific situations. Further, copyright ownership can change through contractual arrangements.

There are special rules for ownership of other subject-matter.

Notwithstanding the ownership of copyright in a work, moral rights always belong to the author of the work. Moral rights cannot be assigned, but they can be waived or passed on upon death.

CHAPTER 8

THE DURATION OF COPYRIGHT

Be ready when opportunity comes. . . . Luck is the time when preparation and opportunity meet.

— Pierre Elliott Trudeau (1919–2000)

A LIMITED DURATION

Unlike physical property, ownership in copyright material has a limited duration. Whereas you can own your house for an indefinite amount of time, you can only own the copyright in your book or sculpture for the period of time stipulated in the Copyright Act.

GENERAL RULE FOR WORKS

There is a general rule concerning the duration of copyright. The general rule applies unless specific provisions exist in the Act for that type of work or situation. These specific provisions are outlined below and should be read along with the general rule.

General Rule

The Copyright Act provides the general rule for the length of copyright protection for published works as "the life of the author, the remainder of the calendar year in which the author dies, and a period of 50 years following the end of that calendar year." Those familiar with copyright often refer to this duration as the life-plus-50 rule. According to the life-plus-50 rule, an author will enjoy copyright in a work he or she creates throughout his or her lifetime, and his or her heirs or assignees will enjoy copyright for a period of 50 years until the calendar year end after the author's death. In certain circumstances, the life-plus-50 rule does not apply. Departures from the general rule are discussed further on.

AUTHOR VERSUS OWNER OF A WORK

It is important, in terms of duration of copyright, to distinguish between the author and the owner of a copyright work. The term of copyright is determined by the life of the author, and not by the life of the owner of copyright. This is relevant where copyright has been transferred, or when certain provisions of the law such as the provision dealing with works made during the course of employment grant copyright to someone other than the author of the work. In these situations, duration of copyright is still determined by the life of the author. Where duration is tied to the life of the author, the date when the work was created or first published is irrelevant with respect to the term of copyright protection.

The determination of the author and owner of a copyright-protected work is discussed in the previous chapter on ownership of copyright works.

CALCULATION OF THE DURATION

Calculation of the duration of copyright is based on the calendar year plus 50 years, as opposed to the actual date of the author's death. For instance, if a writer died on November 26, 1970, copyright in his or her books expires on December 31, 2020. In fact, most creations of the same author (unless any creations are subject to a specific provision other than the general rule of copyright) will be protected for the same amount of time. Therefore, all of our exemplified writer's published books will be protected until December 31, 2020.

Not long ago, copyright in Canada expired 50 years after the exact date of the author's death, and not at the end of the calendar year. Thus, in the above example, copyright in our writer's books would expire on November 26, 2020. The "calendar year" duration applies to all works protected by copyright as of January 11, 1994 (i.e., they were not then in the public domain), no matter when the works were created.

Unexploited Works

The Copyright Act used to distinguish the duration of protection on the basis of whether the work was exploited. The term *exploit* in this situation refers to publication, performance in public (which includes delivery of a lecture), and communication to the public by telecommunication. Published does not mean published in the sense of a book publisher publishing a book. In copyright parlance, "published" is a broader concept that includes making copies of the work available to the public in quantities that satisfy the reasonable demands of the public, taking into account the nature of the work in question. Performance in public means a performance outside a family or quasi-family circle. The meaning of publication, performance in public, and communication to the public by telecommunication are further explored in Chapter 9, "Rights Protected by Copyright."

Previous Law

In order to have perspective on the current law with respect to the duration of copyright in unexploited works, this section explains the previous law. Until relatively recently, unexploited works were protected in perpetuity, or until published or performed in public. Under the previous law, if a work was first published or performed in public after the death of the author it was protected for 50 years from the date of that publication or performance regardless of how long the author had been dead.

The purpose of perpetual copyright protection in unexploited works was to protect authors and copyright owners from derogations of their private rights. For instance, there may be a desire not to publish certain letters, diaries, sketches, and manuscripts. It was believed that if perpetual copyright did not exist, that some authors would destroy their works rather than have them ever fall into the public domain. Perpetual copyright in unpublished works has been a major cause of frustration to historians and researchers who can have access to these works, but may not use them in the copyright sense; for example, they may not reproduce or publish them.

Current Law

Perpetual copyright protection in unexploited works is being phased out; eventually all works including unexploited works will be subject to the general rule of life-plus-50. As of December 31, 1998, the general rule of duration applies to works not published or performed or communicated to the public by telecommunication (or in the case of lectures, delivered) during the life of an author. This applies to any literary, dramatic, or musical work and any engraving. For example, if an author died after December 31, 1998, with an unpublished manuscript or book, the manuscript or book is protected until the calendar year end in which the author dies and for a period of 50 years following that year-end.

Exceptions to the above include Crown or government works, which are protected until published and for an additional 50 years from the date of publication, as well as artistic works (except engravings), which have always been protected for life-plus-50 of the artist regardless of whether the work was published during the artist's lifetime.

Transitional Provisions

The Copyright Act provides a number of transitional provisions relating to unexploited works by deceased authors as of December 31, 1998. In the case of an author who died with an unexploited work that her or her heirs or estate exploited prior to December 31, 1998, the work would be protected for 50 years from the date it is exploited. Where an author died on or after December 31, 1948, and whose works remained unexploited as of December 31, 1998, the work is protected until December 31, 2048. Finally, in the case of an author who died before December 31, 1948, with an unexploited work that remained unexploited as of December 31, 1998, the work would be (and was) protected until December 31, 2003.

MORAL RIGHTS

The Copyright Act specifically states that moral rights last for the same term as the copyright in a work. Accordingly, the general rules and specific provisions set out in this chapter apply equally to the moral and economic rights. Thus, moral rights endure for the life of the author plus 50 years from the calendar year-end of the author's death. Such a term allows heirs to sue on behalf of a deceased author where it seems that a modification to a work resulted in prejudice to the author's honour or reputation, or to protect any other of the moral rights.

The durations of copyright set out in this chapter refer to the "term of copyright," but this expression encompasses the moral rights as well. Thus, any durations of copyright are also the length of protection for moral rights.

SPECIFIC WORKS

Literary, Artistic, Musical, Dramatic, and Choreographic Works

The general rule of life-plus-50 applies to these works, unless specifically provided for otherwise in the following sections.

Photographs

Photographs are subject to the general rule of copyright duration, life of the author plus 50 years following the calendar year-end. This is only true for photographs created on or after November 7, 2012, or still protected by copyright on that date. Recall that only natural persons (and not corporations) can be authors of photographs created after November 7, 2012. If the durations relating to photographs are confusing, reread the section in Chapter 7 on ownership of photographs.

Any photographs that are in the public domain as of November 7, 2012, remain in the public domain. For corporate-authored photographs still protected by copyright on November 7, 2012, the duration of copyright is now life of the author plus 50 years.[1]

Photographs created by authors (and not corporations) prior to November 7, 2012, are subject to the following rules of duration. Photographs created on or before December 31, 1948, or where the author has died more than 50 years ago are in the public domain. Photographs created after December 31, 1948, where the author is still alive or died less than 50 years ago, the photograph is still protected by copyright.

Corporate-authored photographs created before November 7, 2012, are subject to the following rules of duration. If the author of the photograph was a corporation (under the previous law), the photograph is in the public domain if it was created on or before December 31, 1961. For any corporate authored photographs created between January 1, 1962, and November 6, 2012, you must determine the author of the photograph and then determine if copyright still exists in the photograph.

Audiovisual Works (i.e., Movies and Videos)

Scripted Audiovisual Works

Scripted audiovisual works are subject to the general rule of duration, until the calendar year-end 50 years after the death of the author.

Nonscripted Audiovisual Works

Nonscripted audiovisual works made since 1944 are protected for 50 years following the end of the calendar year in which they are first published or made available to the public. If copies are not made available to the public (i.e., they are not published) before the expiration of

50 years following the end of the calendar year of their making, they are protected for 50 years from the calendar year-end of their making.

Nonscripted audiovisual works made before 1944 are subject to protection for 50 years from the date of making.

SPECIFIC SITUATIONS FOR WORKS

Works Made by Two or More Authors

Collective Works

Recall that examples of collective works are anthologies such as encyclopedias or magazines. Two copyrights may exist with respect to collective works. In the case of a magazine, for instance, there is copyright in the magazine as a whole, and there is also copyright in each individual article in the magazine. Thus, there may be two different durations of copyright. In order to determine the term of copyright in each component of the collective work, first determine the author of each one and then apply the general rule of duration on one of the specific provisions. Note that because there are two layers of copyright in a collective work, one copyright may expire while the other one continues to run.

If an individual or other item in a collective work is in the public domain, it is generally possible to copy or otherwise use that individual article or item even though the collection as a whole may still be protected.

Works of Joint Authorship

The term *works of joint authorship* refers to works where there is a single copyright in a work that has been created by more than one author and the contribution of any one author is indistinguishable from that of the other author(s). Copyright in this situation is based on the death of the last living author and for 50 years thereafter until the end of the calendar year.

Authors who are nationals of countries other than Canada, the United States, and Mexico that grant a duration of copyright protection shorter than the one above for works of joint authorship cannot claim a longer term in Canada. See the discussion under "Works of Unknown Authors" in this chapter, where the identity of one of the authors in a work of joint authorship is unknown.

Works First Exploited after an Author's Death

The Copyright Act no longer has specific terms of copyright protection for posthumous works; however, for certain works or subject-matter unpublished, or not performed in public or broadcast prior to March 19, 1998, consult the Copyright Act (section 7) for details about their term of copyright.

Works of Unknown Authors

Since January 1, 1994, the Canadian Copyright Act sets out the term of copyright in works by anonymous and pseudonymous authors. Copyright in anonymous and pseudonymous works lasts for the shorter of 50 years from first publication of the work, or 75 years from the making of the work. However, if during the above term, the identify of one or more of the authors becomes commonly known, copyright subsists for the life of whichever of those authors dies last and for 50 years until the end of that calendar year.

Works Prepared in the Course of Employment

The term of copyright protection for works prepared in the course of employment is subject to the life-plus-50 rule. The life-plus-50 rule is based on the life of the author, and not the life of the employer or the copyright owner. For example, if Frances creates a report for her employer as part of her work duties, her employer owns the copyright in the report; however, the duration of copyright protection is for the duration of the life of Frances and for 50 years thereafter (until calendar year-end.)

Works Owned by the Government

The Copyright Act provides that where a work is, or has been, prepared or published by or under the direction or control of the federal, provincial, or territorial government, the copyright in the work continues for a period of 50 years to the calendar year-end from the date of the first publication of the work.

If the work is not published, then it is protected until publication plus 50 years. Some government works are never published and therefore have perpetual copyright protection.

Arrangements, Adaptations, and Translations

When determining the duration of copyright in a particular work, you should keep in mind that a new work based on a work in the public domain (i.e., copyright protection has expired), may be subject to a "new" term of copyright protection. For example, a translation of a George Walker play or an adaptation of a Mozart concerto would acquire a "new" term of copyright protection. When a work has been arranged, adapted, translated, or the like, the general rule of life-plus-50 applies to the arranged, adapted, or translated work. However, if there is insufficient skill and judgment in that adaptation, there will be no new copyright work and therefore no duration of copyright in that adaptation.

Reversionary Interest Proviso (25 Years after the Author's Death)

Where the author of a work is the first owner of the copyright in it (it is not a situation of employment, Crown works, commissioned engraving, photograph, or portrait), any copyright acquired by contract becomes void 25 years after the author's death. This does not mean that the term of copyright is affected. It means that any subsequent owner of copyright will lose his or her rights (provided the conditions apply) 25 years after the author's death. At this time, the copyright becomes part of the author's estate and only the estate has the right to deal with the copyright.

There is no reversion where the author disposes of the copyright by will for the period following the 25-year limit. Thus, the section may be avoided by bequeathing copyright for the period between 25 and 50 years after the author's death. It also does not apply where a work has been assigned as part of a collective work, or a work or part thereof, that has been licensed to be published in a collective work.

Where a literary, dramatic, or musical work or engraving was not published, performed, or delivered in public prior to an author's death, the date of calculation for the "25 years after the author's death" runs from the date of publication, performance, or delivery in public—25 years from that date.

OTHER SUBJECT-MATTER

Sound Recordings

Copyright subsists in a sound recording for 50 years from the calendar year end in which the first fixation of the sound recording occurred, or if published within 50 years of fixation, for 50 years after publication. According to the Act, a "plate" includes "any stereotype or other plate, stone, block, mould, matrix, transfer or negative used or intended to be used for printing or reproducing copies of any work, and any matrix or other appliance used or intended to be used for making or reproducing sound recordings, performers' performances or communication signals." This 50-year term applies to the original and to various copies pressed from the original.

When determining whether copyright still exists in a sound record-ing, remember that if a literary, dramatic, or musical work is embodied in the sound recording, there may be two different lengths of copy-right to consider. For example, a musical work (composed in 1933) is recorded in 1941. The composer of the musical work dies in 1984. Copyright in the sound recording lasts for 50 years from the fixation of the recording—from 1941 to December 31, 1991. Copyright in the musical work subsists for 50 years after the author's death—until December 31, 2034. The same scenario would apply to any dramatic or literary work on a sound recording.

Performer's Performance

Performances are protected for 50 years after the calendar year-end in which the performance occurs. If the performance is fixed in a sound recording, it is protected to the end of 50 years from the date it was fixed or 50 years from the date of publication of the sound recording if the recording is published within 50 years of fixation.

The moral rights in a performer's performance last for the same duration as set out in the above paragraph. Note that these moral rights only exist in performer's performance on or after November 7, 2012.

Communication Signals

Communications signals are protected for 50 years after the end of the calendar year in which the signal is first broadcast.

PUBLIC DOMAIN WORKS

Once copyright has expired in a work, the work is said to be in the "public domain." The work is no longer protected by copyright and can be used freely, without obtaining permission from or compensating, the copyright owner. For example, works of Mozart and Shakespeare are in the public domain and can be copied freely (provided the works are not adaptations). The duration of copyright cannot be extended or renewed.

Works may be copied freely even where the copyright protection granted by the Copyright Act has not expired, if the copyright owner chooses to let people freely use the work. For example, creators of computer programs sometimes decide not to exercise the copyright in their programs and allow others to freely copy them. Similarly, some blog owners may allow content from their sites to be freely copied. You should never assume that these or any other content can be copied freely unless there is evidence to support it; for instance, when it is clearly indicated on the work in explicit wording or through a licence stating so. Even when it is indicated that a work may be freely copied, determine for what purposes this is permitted. For instance, you may be able to print out a page from a website for personal purposes, but not include it in a print book or make 100 copies for your colleagues. Chapter 14, "Legally Using Content," discusses when permission to use content is necessary.

Once copyright expires, moral rights also expire, and a work may be freely adapted and used without the author's name on it. In some countries, moral rights are in perpetuity and exist even after copyright in a work expires.

SUMMARY

The duration of copyright is according to the life of the author and not owner of a work. The general rule is that copyright and moral rights protection in a work endure for 50 years from the calendar year-end after the author's death. The general rule applies unless there is a specific provision providing otherwise. In addition, there are specific durations for other subject-matter.

CHAPTER 9

RIGHTS PROTECTED BY COPYRIGHT

It's why you create characters: so you can argue with yourself.

—Michael Ondaatje

THE NATURE OF RIGHTS GRANTED BY THE COPYRIGHT ACT

Rights are acts that only a copyright owner may do, or authorize others to do, with protected material. Anyone who exercises a right without the copyright owner's permission is violating copyright and may be subject to a number of remedies set out in the Copyright Act. The remedies are discussed in Chapter 13. Legally using content is discussed in Chapter 14.

This chapter examines three kinds of rights set out in the Copyright Act: economic rights, moral rights, and rights in other subject-matter (called neighbouring rights). Copyright protects the economic interests of the creators and owners of literary, dramatic, musical, and artistic works. Moral rights protect the integrity of a work and the identification of its creator. Neighbouring rights protect the rights of performers (including their moral rights), broadcasters, and makers of sound recordings.

Copyright versus Moral Rights

Moral rights must be distinguished from copyright. In order to do this, think of copyright as economic rights; that is, those rights that can be exchanged for money. An example of economic rights is where an author grants to a publisher the right to publish his or her book in exchange for a royalty payment. These economic rights, or copyright, include a myriad of rights, or a bundle of rights such as the right to publish, reproduce, perform in public, broadcast, translate a work, and so on, as well as the right to authorize or permit any of these acts. An author has the right to "exploit" these rights in any manner he or she chooses, and the right to be monetarily compensated for such exploitation.

Moral rights are different from the economic rights of copyright. The purpose of moral rights is to protect the honour and reputation of a creator. Moral rights are closely related to the personality of an author. Moral rights cannot be exercised by any person other than the author (or an heir), and cannot be exchanged for money.

Often when the term *copyright* is used in this book and elsewhere, it means both economic rights, and moral rights (and may also include rights in other subject-matter). Sometimes, however, copyright means just economic rights. In this chapter (and book), the intended meaning will generally be revealed by the context in which the word copyright is used.

The Rights Set Out in the Copyright Act

The way rights are set out in the Copyright Act is complex. Although the bulk of rights are set out in one section of the Act, the wording is complicated. As a result, this chapter does not follow the exact order of the rights or use the exact terminology as it appears in the Act. This is an important chapter, and care should be taken in understanding the concepts in it.

The rights set out in this chapter are set out as "full" rights and do not always take into account specific provisions in the Act that may be limitations on, or exceptions from, these rights. Chapter 10 deals with these limitations or exceptions.

As you begin to discover the rights set out in the law, you may be surprised to find that certain rights are, in fact, included in the law, and others that you might have thought were rights are not actually so. This chapter examines both these kinds of "rights."

ECONOMIC RIGHTS IN LITERARY, DRAMATIC, MUSICAL, AND ARTISTIC WORKS

This section deals with economic rights in literary, dramatic, musical, and artistic works. In general, copyright owners of literary, dramatic, musical, and artistic works enjoy the same rights. However, there are some specific rights attaching to specific works, for example, the exhibition right in artistic works, and the commercial rental right for computer programs and sound recordings. These are separately discussed below.

The economic rights set out in the Act are the sole and exclusive rights of the copyright owner. Only the copyright owner has the right to exercise these economic rights or to authorize others to do so. Hence, if you want to exercise them, you need the permission of the copyright owner.

Every economic right is independent of all other economic rights. For example, the right to publish a work is distinct from the right to perform the work in public. Likewise, the right to translate a work is distinct from the right to broadcast a work. A copyright holder owns or controls one or more rights within this bundle of rights.

The Right of Reproduction

A copyright owner has the sole and exclusive right to "produce or reproduce the work or any substantial part thereof in any material form whatever." This means that a copyright owner has the initial right to bring a work into existence by producing it and to make subsequent reproductions of it. Reproduction can mean the reproduction of the work in the same format or in another format. For example, you can reproduce a play script by photocopying it or by copying it out by hand or by digitizing it. In addition, reproducing a road map in a different size and format, for example to be included in a calendar, would be considered a reproduction for copyright purposes[1] (and it may also be considered an adaptation).

Like all rights in copyright, the right of reproduction includes digital uses or digital reproductions. If you scan or digitize a photograph, you are making a digital reproduction of it and must obtain permission to do so. Likewise, if you download an article from the Internet and save it on your hard drive or print it, you are making a reproduction of a work. Posting an image or an article on a website exercises the right of reproduction (and entails the exercise of other rights as well—see following discussion).

Digital products are sometimes verbatim reproductions of text, but often the digital products change or enhance the original work. An example of an enhancement would be a DVD of *A Hard Day's Night* in which text, sound, and images are added to the original movie and book, respectively. Where an original work is adapted, or enhanced, it may involve more than reproduction rights—for instance, adaptation rights and moral rights such as the rights of integrity and association. These rights are discussed below.

The terms *electronic rights* or *e-rights* include the reproduction of a work in a digital or electronic format—which in the Copyright Act is encompassed by the right of reproduction. E-rights may also fall under other rights set out in copyright law including the right to perform a work in public and the right to communicate to the public by telecommunication (both of these rights are explained below). E-rights are not specifically mentioned or defined in the Copyright Act and do not have a precise definition. Generally, e-rights are defined in licencing agreements or contracts relating to the licence or assignment of e-rights, and are defined in a manner agreed upon by the parties signing that licence or agreement. Chapter 11, "How Can Rights Be Exploited?" discusses e-rights in more detail.

Browsing or surfing the Internet may technically be a use of the right of reproduction even though we do not necessarily perceive browsing as a reproduction. Deep or inline linking or embedding a website address in another website is likely not considered a reproduction in Canada.[2] Posting content (e.g., a photograph) on social media such as Facebook or Twitter is a reproduction of the image. Reposting an image found online is a reproduction of the image.

What Is a Substantial Part?

The right to produce or reproduce a work applies to copying an entire work or a "substantial part" of the work. Anything less than a substantial part of a work may be copied without authorization. This raises the question, "what is a substantial part?" This concept is not defined in the Act. Many court cases have, however, looked at its meaning.

Basically, there are two factors a court of law would consider when determining whether a certain use of a copyright-protected work constitutes using a substantial part of it. First, the court will examine the quantity of the work, that is, how much of the original work has been copied. Second, the court will examine the quality of the work; that is, was the portion copied "qualitatively" a substantial portion of the work copied. Even the reproduction of a small amount of a work, which is an "important" part of it, may be considered a substantial part of a work. In one case concerning a musical work, 28 bars of a song were played (which equaled 20 seconds of a four-minute song) and these 28 bars were held to "contain what is the principal air of the 'Colonel Bogey' march—the air that every one who heard the march played through would recognize as being the essential air of the 'Colonel Bogey' march."[3]

As you can see, there is no hard and fast rule to determine whether a "substantial" part of a work is being copied. In each situation, you must consider the part of the work being copied and ask whether it is qualitatively and quantitatively a substantial part of a work.

What Is a Material Form?

There is another issue you must consider with respect to the right of reproduction. The reproduced portion of the work must be in "any material form whatever." If the reproduction is not in a material form, then the copyright holder has no right to prevent the reproduction, or to authorize it.

The phrase "any material form whatever" is very broad and would encompass a variety of formats depending on, and appropriate to, the type of work in question. Photocopying a book, photographing a sculpture, or posting an image on a website are all examples of reproducing a work in a material form.

The Right of Public Performance

The right to perform a work in public, or the public performance right, gives the copyright owner the sole and exclusive right to perform the work in public, visually or acoustically. Akin to the public performance right is the right to communication to the public by telecommunication. This is the way that public performances are effected via radio, television, and the Internet. As they are similar rights, both are referred to here as the public performance right.

This right of public performance and the neighbouring right in a performer's performance are two distinct rights that are separately defined in the Copyright Act. Rights in a performer's performance are discussed later in this chapter.

Similar to the reproduction right, the right to perform a work in public is not limited to the performance of an entire work. The copyright owner has the right to authorize the public performance of a "substantial part" of the work. Anything less than a substantial part may be publicly performed without authorization. The question as to what constitutes a "substantial part," is explored above.

The right to perform a work only refers to the "public" performance of the work. Thus, a book may be read aloud at home or a film played in your living room, but if the same occurs in public (whether or not a fee is charged), permission of the copyright holder is necessary.

The term *public* is not defined in the Copyright Act, but has been discussed in a number of court decisions. It seems that when the audience is by nature domestic or quasi-domestic (a family or those living under the same roof), the performance is less likely to be considered a "public" performance. One proposed definition of public is to "include situations where individuals share living quarters by reason of their work, education, vacation or detention."

If the performance takes place in a "non-domestic" setting, it may be considered a "public" performance whether or not an admission fee is charged, or whether there is a small or large audience. In fact, there need not be an audience listening to the performance, as long as the performance is meant for an audience. Note that certain performances for specific audiences, as outlined in Chapter 10, "Limitations on Rights," are allowed under the law.

Examples of a public performance of a copyright-protected work are the presentation of a play at a community centre, the reading of a poem during a rally, the showing of a television program in a restaurant, and streaming an online movie at a health club.

The Right of Publication

The copyright holder has the sole and exclusive right to first publish a work (i.e., an unpublished work), or any substantial part thereof, and to initially make the work available to the public. Publication encompasses online and traditional (offline) publication. Once an author has authorized a work's publication, he or she has no rights on subsequent sales; for example, on resales or rentals, unless reserved by contract or unless it is a commercial rental of computer software or sound recordings. Resales and rentals are discussed below.

What Is "Publication" in Copyright Law?

The right to publish a work is not explicitly defined in the Act, but the Act does state that publication is "in relation to any work, making copies of the work available to the public." According to this provision, publication is not restricted to the publishing of a work in the sense of, for example, a book publisher publishing your next novel. It does include this concept, but goes further than that. Since copies must be made available to the public in order for publication to occur, the fact that many copies of a particular work have been made does not by itself constitute publication of that work. These works (or at least more than one copy of the work) must be available to the public, though the public need not necessarily be in the possession of any of the copies of the work. In this context, the term *public* might be defined to refer to those outside a closed circle such as family, friends, a company, or a restricted group of people.

For purposes of the Copyright Act, publication includes the construction of an architectural work as well as the incorporation of an artistic work into an architectural work.

The following acts do not constitute publication for purposes of copyright law:

- The performance in public of a literary, dramatic, musical, or artistic work or a sound recording.
- The communication by telecommunication of a literary, dramatic, musical, or artistic work or a sound recording (defined later in this chapter).
- The exhibition in public of an artistic work, and the issue of photographs and engravings of works of sculpture and architectural works where associated with the exhibition of such artistic works.

A work or other subject-matter will not be considered to be published, performed in public, or communicated to the public by telecommunication if done without the consent of the copyright owner.

Note

The introductory portion of the provision in the Copyright Act dealing with rights mentions the above rights: the right to produce or reproduce a work, to perform a work in public, and to publish an unpublished work. Following this introduction is a listing of other rights that have been confirmed to be subcategories of these three basic rights.[4] This information is provided to help you understand why some of the rights listed individually below were not included earlier.

The Right of Adaptation

The copyright holder has the right to adapt, or authorize the adaptation of, a work. An example is the adaptation of a play into a film. Also, an author has the right to convert a dramatic work "into a novel or other nondramatic work"; for example, a film into a book, or even an artistic work. Further, the author has the explicit right to convert a novel or other nondramatic work, or artistic work, into a dramatic work. For example, a novel or magazine article could be converted into a film. A painting could be adapted into a dramatic work through a performance. Or the adaptation could be reproducing any literary, dramatic, musical, or artistic work into a film. Manipulating a digital photograph may be considered an adaptation of a work, as may be adding multimedia features to text posted on your blog.

The Right of Translation

A copyright owner has the sole and exclusive right to translate, and to authorize others to translate, a work. A translation might be a translation of a novel (literary work) from French to English. Since the copyright owner has this right, you must obtain his or her permission before translating the work.

The Right of Telecommunication to the Public

A copyright owner has the sole and exclusive right to authorize the use of a work on radio or television, and the transmission of a work via cable, satellite, and telephone wires. More specifically, the Act allows the copyright owner "to communicate the work to the public by telecommunication." Thus, any form of telecommunication requires the permission of the copyright owner. Such telecommunications would include any radio or television broadcast including transmissions by microwave over the airwaves as well as cable transmissions. As defined in the Copyright Act, telecommunications is "any transmission of signs, signals, writing, images or sounds or intelligence of any nature by wire, radio, visual, optical or other electro-magnetic system."

This right includes making content available on the Internet. This is explicitly stated in the Copyright Act as making it available to the public "in a way that allows a member of the public to have access to it from a place and a time individually chosen by that member of the public." Some examples of the "making available" right are: uploading a copy of an article or illustration to the Internet; making a musical work available for streaming from an online music service; and posting a text message on an electronic bulletin board where anyone can dial in with his computer and by pressing the right buttons can access the posted message. In this latter example, the work is being transmitted to the public notwithstanding the fact that each member of the public is receiving the transmission at different times, and on-demand or at his or her own convenience.

The right to communicate to the public by telecommunication extends to communicating works to people who view them in "apartments, hotel rooms or dwelling units situated in the same building" by means of an internal transmission system.

Retransmission Right

The copyright holder has the right to initial telecommunications of copyright materials, as well as the right with respect to subsequent telecommunications of the same materials. This latter right is commonly called the "retransmission right." Any "retransmitters" of "distant signals" (ones that cannot normally be received off-air because the community is located well beyond that signal's good-quality reception area) have to pay a royalty to the respective copyright owners. These retransmitters may be cable TV companies, a master antenna system, a low-power television station, and a direct-to-home system delivering television signals by satellite. Retransmitters may also retransmit signals from radio stations.

One important element of the retransmission right is that copyright holders do not actually authorize this right, but are merely entitled to a royalty payment when their works are used. Further, this payment may only be collected through a "collective" that collects such royalties on behalf of many copyright holders. This is further discussed in Chapter 14, "Legally Using Content."

Copyright owners of works who benefit from the telecommunications rights include producers of television programs and movies; copyright holders of recorded sports events; and copyright holders of musical works that are played on radio stations or on television.

The retransmission regime will be of no direct interest to individuals who must obtain copyright clearances.

THE RIGHT TO PROHIBIT IMPORTATION

There are two distinct elements of this right. First, a copyright holder has the right to ensure that pirated copies of his or her work are not imported into Canada. By obtaining a court order, a copyright owner may enlist the assistance of Canadian customs officials to prevent the importation of such copies. The right only applies where the importer had knowledge that his or her activity violated copyright.

Second, there is a right against parallel imports. The term *parallel imports* refers to both works in general and to books that were legally published elsewhere (i.e., outside of Canada) but have been imported into Canada without the consent of the Canadian rights holder. Both authors of books, and book distributors, can prevent parallel importation of their works, or works they represent through exclusive distribution arrangements. The provision against parallel importation for books is clearer and stronger than for other types of works.

The parallel imports provision for other types of works than books is subject to conflicting interpretations. One interpretation is that a copyright owner can keep out a parallel import produced by a foreign exclusive licensee; and an exclusive licensee cannot keep out a work produced by a foreign copyright owner, but may be able to keep out a work by a foreign exclusive licensee.[5]

The Right of Authorization

You have already seen the term *authorization* used a number of times in this chapter. This is because the right of authorization is one of the exclusive rights of the copyright owner. Thus, only the copyright holder may authorize or permit the use of any of the exclusive rights set out in the Act. It follows that if these rights are used and have not been authorized by the copyright holder, then copyright has been infringed.

A person other than the copyright owner should never authorize others to "use" a work in a copyright sense. Even if you have authorization to use a copyright-protected work, you cannot authorize someone else to use it. For instance, if you have permission to reproduce a book, you do not automatically have permission to authorize someone else to reproduce it, or to perform it in public (for example, to do a public reading of the book).

If a work is used without the permission of the copyright owner, the "user" of that material does not acquire copyright in it, nor does the copyright owner lose any of his or her rights set out in the law.

Economic Rights in Specific Works

The rights described previously apply to literary, dramatic, artistic, and musical works, provided it is possible for such rights to apply. For instance, it may not be possible for the translation right to apply to an artistic work such as a painting. In addition to those rights listed above, there are further rights that apply to specific works like artistic works, musical works, and computer programs. This section discusses further rights as well as the specific rights for sound recordings.

Exhibition Right in Artistic Works

Before examining this particular right, it is important to look at its history in order to understand why the right only exists with respect to artistic works. The exhibition right has existed in the Copyright Act since 1988. Prior to that time, creators of paintings, sculptures, and the like claimed that because of the nature of their works, they could not benefit from many of the rights set out in the Act. For example, a sculpture could not be translated. Creators of artistic works professed that a right should be included in the Act that recognized the unique nature of an artistic work. Thus, the exhibition right was added to the Copyright Act. It gives creators the right to control the use of an artistic work and to be entitled to a royalty payment each time an artistic work is exhibited in public.[6]

The exhibition right is set out in the Copyright Act as the right "to present at a public exhibition, for a purpose other than sale or hire, an artistic work created after June 7, 1988, other than a map, chart or plan." As such, the exhibition right applies to:

- Artistic works, which you will recall include paintings, sculptures, drawings, photographs, and engravings if these artistic works were created after June 7, 1988.

The right does not apply to:

- Maps, charts, and plans.
- Artistic works created before or on June 7, 1988.
- Artistic works that are presented for the purpose of "sale or hire" (for example, sales by commercial galleries, art dealers, or museum sales or shops or rentals by the Canada Council Art Bank, though the exhibition of a rental work would be subject to the exhibition right).

The right applies to "presentations at a public exhibition." Neither "presentations" nor "public exhibitions" is defined in the Copyright Act. Whether a particular situation would constitute a presentation at a public exhibition depends on the facts in each particular case. Some of the factors that a court might take into account when deciding this are:

- The physical location of the work (is it in a gallery or the office of an accountant?).
- The exhibitor's intention to attract attention to the work (are there incentives in the form of lighting, segregated space, posters and information, and/or invitations drawing people to the exhibition?).
- Purpose of exhibition (to show works or mere decoration?).
- The attention given by the public to the exhibit (did people stop to look or did they just walk by?).
- The audience of the exhibit ("public" does not have to include all members of the public, but can include members of a smaller public connected by a common event, interest, or characteristic).
- The size of the audience.
- The charging of an admission fee (free admission is not conclusive that it is public).
- Compensation to the artist.

Keeping the elements of an exhibition in mind, an "exhibition" would probably not include a painting hanging on a living room wall. However, a show at the National Gallery of Canada would be an exhibition.

There are a number of grey areas where it is not always possible to easily determine whether an exhibition is taking place. For instance, an exhibition at a bank may or may not be a public exhibition. Other examples include corporate collections, professional offices, public buildings such as the Parliament buildings, or the corridors of a public library, hotel rooms, and restaurants. Whether an exhibition occurs in these situations would depend on the circumstances in each particular case.[7]

Commercial Rental Right in Computer Programs and Musical Works in Sound Recordings

Until January 1, 1994, once a copyright-protected work had been purchased, the copyright owner had no further rights in the physical property itself, unless the copyright owner and purchaser had agreed otherwise. Therefore, a copyright owner could not prevent the public renting of a copyright-protected work. This meant that every time you rented a musical work or computer program on a CD from a store, the copyright owner did not receive any royalties from the rental of that musical work or computer program.

Since January 1, 1994, a right has existed in the Copyright Act for the commercial rental of a sound recording of the musical work embodied in the sound recording, and of a computer program (regardless of when the sound recording or computer program was created). As a result, rental stores have either closed or must obtain permission from copyright holders to rent sound recordings and computer programs. All other copyright-protected works can be rented without permission from, or payment to, the copyright holder.

When the rental right was first introduced in 1994, its beneficiaries were authors of computer programs and producers of sound recordings. The rental right in musical works and sound recordings has been expanded and currently benefits composers, lyricists, and performers of any musical works embodied in sound recordings.

The commercial rental right applies where there is a "motive of gain" in the overall operations of the person who rents out the computer program or sound recording embodying a musical work. For instance, the activities of a public library would not in substance constitute a rental nor would they be considered to have a motive of gain; libraries are able to rent computer programs and musical works in sound recordings without the permission of the copyright owner, even if an administrative fee or other cost is charged. Also, since a court would look at the overall operations for a motive of gain, there could be a gain where the rental is a "loss leader" to the establishment renting it. In general, there is no motive of gain where no more than costs, including overhead, are recovered. Of course, if an infringement of this right is claimed, a court of law would look at all of the surrounding circumstances.

For purposes of the commercial rental right, the right applies to any sort of protected musical work embodied on a sound recording.

However, only certain computer programs are subject to the rental right. Generally, the right is for stand-alone computer programs like word processors and accounting programs. The Copyright Act refers to eligible computer programs as ones that can be reproduced in the ordinary course of their use; this excludes computer programs reproduced when used in a machine, device or computer, such as an elevator or car. Also, the right does not apply to "copy-protected" software, that is, software that cannot be reproduced in the ordinary course of its use.

When you rent copyright-protected works, you must still respect the rights of the copyright holder. For instance, you cannot reproduce any rented copyright-protected work or show it in public without the permission of the copyright holder.

Infringement of the rental right is subject only to civil remedies and not to criminal remedies. Civil and criminal remedies are discussed in Chapter 13, "What Are the Remedies for the Infringement of Copyright?"

Right of Distribution

A copyright owner has the right to sell or otherwise transfer ownership of any work that is in the form of a tangible object. This is on the condition that ownership has not been previously transferred in or outside Canada with the owner's permission.

Right to Make a Sound Recording

Due to the complexity of the right to make a sound recording, it is separately dealt with in this section.

Mechanical Right

A copyright holder has the right to make an audio recording of a work, or authorize others to do so. According to the Copyright Act, a copyright holder has this right, "in the case of a literary, dramatic or musical work, to make any sound recording, cinematograph film or other contrivance by means of which the work may be mechanically reproduced or performed." For example the copyright owner of a song or play has the right to make or authorize the making of a sound recording of that song or play. The music industry refers to this right as the mechanical right.

Where a work is in the public domain, anyone may make a sound recording of that work. Thus, anyone may make a recording of Vivaldi's "Four Seasons."

Synchronization Right

The right to make a sound recording includes the "synchronization right." The synchronization right is not specifically mentioned in the Copyright Act, but is a term used worldwide in the film and television industry, as well as in the commercial advertising industry. This term describes the rights used when making a film or television program, music is synchronized with the picture in the film or television program. The synchronization right does not concern itself with the making of a sound recording per se, but comes into play when sound is matched with pictures. The pictures on a film are on the video track of the production, and the sound is recorded on what is called the soundtrack of a production. The two elements must be matched, so if someone is playing a violin, the sound of the violin is heard, and the auditory and visual action correspond. Permission of the copyright holder of the musical work is necessary when synchronizing it with a film or television program.

The synchronization right is usually dealt with by contractual arrangements and is perceived as a right separate from the mechanical right. Separate permissions must be obtained for the use of the mechanical and synchronization rights.

It should also be noted that, if the original sound recording embodying a musical work is used in a film, TV program, or TV commercial, the owner of the sound recording must also authorize its "synchronization" in such medium. The industries refer to a licence of a sound recording as a "master use" licence.

MORAL RIGHTS

Since moral rights are an integral part of the Copyright Act, there are portions throughout this book dealing with moral rights. This section will set out a full description of the various components of moral rights.

Moral rights protect the personality or reputation of an author. Because these rights attach to the personality of an author, an author retains them even after he or she has assigned the copyright in a work. This is a very important concept. An older English case described the moral rights concept in the following phrase "to protect the copy after publication."[8] Another case described the same concept stating that "after the author has parted with his pecuniary interest in the manuscript, he retains a species of personal or moral right in the product of his brain."[9] Since moral rights are so personal to an author, they cannot be assigned to subsequent copyright owners to exercise. However, they can be inherited upon the death of an author.

Notwithstanding that moral rights cannot be assigned, authors can agree not to exercise their moral rights by means of a waiver.

Moral rights can be divided into three categories:

1. Right of paternity
2. Right of integrity
3. Right of association

Right of Paternity

An author has the right, "where reasonable in the circumstances, to be associated with the work as its author by name or under a pseudonym and the right to remain anonymous." An author has this right whenever he or she has economic rights in a work, and this right applies in relation to uses covered by those economic rights. For example, when reproducing a magazine article, the author of the article has the right to have her name appear on the article.[10] The author of an e-book has the right to have her name appear on her e-book.

According to this section, an author has the following rights.

Right to Claim Authorship

An author has the right to have his or her name associated with a work. For example, a writer has a right to have her name appear on the cover of her book or in association with a photograph posted on a social networking site.

Right to Remain Anonymous

An author has the right to remain anonymous with respect to a work. Thus, an author could request that his or her work be presented to the public without any name appearing on it as its author.

Right to Use a Pseudonym

An author has the right to use a pseudonym or a pen name.

The above three elements of the right of paternity are subject to the condition "where it is reasonable in the circumstances." It would be reasonable to have a book published with the author's name on it; however, a court may not consider it "reasonable in the circumstances" to have a composer's name mentioned when music incidental to a broadcast is played within that broadcast. The question of "reasonableness" is a matter for a court to decide, depending upon the circumstances of each case.

Right of Integrity

A second component of moral rights is the right of integrity. According to the Copyright Act, the author's right to the integrity of a work is violated if the work is, to the prejudice of the honour or reputation of the author, distorted, mutilated or otherwise modified.

Right to Prevent Changes to a Work

An author has the right to prevent any distortion, mutilation, or other modifications to his or her work. But this distortion, mutilation, or other modification must be prejudicial to the honour or reputation of the author. Whether something is prejudicial in this manner is a question of fact that can be determined through the testimony of witnesses. For example, manipulating a scanned photograph could be an infringement, provided it is prejudicial to the honour or reputation of the author of the photograph.

One of the more well-known Canadian moral rights cases concerns the artist Michael Snow's sculpture, *Flight Stop*, of 60 geese hanging in the Toronto Eaton Centre.[11] In this case, the Eaton Centre had tied ribbons around the necks of the 60 geese in the sculpture as a Christmas decoration. The artist, Michael Snow, had no knowledge of this and did not consent to this decoration. The Court said "the plaintiff is adamant in his belief that his naturalistic composition has been made to look ridiculous by the addition of ribbons and suggests it is not unlike dangling earrings from the Venus de Milo. While the manner is not undisputed, the plaintiff's opinion is shared by a number of well-respected artists and people knowledgeable in his field." The Court held that the attachment of the ribbons to the sculpture was prejudicial to the artist's honour or reputation and ordered that the ribbons be removed.

Special Treatment of Artistic Works

As mentioned previously, the right of integrity, with respect to distortions, mutilations, or other modifications of a work is always subject to the factual question as to whether there is a resulting prejudice to the honour or reputation of the author. There is one exception to this "prejudicial" condition. This exception applies in the case of a painting, sculpture, or engraving. With respect to these works, the prejudice is "deemed to have occurred as a result of any distortion, mutilation or other modification of the work." Thus, there need be no proof of the prejudice. For example, painting a moustache on the *Mona Lisa* (if the *Mona Lisa* were still protected by copyright) would be an infringement of Leonardo da Vinci's moral rights.

Paintings, sculptures, and engravings are given this preferential treatment because these types of works are often unique and one-of-a-kind.

Any change to them would be automatically prejudicial to a creator's honour or reputation.

Right to Prevent Use of a Work in Association with a Product, Service, Cause, or Institution

A further component of moral rights is the right of association. An author has the right to prevent anyone else from using his or her work "in association with a product, service, cause or institution." This right is subject to the distortion, mutilation, or other modification being prejudicial to the honour or reputation of the author. Whether something is prejudicial in this manner is a question of fact that can be determined through the testimony of witnesses.

An example of this right might be an art exhibit sponsored by a tobacco company where the artist's reputation rides on the fact that he is a no-smoking advocate.

Other "Moral Rights"

As is evident, the Canadian Copyright Act does not specifically deal with such things as the right to withdraw a work (once being exhibited, performed, etc.) or the right to revoke a licence to use a copyright-protected work where a licenced right has not been exercised. It also does not explicitly deal with the right to prevent the destruction of a copyright-protected work, though this is arguably a "modification" that is prejudicial to the honour or reputation of a creator, or could be protected by other areas of law.

Certain rights that may or may not be considered moral rights may be secured by contract in order to ensure certainty in a particular situation. These include the situations set out in the above paragraph. Another example may be a choreographer who wants to protect her integrity by contracting in advance the right to approve casting, costumes, stage designs, settings, and lighting for a particular choreographic work.

OTHER SUBJECT-MATTER

In this book, the term *other subject-matter* is used interchangeably with *neighbouring rights*. In this chapter on rights protected by copyright, the term *neighbouring rights* is predominantly used as a way to explain how these rights work in relation to copyrights. Neighbouring rights protect the rights of performers (actors, singers, and the like), record producers, and broadcasters. Neighbouring rights are rights akin to copyright, but are distinct from copyright. In basic terms, copyright can be described as those rights granted to creators of copyright-protected works, whereas neighbouring rights are rights granted to users of those copyright-protected works. For example, copyright protects the composer of a song whereas neighbouring rights would protect the performer of the song. Another way of putting it is that a performer performs music to produce a "neighbouring" work called a performer's performance. Neighbouring rights can sometimes be obtained through contractual agreements. Neighbouring rights are sometimes referred to as rights in nontraditional copyright material, and the Copyright Act refers to neighbouring rights as "other subject-matter."

As is evident from discussions throughout this book, most of the neighbouring rights are relatively new to the Canadian Copyright Act. These newer rights include a right in performers' performances, expanded rights in sound recordings, and rights in broadcasts. In addition, there is a right for performers to enforce contractual obligations.

Performer's Performance

Performers who perform in Canada are entitled to a number of rights. Performances that do not take place in Canada but that would qualify for protection in Canada due to international relationships via the WPPT, WTO, or Rome Convention may have more limited protection in Canada. The rights granted to performers for performances in Canada and other countries are dependent on whether the performance took place in a WPPT, WTO, or Rome Convention country.

For performances in Canada and in WTO countries, since January 1, 1996, the Canadian Copyright Act protects performers against unauthorized fixation (i.e., recording) of their live performances, as well as reproduction or broadcast of their live performances. This is now extended to WPPT countries. Thus, a performer has the right to authorize any recording of his or her live performance (including improvisations and performances of public domain works), any reproduction of the audio or video recording, as well as any broadcast of it on radio or television. Eligible performances are discussed in Chapter 3, "Is Your Creation Eligible for Copyright Protection?"

Since September 1, 1997, performances in Canada or in a Rome Convention country have the above rights plus wider rights that include rental, public performance, broadcast, and authorizing any of these rights. These rights have been extended to performances in WPPT countries. Eligible performances are discussed in Chapter 3.

In addition, for performances on or after November 7, 2012, a performer has certain moral rights in his performance. A performer of a live aural performance or of a performance fixed in a sound recording has the right to the integrity of the performance. These moral rights attach to any performer who is entitled to remuneration, and where it is reasonable in the circumstances. In those situations, the performer has the right to be associated with the performance as its performer by name or under a pseudonym and the right to remain anonymous.

Performers Enforcing Contractual Obligations

Performers in cinematographic works experience a unique problem. These performers have had extreme difficulty enforcing their rights in contractual agreements where the rights are no longer owned by the person or company who signed the original agreement. These contractual arrangements lose their power when assigned to others than the original producer because these others do not "assume" the original obligation to performers. For example, performer Lawford signs an agreement to appear in producer Ken's film. Subsequently, Ken sells his right to distributor Shelley. Lawford has no agreement with Shelley and therefore cannot obtain payment when the film is shown.

A provision in the Act specifically provides performers the right to exercise their contractual right to remuneration against the original producer, assignees of the original agreement, and subsequent rights holders.

Rights for Performers and Producers in Sound Recordings

Pubic Performance and Broadcast

Sound recording performers and producers are entitled to receive royalty payments from those who use their sound recordings for public performance or broadcast. The radio broadcasting industry and commercial establishments that use sound recordings are responsible for paying these "neighbouring-rights royalties. The royalties are collected by a single copyright collective Re:Sound, which is discussed in Chapter 14, "Legally Using Content." However, Re:Sound will not distribute these royalties to individuals, rather, they are distributed to its five member collectives, three of which represent performers, and two of which represent sound recording "makers" (producers). The Copyright Act requires that makers and performers share these royalties equally.

Canadian performers and producers are also eligible to receive royalties when their sound recordings are performed or broadcast in the more than 90 other countries that have agreed to abide by the Rome Convention (discussed in Chapter 5). The exchange of neighbouring rights royalties is handled through international agreements among societies that operate in the major territories. Exceptionally, the United States is not a member of the Rome Convention, and thus its performers and producers are not entitled to collect these royalties in the United States or from other countries, nor are Canadian performers and producers able to collect these royalties from the United States, at least from regular broadcast radio stations. However, U.S. legislation does require satellite and Internet radio stations to pay such royalties and, although a small portion of the U.S. broadcasting industry, these broadcast segments generate a large amount of royalties for Americans as well as for record companies and performers from other countries, including Canadians.

As of November 7, 2012, performers and makers of sound recordings have the right to make a sound recording available to the public over the Internet, prevent others from doing so without their permission, and to sell or transfer the ownership in a physical record. Once that sound recording is made available to the public, it is then considered published for copyright purposes. This making available right allows rights holders to authorize or prohibit the dissemination of their protected material on the Internet and other interactive networks (for example, on iTunes).

Private Copying

Authors (composers and lyricists), producers, and performers of musical works in sound recordings are entitled to monies collected as the blank audio recording media levy on media made or imported and sold in Canada. Those media include cassettes and CDs, but cassettes have virtually disappeared from the marketplace, and CDs are on the decline. As a result, the substantial revenue realize in the early 2000s has dwindled to a small amount. The levy was originally intended as compensation for lost sales due to private copying of sound recordings, which is permissible under Canadian copyright law. The levy is collected by a single copyright collective, which in turn distributes the royalties to its member collectives for further distribution to their individual members.

Broadcasts

Broadcasters have the right to "fix" their transmissions, to enforce reproduction rights on unauthorized fixations, to performance rights in television programs played in premises where the public pays an entrance fee to view them, the right to authorize any of these rights, and a right to authorize simultaneous retransmission by other broadcasters. Further, broadcasters have the right against unauthorized distribution and importation of fixed communication signals.

RIGHTS NOT CURRENTLY IN THE COPYRIGHT ACT

Public Lending Right

A public lending right in the Copyright Act would compensate authors when their books are lent to the public in a library. Without such a right, an author does not receive a royalty when his book is loaned by a library (although the author does receive a royalty from the sale of the book to the library). The underlying principle for a public lending right is that a book is borrowed from a library instead of being purchased and therefore an author loses out on royalties from sales each time that book is loaned.

In Canada, the public lending right (PLR) is not a right in the Copyright Act. Rather, it is a federal government program in which eligible authors are given annual payments to compensate for the free public access to their books in public libraries in Canada.

For more information on the PLR, contact:

Public Lending Right Program
350 Albert Street
P.O. Box 1047
Ottawa, Ontario K1P 5V8
Telephone: 1.800.521.5721 or 613.566.4378
Fax: 613.566.4418
E-mail: plr@canadacouncil.ca
Web: http://plr-dpp.ca

Right of Resale

The Copyright Act does not have a right of resale. Therefore, a copyright holder has no rights in the resale of a work, unless such rights have been reserved by contract.

An example of this concept occurs when an author cannot stop the resale of a book in a used bookstore and an author is not entitled to any royalties from the resale of a book. Keep in mind, however, that the author still has copyright in that book notwithstanding the fact that it is physically owned by its original purchaser or by a subsequent purchaser. Thus, the author can claim any rights under the Copyright Act and can, for example, prevent the reproduction of the book, or the use of it in association with a service, product, cause, or institution, if that use is prejudical to the honour or reputation of the author.

Droit de Suite

Recognized in many foreign countries, the droit de suite is the right of an artist to participate in any proceeds from a resale of the "physical" (as opposed to the copyright) aspect of a work. Thus, a droit de suite would enable creators of original artistic works to share in the proceeds from resales and to claim a share of any increase in the value of a work of art such as a painting each time that it is resold. The current Copyright Act does not contain a droit de suite. An artist, however, may negotiate a term in a purchase and sale agreement of a piece of art that is similar to a droit de suite and that would enable the artist to benefit from increases in the value of a work.

SUMMARY

Copyright holders are entitled to a bundle of rights, such as the right to publish, reproduce, and perform in public a copyright-protected work, or to authorize others to do so. Authors of copyright-protected works also have moral rights in their creations. In addition, there are rights in performers' performances, sound recordings, and broadcasts. The rights described in this chapter are subject to limitations set out in the next chapter.

CHAPTER 10

LIMITATIONS ON RIGHTS

Seek advice but use your own common sense.

—Yiddish Proverb

WHAT ARE LIMITATIONS ON RIGHTS?

In Chapter 9, we dealt with the rights of authors and copyright holders. This chapter covers limitations on, or exceptions from, these rights. Basically, these limitations are certain provisions in the Copyright Act that allow people to use copyright materials without obtaining the permission of, and/or paying compensation to, the copyright holder. The Act sets out many limitations as well as many conditions on these limitations; this chapter highlights these limitations but does not comprehensively discuss each limitation and all conditions relating to these limitations.

FAIR DEALING

What Is Fair Dealing?

The fair dealing[1] provision was originally included in the Canadian Copyright Act in 1921, at a time when reproducing copyright materials meant copying out by hand. At the time, the fair dealing provision applied to the use of quotes and "small" passages for purposes of private study, research, criticism, review, or news reporting. Of course, the concept of photocopiers, computers, computer scanners, and the Internet was not envisioned. However, like other terms and provisions used in the Copyright Act, fair dealing is being interpreted to meet the technology of the time.

The term *fair dealing* is not defined in the Copyright Act. The wording used in the Act, which may seem straightforward, cannot be interpreted on its face. Some court cases have dealt with this concept, but no single court case clearly establishes what exactly constitutes fair dealing; this goes to the very nature of fair dealing, which must be determined on a case-by-case basis on the specific factors in each case. There is confusion and discussion as to which activities may be considered fair dealing. The Act does not set out a percentage of use that is acceptable under fair dealing. Because of the uncertain nature of fair dealing, users of copyright material such as librarians, educators, researchers, copyright compliance officers, and even creators, all of whom are not copyright experts, must decide for themselves as to whether their activities would be considered fair by a judge in a court of law.

Although the law in this area must be interpreted on a case-by-case basis to your particular circumstances, there is some guidance as to what constitutes fair dealing. To begin, in order for something to constitute fair dealing, it must fit under one of the purposes listed in the fair dealing provision of the Act: research; private study; education; parody; satire; criticism; review; or news reporting. If the use falls within one of the purposes, the next step is to assess whether the dealing is "fair."

Determining Whether Fair Dealing Applies to Your Situation

To make a determination as to whether or not a certain activity might constitute fair dealing, you should first consider whether a substantial part of a work is being copied. One must first establish this factor because all the rights in the Act apply to using a substantial part of a work. If anything less than a substantial part of a work is being used, then the copyright owner has no right to prevent its use. Remember that what constitutes a substantial part of a work is not defined in the law; it depends on the nature of the reproduction, and it is also a matter of degree, in terms of both quality and quantity of the work used.

If a substantial part of a work is being copied, you must then determine whether the dealing is for one of the allowable purposes set out in the Act. The purposes are:

- Research
- Private study
- Education
- Parody[2]
- Satire
- Criticism
- Review
- News reporting

These purposes are not further elaborated in the Act and are open to interpretation by the courts.[3] Education, parody, and satire have been part of the Act since November 2012 and are not subject to interpretation by the courts at the time of writing.[4] Note that the term *education* in the fair dealing provision is not related to the definition of *educational institution* or the specific provisions for educational institutions discussed in this chapter. Although a use must fit within one of the defined purposes, that alone does not determine that the use falls within fair dealing. One must then assess the fairness of the use.

To assess the fairness of the dealing, the Supreme Court of Canada has set out factors that should be taken into account.[5] These factors are:

- The purpose of the dealing
- The character of the dealing
- The amount of the dealing
- Alternatives to the dealing
- The nature of the work
- The effect of the dealing on the work

In addition, the Supreme Court has said, "There may be factors other than those listed here that may help a court decide whether the dealing was fair."

Making a Fair Dealing Determination

Fair dealing is a defence to a claim of unauthorized use of copyright materials. Once a copyright owner establishes ownership of his or her work, it is up to the user of those materials to establish that that use does not infringe copyright because it falls within fair dealing. To utilize the defence of fair dealing in any specific circumstance, you must establish that your use fits within one of the allowable purposes in the Copyright Act. If it does, then you must assess whether the dealing is fair according to various factors. So, how does one make this judgment? What do all these words and terms mean? How does your own situation fit within the purposes and factors? Throughout this determination, keep in mind that fair dealing is intentionally ambiguous and that in each situation you must apply the law to your particular facts. At the end of the day, although you may make your own fair dealing determination and choice of content based on your determination, the ultimate decision of fair dealing rests in a court by a judge.

As one court expressed, "[Y]ou must consider first the number and extent of the quotations and extracts. Are they altogether too many and too long to be fair?" The case went on to consider the proportions of the work taken. "To take long extracts and attach short comments may be unfair. But, short extracts and long comments may be fair. Other considerations may come to mind also. But, after all is said and done, it must be a matter of impression."[6]

Some background on the development of the interpretation of fair dealing may assist when making your own determinations.

The year 2004 marked a significant change in the interpretation of fair dealing. For example, prior to 2004, it was likely that private study or research did not extend to multiple copies for classroom use.[7] Criticism usually referred to quotes and extracts from a work to illustrate a commentary on it. One court case had stated, "[A] critic cannot, without being guilty of infringement, reproduce in full, without the author's permission, the work which he criticizes."[8] However, a critic writing about a particular painting may argue that reproduction of the entire painting in a newspaper article is necessary for review purposes. A 1995 court case held that the reproduction of a magazine cover by a newspaper where a photograph on the cover was predominant was not fair dealing of the photograph.[9]

In 2004, the Supreme Court of Canada broadened the scope of fair dealing. The Court used such expressions as "users' rights," a concept that had never been part of Canadian copyright law. The Court stated, "'Research' must be given a large and liberal interpretation in order to ensure that users' rights are not unduly constrained, and is not limited to non-commercial or private contexts." In addition, the Court stated, "This case requires this Court to interpret the scope of both owners' and users' rights."[10]

In 2012, the Supreme Court provided further clarification on the interpretation of fair dealing.[11] The court stated that the term *private study* includes students in a classroom setting. The word *private* does not mean that users have to view copyright materials in isolation; studying and learning are essentially personal endeavours, whether in solitude or with others. Note that this decision was prior to "education" being added as one of the purposes in fair dealing in the Act.

In another 2012 Supreme Court decision, the court held that fair dealing covered listening to previews of songs on services such as iTunes. The court stated that research is not limited to creative purposes, and research includes listening to preview to identify which music to purchase.[12]

Citing the Source

If you are using a work under the fair dealing provision for purposes of criticism, review, or news reporting, in your use you must mention the source and the author's name if it is given in the source. The performer must be mentioned in the case of a performance, the maker in the case of a sound recording, and the broadcaster in the case of a broadcast signal.

SPECIFIC EXCEPTIONS

Noncommercial User-Generated Content

An exception for the use of noncommercial user-generated content was added to the Copyright Act as part of the 2012 amendments. This exception is sometimes called the YouTube or mashup provision. However, these exact words are not used in the actual wording in the provision, nor does the wording of the exception limit its scope to online or digital uses.

This new provision states that it is not illegal for an individual to use an existing work or other subject-matter in order to create a new work or other subject-matter and to share that new work. The following conditions apply:

- The existing work has been published or otherwise made available to the public.
- The use of the new work is done solely for noncommercial purposes (*noncommercial* is not defined in the Copyright Act).
- The source of the existing work is included and also the name of the author, performer, maker, or broadcaster (if these are in the existing work), if it is reasonable to include in the new work.
- The individual had reasonable grounds to believe that the existing work is not itself infringing copyright.
- The use of the work does not have a substantial adverse effect, financial or otherwise, on the current or future exploitation of the existing work or copy of it, and is not a substitute for the existing work.

The individual may by himself or herself or with the aid of a member of his or her household use the new work or other subject-matter or authorize an intermediary to disseminate it. An intermediary is a person or entity "who regularly provides space or means for works or other subject-matter to be enjoyed by the public." An example of an intermediary is YouTube or Vimeo.

The term *use* refers to all of the rights as set out in the Copyright Act that solely belong to a copyright owner (except for the right to authorize).

The scope of this provision can only be determined by interpretation in the courts. However, in its information about this provision, the Canadian Government describes it in the following words: "Examples include making a home video of a friend or family member dancing to a popular song and posting it online, or creating a 'mash-up' of video clips. This provision would not permit such activities as simply adding a few lines to an e-book or a brief introduction to a song and then posting the copy for free online, or re-ordering the tracks on an album and selling CDs at a flea market."[13]

Private Copying of Sound Recordings

An individual may make for his or her own private purposes a copy of a musical work in a sound recording, a performer's performance of a musical work in a sound recording, onto an audio recording medium such as a CD. As discussed in Chapter 11, there is a levy on blank audio recording media made or imported, and sold in Canada. The proceeds of this levy are distributed to eligible composers, lyricists, performers, and producers of sound recordings through their professional associations or copyright collectives.

The private copying provision only applies if the copy is not sold, rented, distributed, communicated to the public by telecommunications, or performed in public.

The Copyright Act grants one exemption to paying this levy, to associations representing persons with perceptual disabilities.

Format Shifting

The provision for format shifting does not apply to the *copy* of a musical work made onto an audio recording medium as discussed in the above section.

This new provision for format shifting became part of the Copyright Act in November 2012. It allows an individual to reproduce a non-infringing copy of a work or other subject-matter or a substantial part of it in specific circumstances. For example, an individual may reproduce a song onto a smartphone or iPod. The copy of the work or other subject-matter must not be borrowed or rented, and the individual must own it or be authorized to use and own the medium or device on which it is reproduced. There must be no circumvention of technological protection measures. The reproduction may only be used for the individual's private purposes and may not be given away. The Act defines a medium or device to include "digital memory in which a work or subject-matter may be stored for the purpose of allowing the telecommunication of the work or other subject-matter through the Internet or other digital network." This could include a MP3 player, iTouch, or online storage.

Reproduction for Later Listening or Viewing

The provision for "private" reproductions, or for time-shifting purposes, became part of the Copyright Act in November 2012. The term *time shifting* refers to recording a program or movie to watch at a later, more convenient time.

An individual may reproduce a work or sound recording that is being broadcast, or record or reproduce a performer's performance that is being broadcast, for the purpose of listening to or viewing it at a later time as long as the individual receives the program legally, no technological protection measures have been circumvented, and only one recording is made. The individual may only keep the recording for as long as is reasonably necessary to listen or view it at a more convenient time, cannot ever give the recording to others, and may only use the recording for the individual's private purposes. This provision allows individuals to record television, radio, and Internet broadcasts. This exception does not apply where the work, performer's performance, or sound recording is received on an on-demand service (a service that allows the individual to choose to receive the work, performer's performance or sound recording).

Temporary Reproductions for Technological Processes

Temporary reproductions of works and other subject-matter are permissible if the reproduction is an essential part of a technological process, the reproduction's only purpose is to facilitate a use that is not an infringement of copyright, and the reproduction exists only for the duration of the technological process.

Backing Up Copies of Content

Owners of legal copies of all works and subject-matter, as well as licensees of these materials, may make back-up copies in specific circumstances. An owner or licensee of noninfringing materials may make back-up copies solely for the purpose of replacing a possible lost, damaged, or otherwise unusable copy. The copies must be made without circumventing any technological protection measures. The copies must not be given to others. The owner or licensee must be able to prove that any back-up copies are destroyed as soon as he or she ceases to be the owner of, or have a licence to use, the original work or subject-matter. The copies may be on online or cloud-based back-up services.

Computer Programs

Back-Up Copy

The Copyright Act allows owners of legal copies of computer programs, as well as licensees of computer programs, to make reproductions of these programs in specific circumstances. These provisions apply to owners of programs, whether original or subsequent owners, and not to borrowers of programs, whether borrowed from a friend or office, or for a rental fee from a store.

An owner of a legitimate copy of a computer program and a licensee may make back-up copies of that program. The back-up copies must be solely for the purpose of replacing a possible lost, damaged, or otherwise unusable copy. The copies must be made without circumventing any technological protection measures. The copies must not be given to others. The owner or licensee must be able to prove that any back-up copies are destroyed as soon as he or she ceases to be the owner of, or have a licence to use, the original computer program.

Copying for Purposes of Adaptation, Modification, Conversion, or Translation

An owner of a legitimate copy of a computer program, as well as a licensee, may make a single copy of that program by adapting, modifying, or converting the computer program or translating it into another computer language, provided that the person can prove the following:

- The reproduction is essential for the compatibility of the program with a particular computer,
- The reproduction is solely for the person's own use,
- The copy is destroyed when the person ceases to be the owner of the copy of, or licensee of, the program from which the copy was made.

Copying for Purposes of Interoperability

An owner of a legitimate copy of a computer program, as well as a licensee, may reproduce the program for the purpose of obtaining information that would allow the person to make the program and another computer program interoperable.

Public Domain Software

Using public domain or shareware software is not an "exception" under the Copyright Act. In these cases, the particular copyright owners are allowing the use of these programs, either for free or subject to a "voluntary" payment. This is a choice made on an individual basis by each copyright holder.

Encryption Research

A lawfully obtained work or other subject-matter may be reproduced for purposes of encryption research if it would not be practical to carry out the research without the reproduction, and the owner of the work or other subject-matter has been informed. Note that there are further specific provisions in the Act where this research relates to the use of computer programs and to the assessment of the vulnerability of a computer, system, or network or of correcting any security flaws.

Public Recitation of Extracts

It is not illegal for a person to read or recite in public any reasonable extract from any published work. Without this exception, such a reading would infringe the right of public performance in the work.

Legislative, Judicial, and Administrative Proceedings

The Copyright Act does not explicitly provide any exceptions for the use of copyright materials during legislative, judicial, or administrative proceedings, or for the use of the reports of such proceedings. The discussion under "Applying for Crown Copyright Clearance" in Chapter 14 will guide you through the permissions process for the use of materials of the federal government, and provincial and territorial governments.

Reusing Molds, Casts, and So Forth of Artistic Works

An author may reuse any mold, cast, sketch, plan, model, or study used to make an artistic work, even if the author no longer owns the copyright in the artistic work, as long as the author does not thereby "repeat or imitate the main design of that work."

Works Permanently Situated in a Public Place

Certain works that are permanently located in public places may be reproduced in certain manners without violating copyright. A painting, drawing, engraving, photograph, or cinematographic work can be made of any sculpture or work of artistic craftsmanship if the sculpture or work of artistic craftsmanship is permanently situated in a public place or building. The painting, drawing, engraving, or photograph may also be published. Always keep in mind that this provision refers to works permanently situated in public places or buildings. A painting that travels from one public art gallery to another would probably not be permanently situated in a public place.

This provision also extends to architectural works. You can publish and reproduce paintings, drawings, engravings, or photographs of architectural works in public places as long as the paintings, drawings, and so forth are not architectural drawings or plans.

The purpose of the provision for works permanently situated in a public place is to allow tourists to photograph a statute or monument in a public place, or to allow a person to sketch the outside of a building.

Incidental Use of Copyright Materials

There is an exception in the Act for the incidental inclusion of copyright-protected works and other subject-matter in other copyright material. However, in order for this use not to infringe copyright, it must be incidental and not deliberate. For example, this would allow a news camera crew to incidentally and not deliberately film a street scene in which music is playing in the background.

Public Lectures

There is a provision in the Act that allows a person, for purposes of news reporting or news summary, to report a public lecture without clearing copyright permission. The following conditions must be met for this provision to apply:

- The lecture must be delivered in public (broadcast to the public is probably not acceptable).
- There must be no conspicuous written or printed notices prohibiting the report affixed before and maintained during the lecture at or about the main entrance of the building where the lecture is given, and in a position near the lecturer.

Political Speeches

Any person may publish a report for purposes of news reporting or news summary of an address of a political nature delivered at a public meeting.

Commissioned Photographs or Portraits

An individual may use a photograph or portrait he or she commissioned if it was made for personal purposes (e.g., a wedding) and for valuable consideration, unless the individual and photographer/artist have agreed otherwise. This exception is for an individual to use for private or noncommercial purposes or to allow others to use the works in the same circumstances. Another person in the photograph who did *not* commission the photograph may not benefit from this exception.

Importation of Works

Any person may import two copies of a work or other subject-matter for personal use. Any number of copies of a work or other subject-matter may be imported for use by a federal or provincial or territorial government department. In addition, any number of used books may be imported into Canada. A single copy of a book, or any number of copies of a work or other subject-matter, may be imported for use by any nonprofit library, archive, museum, or educational institution at any time before the work is made in Canada. See below for the definition of nonprofit library, archive, museum, or educational institution.

This exception applies only with respect to works that were made with the consent of the copyright owner in the foreign country where they were made. Thus, it is a limit on the protection that certain rights owners have against parallel importation.

A person may also import a work that could have been made by the person who made it under a limitation or exception in the Canadian Copyright Act, even if no such exceptions exists in the country where it was made. For example, a work that could have been made under the parody fair dealing purpose can be imported into Canada even if there is no parody exception or defence in the country where it was made.

EXCEPTIONS IN SPECIFIC SITUATIONS

The exceptions described below under the headings schools, libraries, and so on, are exceptions in the Act that specifically refer to these headings. Other provisions—for example, fair dealing or specific exceptions such as the ones for computer programs—may also apply with respect to schools, libraries, or in any other of the specific situations listed below.

Meaning of *Commercially Available*

The term *commercially available* arises in many of the school and library, archive and museum exceptions. It is defined as "available on the

Canadian market within a reasonable time and for a reasonable price and may be located with reasonable effort," or where there is a licence available from a copyright collective "within a reasonable time and for a reasonable price and may be located with reasonable effort." The available licence would be for the purpose of reproduction, performance in public, or communicating to the public by telecommunication.

Educational Institutions

The Copyright Act includes several exceptions specifically for non-profit educational institutions at all levels including preschool, elementary, secondary, and postsecondary education, as long as they are licensed or recognized by or under federal or provincial legislation. The exceptions apply to continuing, professional, or vocational education or training where the nonprofit institution is directed or controlled by a board of education regulated by or under provincial legislation. They apply to any government department or agency or nonprofit body that controls or supervises the education or training mentioned above. Further, the government may include other nonprofit institutions to this list by regulation. In addition, the exceptions apply to any library, archive, or museum that forms part of an educational institution.

Each of the exceptions is described next. For purposes of this book, the terms *educational institution* and *school* are interchangeably used.

The premises of an educational institution are a place where education or training is provided, controlled, or supervised by the educational institution.

Educational Institutions and Copying for Education

As of November 2012, "education" is a purpose under fair dealing. This means that anyone (and not just educational institutions) may claim the defence of fair dealing when using copyright materials for the purpose of education. It does not mean, however, that any use for education by anyone or by any educational institution is automatically allowed without permission from the copyright owner. If copying is for the purpose of education, then one may consider the fair dealing defence and make a fair dealing analysis as discussed earlier in this chapter. For purposes of this section of this chapter, educational institutions should review the fair dealing provision as well as the specific exceptions following.

Instruction/In-Class Display

In order to display a work, educational institutions may make a copy of a work (or undertake other necessary acts). This exception is technology neutral and includes reproduction of a work onto a dry-erase board, flipchart, or other similar surface, using an overhead or slide projector, a smartboard, or other computer projection. The display must be done for the purposes of education or training on the premises of the educational institution. Any person under the authority of the educational institution may undertake the reproduction. Except in the case of manual reproduction, this exception does not apply if the work is commercially available in an appropriate medium. In this context, "commercially available" does not include the availability of a licence from a collective.[14] Also, there must be no motive of gain. *Motive of gain* is defined as recovering no more than the costs, including overhead costs, associated with doing the specified act. The copies may not be archived for storage purposes.

Tests and Exams

An educational institution (or any person acting under its authority) may reproduce, translate, or perform in public or broadcast a work or other subject-matter on a school's premises "as required" for a test or exam. Except in the case of manual reproduction, this exception does not apply if the work or other subject-matter is commercially available in an appropriate medium. In this context, "commercially available" does not include the availability of a licence from a collective. Also, there must be no motive of gain.

Performances

Certain performances for and by students are allowed. The performance must take place on the school's premises for education or training purposes and not for profit. The audience must consist primarily of students of the school, instructors, or any person who is directly responsible for setting a curriculum for the school. This would not therefore include a school play in which the audience consisted primarily of family and friends. There must be no motive of gain. Allowable performances are:

- Live performances in public, primarily by students, of a work such as a play or music.
- Playing sound recordings (that are legal copies or the person responsible for the playing of the sound recording has no reasonable grounds to believe that it is an infringing copy).
- Playing radio or television programs live while being broadcast.
- Playing cinematographic works (that are legal copies or the person responsible for the playing of the sound recording has no reasonable grounds to believe that it is an infringing copy).

Taping Radio and Television Programs

In both of the following situations, certain use is permitted for lawful materials. For instance, if you receive a pay-per-view signal via illegal means, then the off-air taping exceptions do not apply.

Taping Off-Air for Classroom Use   An educational institution or person acting under its authority may tape off-air a single copy of a news program or a news commentary program at the time the program is aired. This must be done for the purposes of playing the copy to students for educational or training purposes. This exception does not apply to documentaries. The copy may be shown to students on the premises of an educational institution for educational or training purposes.

Taping Off-Air for Evaluation Purposes   An educational institution or person acting under its authority may tape a single copy of any work from a radio or television broadcast at the time the program is aired, and keep it for up to 30 days to determine whether or not to play the copy for educational or training purposes. At the end of the 30 days, the copy must be destroyed, or royalties paid as set by the Copyright Board, and use is then subject to the Board's terms and conditions. In addition, the educational institution must keep any records prescribed by regulation in relation to the making of the copy, the destruction of it, or any performance in public of it for which royalties are due, as well as mark the copy in the manner prescribed by regulation. The applicable Regulation SOR/2001–296 and required record-keeping is set out in Appendix V.

Public Performance of Musical Works

A religious organization or institution or educational institution (as defined above) may publicly perform a musical work in furtherance of a religious, educational, or charitable object without payment royalties to the copyright holder of the musical work. This includes a live performance in public of a musical work, and the performance in public of a sound recording embodying a musical work or a performer's performance of a musical work (and the performance in public of a communication signal carrying these performances). In order for this provision to apply, the performance must be closely connected to the "object." For example,

> Singing or performing music in and as part of a church service is directly furthering that service, itself a charitable object; an educational meeting with musical interpolations is carried on in a charitable sense and is itself such an object; and in the relief or amelioration of poverty, the accompaniment of the music of an orchestra at a Christmas dinner given to the poor through the means of voluntary contributions is equally so.[15]

However, the provision will not apply where the music is performed in a school or religious organization for purposes of entertainment, for instance, at a social dance, though it may apply with respect to an assembly undertaken for religious, educational, or charitable purposes.

Note that this provision merely exempts the payment of royalties. The copyright owner still has the right, by obtaining a court injunction, to stop the performance in question.

Publication of Short Passages in a Collection

The Copyright Act allows the publication of short passages in collections for school use without infringing copyright. However, a number of conditions apply:

- The collection must be mainly composed of noncopyright matter.
- The collection must be intended for the use of schools and must state this in the title and in any advertisements issued by the publisher.
- The passages must be from published literary works not themselves published for the use of schools.
- Not more than two passages from works by the same author may be published by the same publisher within five years.
- The source from which the passages are taken must be acknowledged.
- The name of the author, if given in the source, must be mentioned.

Distance Learning

The term *distance learning* refers to the transmissions of lessons with copyright materials over the Internet in an online course. If copyright material in a lesson is used according to an exception in the Act, an educational institution may share that lesson in an online course.

Specifically, since November 2012, an exception exists in the Copyright Act that permits an educational institution to communicate by telecommunication a lesson, test, or examination containing copyright materials. It must be for educational or training purposes and shared only with students who are enrolled in the course of which the lesson forms a part, or to other persons acting under the authority of the educational institution. The educational institution or person acting under its authority may make a "fixation" of the lesson, test, or examination or do any other act that is necessary for the purposes set out in this paragraph.

The student may reproduce the lesson in order to be able to listen to or view it at a more convenient time. However, within 30 days after receiving their final course evaluations, the student must destroy any copies of the lesson. The educational institution must also destroy any fixation of the lesson within 30 days.

The educational institution must take measures that can reasonably be expected to limit the communication by telecommunication of the lesson to students only, and prevent the students from fixing, reproducing, or communicating the lesson other than permitted under these provisions, and to comply with any other measures prescribed by regulation.

Digital Copying by Educational Institutions

If an educational institution has a reprographic reproduction (i.e., photocopying) licence with a copyright collective for an educational or training purpose, the institution may make a digital reproduction of a print version of the work, and share that digital version online for an educational or training purpose to persons acting under the authority of the institution. A person working under the authority of the educational institution may print one copy of the digital reproduction. For these activities to be an exception from copyright, the educational institution is subject to a number of conditions including paying the copyright collective royalties that would be payable for a photocopy of the same work, complying with the reprography licence terms and conditions, and taking measures to prevent the digital reproduction from being electronically shared with those not acting under the authority of the institution.

The above paragraph does not apply if the educational institution has a digital copying agreement with a copyright collective, a tariff has been approved by the Copyright Board, or the copyright owner refuses to authorize the digital reproduction of the work.

Copyright Materials Available Online

Online content that is protected by copyright may be freely used by educational institutions (or a person acting under their authority) for educational or training purposes under certain conditions. The institution may reproduce the materials and share them online with students and others acting under the authority of the educational institution. There must be mention of the source, and if given in the source, the name of the author, performer, maker, or broadcaster. This provision does not apply if the website or material is restricted by a technological protection measure, or permitted acts of reproduction, performance in public, and communication to the public by telecommunication are restricted by technological protection measures on the website or material, or there is a clearly visible notice (not merely a copyright symbol) prohibiting that act is posted on the website where the material is posted or on the material itself.

The protected materials must be legally available on a website open to the public—in other words, the materials are posted with the copyright owner's permission.

COPYRIGHT COLLECTIVES

Because the use of copyright materials is so widespread in certain organizations and institutions and often immediate access is required to reproduce those materials, copyright collectives (groups of copyright holders that administer their copyrights as a whole) have formed for different rights and materials to provide permissions. Collectives are discussed in Chapter 11, and contact information for various copyright collectives is in Chapter 14.

LIBRARIES, ARCHIVES, AND MUSEUMS

The Copyright Act has a number of exceptions for libraries, archives, and museums. These exceptions are grouped together for any eligible library, archive, or museum (though there are some additional exceptions for archives as set out below.) An eligible library, archive, or museum (LAM) is one that is not established or conducted for profit, and not part of, not administered, and not directly or indirectly controlled by, a body that is established or conducted for profit. Also, the LAM must hold and maintain a collection of documents and other materials that is open to the public or to researchers. The Canadian government may include other nonprofit institutions by regulation.

Management and Maintenance

A LAM may make a copy of a work or other subject-matter for the maintenance or management of its permanent collection. This applies to both published and unpublished works. It applies to works in the LAM's permanent collection or the permanent collection of another LAM. This exception applies in the following circumstances:

- If the original is rare or unpublished and it is deteriorating, damaged, or lost, or at the risk of deteriorating or becoming damaged or lost (if a copy is not commercially available).
- For on-site consultation purposes if the original cannot be viewed, handled, or listened to because of its condition or because of the atmospheric conditions in which it must be kept (if a copy is not commercially available).
- In an alternative format if the LAM or a person acting under its authority considers that the original is currently in a format that is obsolete or becoming obsolete, or the technology required to use

the original is unavailable or is becoming unavailable (if a copy is not commercially available).

- For internal record keeping and cataloguing.
- For insurance purposes or police investigations.
- "If necessary for restoration."

The term *commercially available* is defined above, and in these LAM provisions also refers to an appropriate copy being available in a medium and of a quality that is appropriate for the management and maintenance of the LAM's collection.

Any intermediate copies made for making the above preservation copies must be destroyed as soon as they are no longer needed.

Fair Dealing

A LAM (or someone acting under their authority) may do anything on behalf of a person that the person would be permitted to do under the fair dealing provision. There must be no motive of gain.

Single Copies of Articles for Research, and So Forth

Certain articles from magazines and periodicals may be copied under the LAM provisions. The exception applies to an article in a "scholarly, scientific or technical periodical"—a term that is not defined in the Act. It also applies to an article in a newspaper or periodical if that newspaper or periodical was published more than one year before the copy was made. Therefore, on May 1, 2014, you may not use this exception to copy an article in a newspaper published on January 1, 2014, but you may use it to copy an article in a newspaper published on January 1, 2013. "Newspaper or periodical" is not specifically defined but is one other than a scholarly, scientific, or technical periodical. An article in a newspaper or periodical does not include a work of fiction, poetry, or a dramatic or musical work.

For any reproduction of works that occurs under the above exception, the following conditions must be met:

- The library may only provide the patron with a single copy of the article.
- The LAM must inform the patron that the copy is to be used solely for research or private study and that other uses may require permission from the copyright owner.
- The copy must be made by "reprographic reproduction," which is generally photocopying and does not include, for example, scanning the article into a computer.
- There must be no motive of gain.

See the record-keeping requirements below.

Interlibrary Loan

One LAM may make a single copy of an article as described above for a patron of another LAM. The copy sent can be a reprographic reproduction.

A LAM may provide a copy in digital form to a person who has requested it through another LAM in certain circumstances. The providing LAM must take measures to prevent the receiving/requesting person from making any print or digital copies of it (except for one print copy); communicating the digital copy to others; and using the digital copy for more than five business days from the day on which the person first uses it. If a LAM makes any temporary copies in order to give the copy to a patron, that temporary copy must be destroyed.

See the record-keeping requirements below.

Record Keeping

There are regulations (Regulations SOR/99–325) set out in Appendix VI that prescribe record-keeping details whenever a LAM reproduces a single copy of an article for research and so forth. Note that the record keeping only relates to the right of reproduction. So, if a LAM performs a work in public, record keeping is not necessary. The LAM must record the following information for each copy of each article made under this provision. Note that if the LAM has a licence with Access Copyright or Copibec and that licence covers this kind of copying the LAM may copy under the licence and therefore would not be required to keep these records. Records required are:

- The name of the LAM making the copy.
- If an interlibrary loan, the name of the requesting LAM (see below).
- The date of the request.
- Sufficient information to identify the work being copied such as title, ISBN, ISSN.
- If applicable, the name of the newspaper, periodical, or scholarly, scientific, or technical periodical in which the work is found.
- If applicable, the date or volume and number of the newspaper, periodical, or scholarly, scientific, or technical periodical.
- The numbers of the copied pages.

The LAM must keep a copy request form with the above information or may keep the information in any other manner that may be accessed in a readable form within a reasonable time, for example in an electronic database. Such records must be kept for at least three years. The records must be accessible to the copyright owner, his or her representative, or a copyright collective in manners specified in the regulations.

USE OF COPYRIGHT WARNINGS

There is a provision in the law that states that an educational institution, library, archives, or museum does not infringe copyright if a copyright warning is posted near a photocopying machine on its premises. For this provision to apply, the following conditions must be met:

- The photocopier is installed by or with the approval of the school or LAM on its for use by students, instructors, or staff at the school, or by persons using the LAM.

- The school or LAM has a licence with Access Copyright or Copibec or is in the process of negotiating one, or the school or LAM is paying a collective under a certified tariff or the collective has filed a proposed tariff with the Copyright Board.
- A notice warning of infringement of copyright is affixed to, or within the immediate vicinity of, every photocopier in a place and manner that is readily visible and legible to persons using the photocopier.
- The notice must contain at least the following information:

WARNING!

Works protected by copyright may be copied on this photocopier only if authorized by

(a) the Copyright Act for the purpose of fair dealing or under specific exceptions set out in that Act;

(b) the copyright owner; or

(c) a licence agreement between this institution and a collective society or a tariff, if any.

For details of authorized copying, please consult the licence agreement or the applicable tariff, if any, and other relevant information available from a staff member.

The Copyright Act provides for civil and criminal remedies for infringement of copyright.

The Act does not provide a similar provision for other equipment such as scanners, or computers with Internet access, on a school or LAM premise, which may be used to infringe copyright. As such, following the above is no guarantee that a school or LAM may be exempt from infringement for illegal copying taking place on this equipment. However, it may be prudent to post similar warnings near such equipment.

ARCHIVES ONLY

In addition to the provisions for LAMs, there is a special provision for archives to copy an unpublished work that is deposited in the archive.

In order for this exception to apply, a number of conditions must be met:

- The person who deposited the work is given notice that the work may be copied according to this provision.
- The person who deposited the work, if a copyright owner, did not prohibit its copying.
- Copying has not been prohibited by any other owner of copyright in the work.

A person may be provided with a single copy of the work if the archive informs the person that the copy is used solely for research or private study; otherwise permission is required.

Note that donors can deposit works with archives even if they do not own the copyright in the works. This is because it is the physical property that donors give to the archives, and not the authorization to make any copyright uses with the materials. If a donor does own copyright, he or she can grant it to the archives. Whether or not the donor owns copyright in the deposited materials, the donor can request a deposit agreement with the archives that limits copyright and noncopyright uses by the archives. Thus, the Copyright Act does not always govern the use to which copyright material deposited with an archive may be put.

In addition, there are some specific provisions in the Act for copying by the National Archives of Canada.

BROADCASTERS

In addition to the general exceptions in the Copyright Act that may arguably apply to broadcasters, there is a specific exception for broadcasters for "ephemeral recordings." Under the ephemeral recordings exception, broadcasters may make a temporary copy of a performance, or an event, for later broadcast without payment to or authorization from the copyright owner. A broadcaster may, for example, tape a live figure-skating competition that includes musical accompaniment. For a 30-day period following the making of the copy, it may be used as many times as desired by the broadcaster. Further, the exception allows a broadcaster to transfer a sound recording to a format more technically suitable for broadcasting. For example, a broadcaster may copy a CD onto a computer hard drive; this may be kept and used an indefinite amount of times during the 30 days after the making of the copy. In both of the above circumstances, with the permission of the copyright owner, the broadcaster may retain the copy for more than 30 days following its making.

NETWORK SERVICES

As discussed in Chapter 12, "How Is Copyright Infringed?" Internet service providers, search engines, and cloud computing services are not liable for copyright infringement by their users. Those who provide services relating to the operation of the Internet or other digital networks are not liable for infringement when they act solely as intermediaries in communication, hosting, and caching activities. Also, a web hosting service is exempt from liability for storing infringing content, unless the web host knows of a court decision holding that the stored material infringes copyright.

PERSONS WITH PERCEPTUAL DISABILITIES

Under the Copyright Act, perceptual disability is defined as "a disability that prevents or inhibits a person from reading or hearing a literary, musical, dramatic or artistic work in its original format" and includes disabilities from severe or total impairment of sight or hearing or the inability to focus or move one's eyes; the inability to hold or manipulate a book; or an impairment relating to comprehension.

If a person with a perceptual disability or a nonprofit organization acting on his or her behalf, requests it, a person may make a copy or sound recording and/or translate, adapt, or reproduce in sign language, a literary, musical, artistic, or dramatic work (though not a cinematographic work) in a "format specially designed for persons with a perceptual disability." Also, if so requested, a person may perform in public a literary or dramatic work (though not a cinematographic work) in sign language, either live or in a "format specially designed for persons with a perceptual disability." These exceptions do not allow the making of a large print book. Also, the exceptions do not apply where the copyright-protected material is commercially available in a format specially designed to meet the needs of the requesting person.

For any other uses of copyright materials (e.g., large print book version) for persons with perceptual or other disabilities, permission must be obtained from the copyright owner to produce special format materials.

In certain circumstances, it is also possible to export material for print-disabled persons to organizations in other countries. This only applies to accessible material based on works by Canadian authors or authors of the country of reception.

OTHER EXCEPTIONS

Cultural Property Export and Import Act

Permission of the copyright holder is not needed to make a copy of an object referred to in section 14 of the Cultural Property Export and Import Act, for deposit in an institution provided for in that section.

Access to Information Act

Permission of the copyright holder is not needed to disclose, under the Access to Information Act, "a record within the meaning of that Act, or to disclose, pursuant to any like Act of the legislature of a province, like material." However, this section does not authorize any person to whom a record or information is disclosed to do anything that only a copyright owner has the right to do. For example, the person has no right to reproduce or publish the disclosed information.

Privacy Act

Permission of the copyright holder is not required to disclose, under the Privacy Act, "personal information within the meaning of that Act, or to disclose, pursuant to any like Act of the legislature of a province, like information." However, this section does not authorize any person to whom a record or information is disclosed to do anything that only a copyright owner has the right to do.

Broadcasting Act

Permission of the copyright holder is not necessary to make a fixation or a copy of a work or other subject-matter if necessary to comply with the Broadcasting Act or any rule, regulation, or other instrument made under it. However, that copy must be destroyed immediately when it is no longer required. For example, if the Broadcasting Act required that a copy of every broadcast be kept for 30 days, permission of the copyright owner would not be necessary for the making of this copy, and that copy would have to be destroyed at the expiration of the 30 days.

EXCEPTIONS FROM MORAL RIGHTS

The Copyright Act provides some specific exceptions from moral rights. These are listed below. The following acts do not, by that act alone, constitute a distortion, mutilation, or other modification of the work:

- A change in the location of a work.
- The physical means by which a work is exposed or the physical structure containing a work.
- Steps taken in good faith to restore or preserve a work.

SUMMARY

The Copyright Act grants copyright holders a number of rights; however, the Act places certain limitations on these rights that may act as exceptions for those using copyright materials. These exceptions, as set out in the Act, are for specific purposes and specific situations.

CHAPTER 11

HOW CAN RIGHTS BE EXPLOITED?

I skate to where the puck is going to be, not where it has been.

—Wayne Gretzky

HOW THE COPYRIGHT ACT WORKS

One of the main purposes of copyright law is to confer rights upon creators, which they may then exchange for money. This is how the Copyright Act works. Take the example of the author of a book. The author negotiates with a publisher to publish the book. In exchange for the right to publish the book, the publisher generally pays the author royalties, which are a percentage of the selling price of the book. If the author then sells the rights to make a film adaptation of the book, the purchaser of those rights pays the author for their acquisition. The same is true if the author authorizes the translation of the book, and so on. The same scenario applies with respect to all works protected by the Copyright Act and all rights exploitable by their owners.

Now that you know the types of materials protected by copyright law, and you know the sort of rights that belong to copyright owners, you must learn how, as a creator and/or owner, you can exploit these rights and benefit from that exploitation, and how as a consumer of copyright materials, you can obtain the required access to copyright materials.

If you are involved in exploiting rights or obtaining permission to use rights, you must understand certain fundamental concepts about the nature of the rights granted by the Copyright Act and the type of exploitation permitted by the law.

Rights Are "Distinct" and "Exclusive"

One of the most important concepts concerning the nature of the rights set out in the Copyright Act is that these rights are exclusive and distinct. *Exclusive* means that the copyright owner has the "sole right" to do what he or she chooses with a work. No one else may use a copyright-protected work without the permission of the copyright owner. *Distinct* means that each right is separate or independent from any other right and therefore may be dealt with separately by the copyright owner. The concept of "distinct" allows a writer to assign the right to publish a book to a publisher, and the right to make a film of the book to a film producer, and the right to translate the book or publish a print book in an electronic format to someone else.

Since a creator has the sole rights in his or her creations, even where a publisher or film producer has the right to publish a print book or make a movie of a book, that publisher or film producer has no subsequent rights, such as making a translation of the book or publishing an e-book, without further permission of the copyright owner. In other words, the copyright owner must consent to each and every copyright use of a work.

Copyright Is Separate from the Physical Object

Another important concept to keep in mind is that copyright is separate from the physical object in which copyright exists. This means that ownership of copyright does not necessarily follow the physical embodiment of that copyright. For instance, the sale of a painting does not necessarily entail the abandonment of copyright by the copyright holder (or the transfer of copyright in the painting to the owner of the physical painting). Similarly, the purchase of a video does not necessarily mean that any use can be made of that video. If that video is to be shown in public, the right to perform it in public must be cleared from its copyright owner.

Copyright and Moral Rights Are Separate

Remember that copyright and moral rights are separate. Thus, a contract dealing with one does not automatically deal with the other, though in certain circumstances the contract concerning copyright may also include a waiver of moral rights.

WHO CAN PROVIDE PERMISSION TO USE A WORK OR OTHER SUBJECT-MATTER?

In order to authorize someone to use a copyright-protected work, you must have the right to do so. The general rule is that you should be an owner of copyright (see Chapter 7, "Who Owns Copyright?") or have been granted permission by the copyright owner to deal with the authorization of any right set out in the Copyright Act.

The following people or organizations may have the right to grant others to use copyright-protected works or other subject-matter:

- The author of a work, provided this author is also the first owner of the copyright in the work.
- A copyright owner other than the author, by virtue of one of the provisions in the Act granting this status, where, for example, there is an employment situation or where the work is made for the Crown.
- The owner of other subject-matter.
- A legal representative such as heirs, executors, administrators, successors, and assigns, or agents or attorneys as long as they are authorized in writing. In other words, someone to whom the author or copyright owner has given such rights in writing.

- A "duly authorized agent." The Act does not specify that a duly authorized agent must have authority in writing as is the case for a legal representative.

HOW TO EXPLOIT A WORK

Licences and assignments are two ways to allow others to use a copyright-protected work.

In an assignment situation, you "assign" your right thereby permanently giving your copyright, or a part thereof (see divisibility of copyright, below), to someone else. The Act provides that the person who receives the assignment, the assignee of rights, steps into the shoes of a copyright owner with respect to those assigned rights. The assignee may use those acquired rights in the same manner as a copyright owner, within the limitations of the agreement setting out the assignment. A full or partial assignee may also take any legal action that would be open to an owner of copyright to protect those rights.

The person who is giving away certain rights—the assignor—is treated as a copyright owner for any rights that have not been assigned. Thus, the assignor can continue to exercise copyright in certain manners.

Whereas an assignment is like a sale or transfer of rights, a licence is comparable to a lease of rights. In a licence situation, you "license" a piece of your copyright thereby temporarily permitting someone else to use your copyright material.

Using the words "assignment" or "licence" will not by itself guarantee the type of grant of rights you wish to make. The wording of a licence agreement could be such that, in practice, it has a similar effect to an assignment. An important concept to understand is that the rights set out in the Copyright Act may be exploited without necessarily being sold.

In the case of an assignment, you grant an interest in the copyright material or in a specific right in that material. This interest is exclusive and cannot be granted to anyone else. In the case of a licence, there could be a grant of an interest or merely permission to use the right. Generally, this is the difference between an exclusive and a nonexclusive licence. If the licence is exclusive, only one person may benefit from the right in question during a specified period of time. If it is nonexclusive, one or more persons may benefit from the exact same right during the same period of time.

For example, a non-exclusive licence may be given to many movie theatres to show a particular film. Another example is an author of an article providing the right to three different websites to post his article on those sites. A licensee should be aware when he or she is obtaining a nonexclusive licence that others may make the same use of the material. Several people may exercise the same rights in a licence situation (as opposed to an assignment situation) because there is no grant of interest, merely a permission to use the material.

Copyright may be assigned or licensed in a number of ways. The following discussion outlines ways that are specified in the Copyright Act. Although the following discussion may specifically refer to an assignment of copyright, the same rules generally apply to a licence.

By Rights

The Act states that the copyright owner of a work may assign a right "Either wholly or partially." Thus, rights such as publication, reproduction, and performance in public can be divided up for purposes of authorizing others to use the work. What this means is that an artist may assign the right to reproduce a painting to X, and may assign the right to exhibit the painting to Y, and perhaps retain all other rights.

The rights can be divided even more specifically. For instance, an artist may assign the right to reproduce a painting in a book to X, to reproduce the painting in a video to Y, to exhibit the painting in gallery ABC to Z, to exhibit the painting in gallery XYZ to A, to digitize it and include it in a DVD, and so on.

Or a writer could give her publisher the right to publish, translate, make magazine serializations of portions and an audio version, of a book, but she may retain the right to make an e-book or a film version.

In a further example, the right of translation of a book into French could be granted to Jacques, the right to translate it into Italian to Maria, and the right to translate it into Hebrew to Mordecai. All other translation rights could be retained by the copyright owner for the time being.

The ways in which rights can be divided are many and varied under the Canadian Copyright Act. This leaves open the possibility of customizing the division of rights, which underlines the importance of negotiating the rights and related issues in any licence or assignment.

When dividing rights, it is not necessary to use the exact wording found in the Copyright Act. In one court case, an assignment included the right to "manufacture, produce, advertise, publicize, sell, distribute, license or otherwise use or dispose of the copyright material."[1] These words are not all specifically used in the copyright legislation. You can use any language that both parties to the licence or assignment agree upon.

By Time

The Copyright Act states that a copyright owner may assign copyright for the whole term of copyright, or for any part of the duration of copyright. Obviously, the longest length of time that an assignment may endure is for the full length of the copyright protection, that is, 50 years until the calendar year-end after the author's death. There is no minimum length of time for which an assignment may endure.

Different assignments can last for varying lengths of time. For instance, an assignment to X to exhibit a work can last for 15 years, after which time Y may exhibit the work for the next 15 years; at the same time, Z may have the right to reproduce the work for 25 years.

By Territory

A copyright owner may assign a right either generally or subject to territorial limitations. This means that an author may grant a right "worldwide" (for use in the entire world) or "globally," or limited to certain territories. Examples of territorial limitations are North America, Canada, or the West Indies. The size of the territory is irrelevant. Also, there are no restrictions on the segmentation of geographical location to which a copyright can be assigned. In practice, it is rare to divide copyright among a jurisdiction smaller than a country, although "English Language throughout Canada" or "French Language throughout Canada" is an exception to this practice.

Note that the territorial grant of a right does not by itself give the right to control the distribution of legally made copies once these are available in the marketplace. Such protection is made through the specific provisions of the Act that prevent the importation or sale of certain foreign editions.

REGISTERING A GRANT IN INTEREST

The Copyright Act allows for the (voluntary) registration of any "grant of interest" or change in ownership of copyright, or a part of copyright. This registration is through the same registration system for the initial registration of a copyright-protected work, at the Canadian Intellectual Property Office (CIPO), as discussed in Chapter 4. The registration of a subsequent owner of a whole or part of a work protected by copyright can be extremely important to a grantee of a right in copyright. This is because any grantee who has registered a grant of interest will have priority over any other similar grantee of interest if that other interest has not been registered. For instance, if X and Y are both granted an interest in a work protected by copyright and only Y registers this interest, Y may have priority over X with respect to his or her rights in the work. The same is true if A is granted an interest on January 1, B is granted the same interest on February 1, C is granted the same interest on March 1, and D is granted the same interest on April 1, all in the same year. If only C registers this interest, C will have priority over all other claimants in that interest.

Registering a change in ownership of copyright can help new copyright owners be more easily located by those seeking copyright permissions.

Reversionary Interest

There is one statutory limitation on the assignment of copyright that is commonly referred to as the reversionary interest. This provision limits certain assignments to a maximum period of 25 years. Where an author of a work is the first owner of the copyright in it (e.g., it is not a situation of employment or Crown works), any copyright acquired by contract becomes void 25 years after the author's death. Thus, any assignee or licensee of copyright loses his or her rights 25 years after the author's death. At this time, the copyright becomes part of the author's estate and only the estate has the right to deal with the copyright. Note that there is no reversion where the author disposes of the copyright by will for the period following the 25-year limit to the assignee who is already assigned the copyright. Thus, the reversionary interest provision may be avoided by bequeathing copyright for the period between 25 and 50 years after the author's death (but only if the bequeath is to the assignee and not some other person). It also does not apply where a work has been assigned as part of a collective work or a licence has been granted to publish a work or part thereof in a collective work.

Testamentary Dispositions

Like "tangible" property, intellectual property—namely copyright—can be passed on, upon death, to other persons through a will. A person inheriting the physical property (e.g., real estate, furniture, and jewelry) of an author will not necessarily inherit the intangible rights of copyright. However, if there is no specific inclusion or exclusion of copyright in a will, then upon the death of a copyright owner, copyright would pass to the heirs of the copyright owner's tangible property.

A copyright holder who, upon his or her death, would like copyright in some or all of his works to pass on to specific persons, should specify this in his or her will. Such copyright holders should consider appointing a copyright executor, that is, someone with special knowledge in the area and someone who understands the copyright holder's desires.

It is important that the copyright executor be in a position that enables him or her to carry out the desires of the copyright holder, and is not in any position that may give rise to a conflict of interest. For example, a publisher may be in an awkward position to be an executor for a writer who publishes with that publisher's firm. A copyright holder is not limited to specifying one specific copyright executor. For instance, two people may jointly be the executor, or there may be different executors for different works or with respect to different rights in the same work.

COPYRIGHT IN FUTURE WORKS

The current Copyright Act only deals with the granting of rights in existing works. There is no specific mention of assignments or licences of creations to be made in the future. One case has held that there can be an assignment in future works in the form of an agreement to assign.[2]

In practical terms, assignments in future works often take place. For example, a writer signs a publishing contract with a publishing house for a yet unwritten book. The same is true with respect to music publishing contracts.

Some licence and assignment agreements for digital content request the rights for any medium whatsoever whether currently existing or as yet to be "discovered." Copyright owners should carefully think about giving away such broad rights. For instance, a copyright holder who published a book 20 years ago may still have the electronic rights to that book; however, if 20 years ago, he signed an agreement to publish the book in any medium whatsoever whether then existing or to be invented in the future, he likely already gave away his electronic rights.

If a copyright holder is given an offer to assign future rights to a work, the copyright holder should consider whether the sum of money is worth the value of "unknown" rights and whether he or she should retain and negotiate those rights at a later date. Copyright holders must always keep in mind that each right has a value attached to it. Persons and organizations obtaining electronic rights should, on the other hand, ensure that they have all the necessary rights to be able to create and distribute an electronic product.

The Value of Rights and Structure of Payment

Like most things in an agreement concerning the use of copyright materials, the value or permission to use the materials is a matter of negotiation to be agreed upon by the involved parties. The Copyright Act does not set out the amount of money or other compensation for which a work may be negotiated. The Act sets out the rights of a copyright holder; then it is up to that copyright holder, or a representative, to place a value on that right when permitting particular uses in particular circumstances.

The value of a right will depend on many factors, including the nature of the copyright material, the popularity of the creator, the use(s) to which the material is to be made, and the demand in the marketplace. A copyright holder and anyone wishing to use copyright material must come to terms on the value of any assignment or licence. In some circumstances, professional associations may have information on compensation rates, which may be helpful for both creators and users when determining such rates in particular cases.

When the value of a right is based on monetary compensation, the copyright holder may receive a one-time flat fee or ongoing payments based upon the quantity of copies sold, or more often, based upon the revenue received, from the use of the copyright material. These ongoing payments are referred to as royalties.

A "royalty advance," which is usually "recoupable" against future earnings, can also be negotiated. For instance, a writer may get a lump sum payment upon signing a contract with a book publisher. This is called a royalty advance. When the book is published and sold in the marketplace, the writer may be entitled to royalties based upon a percentage of the same price of the book. Before paying the writer any royalties, the publisher will first deduct any royalty advances made to the writer. In that sense, the advance is recoupable. The manner in which royalties and advances are set out in an agreement varies in each industry such as film, book publishing, digital media, and the visual arts. Specific industry associations may be able to guide you on these matters.

Compensation for, and structure of payments for, electronic rights may vary from traditional rights. Some electronic works are *nonlinear* and do not have beginnings and endings per se, and the works are accessed and used by consumers or end users in manners that make it difficult to measure. Some questions to consider in establishing a structure of payment for electronic rights include the following: Will there be a lump sum fee or a royalty based on a percentage of sales? If the electronic product is distributed electronically, will the compensation be defined by the number of people who access the work and/or amount of time people access the digital works? As with traditional works, issues relating to payment are negotiable.

ASSIGNMENT MUST BE IN WRITING

The Copyright Act specifically states that no assignment or grant is valid unless it is in writing and signed by the owner of the right in respect of which the assignment or grant is made. Thus, where there is an assignment of copyright or a licence granting an interest in copyright, there should be a written agreement to this effect signed by the copyright owner and the person obtaining any rights. A verbal agreement is not adequate unless it is confirmed in writing. If there is no written agreement regarding the assignment of copyright, ownership of copyright is determined by the rules set out in the Act.

Exclusive and nonexclusive licences that do not entail a proprietary interest, and involve mere permission to use copyright materials, may be granted orally. The fact that a written agreement is not mandatory should not prevent the making of one. A written agreement can clearly set out the terms and conditions of any agreement and can provide clarity and proof in any situation.

What Is an Implied Licence?

In specific circumstances, permission can be implied by the conduct of the copyright owner. However, to determine an implied licence, one has to examine all of the surrounding circumstances, and it will never be as clear as explicit permission or written permission. Since an implied licence is not explicitly granted, its existence is usually alleged as a defence to a claim of copyright infringement.

What Is a Valid Contract?

The Copyright Act does not specifically deal with the legal parameters of contracts. However, since the rights in the Copyright Act may be licensed or assigned, those creating or using copyright materials must have an understanding of the basic requirements of a valid contract. As a basic rule, a valid contract or agreement has three components:

1. Offer
2. Acceptance of the offer
3. Consideration

An offer is a proposal, and manifestation of willingness, by one person (the offeror) to enter into a contract with another person (the offeree), based on certain terms and conditions. The offer must be communicated by the offeror, and the offeree must have the chance to be able to reject or accept it. The offer must be one that is capable of being accepted. Acceptance of the offer means that the offeree has agreed to enter into the contract. The acceptance can be in the form of conduct or by words.

A valid contract must include the element of consideration. Consideration is something that is of some value in the eyes of the law. Money is one example of consideration. *Black's Law Dictionary* defines consideration as "The inducement to a contract. . .[s]ome right, interest, profit or benefit accruing to one party, or some forbearance, detriment, loss, or responsibility, given, suffered, or undertaken by the other."

A contract is valid only between the parties who agreed to it. Any terms and conditions to which the parties agree, provided they do not contravene any specific laws, may be included in the contract. A contract need not take a specific form or be drafted by particular people. It can be written on a napkin by the parties involved or be prepared by a lawyer. In most situations, there is no requirement that the contract be in writing, with the notable exception for an assignment or grant of interest in copyright. Although an oral contract may be valid in many circumstances, it is always a good idea to have a written contract since, if the parties to the agreement ever end up in court, a written agreement will be easier to prove than an oral agreement.

Contracts vary from industry to industry and in each particular circumstance depending on the negotiated terms and conditions. Standard contracts, for example for book publishing, screenplay options, art exhibitions, website content, and so on, are available in various books and publications, online, and through professional organizations. These contracts will highlight points you need to address in your own situation; however, they should be thoroughly examined and customized to meet your particular circumstances. Contract law is a provincial and territorial matter, and the requirements for a valid contract may vary in each province or territory.

This book aims at providing with you an understanding of the rights set out in the Canadian Copyright Act and how you can license and assign these rights. If you are involved with licensing your own rights, negotiating licence agreements, and using the content of others according to a licence agreement, there is much information online and in written materials to help you navigate through a variety of agreements.[3]

MORAL RIGHTS

Moral Rights Not Assignable

Moral rights cannot be assigned. This is because moral rights protect the reputation of an author and are therefore a personal right.

Waiving Moral Rights

Although moral rights cannot be assigned, an author can decide not to exercise these rights, and may waive the exercise of them. Moral rights may be waived in whole or in part. An author, then, may agree not to exercise certain moral rights and can still retain other moral rights. For example, an author could waive the moral right to have his or her name appear in association with a work, but retain the right to use a work in association with a service, cause, or institution. Further, there is nothing in the Act to prevent an author from waiving rights in favour of one person in one arrangement and not waiving them in agreements with other persons.

If an author chooses to waive a moral right in a work, it should be expressed clearly, and the author should understand what he or she is doing. The mere fact that an author is assigning copyright in a work does not mean that the author is also waiving the moral rights. If you waive moral rights, you will not be able to stop any "harmful" changes or manipulations to images, text, music, and so forth, including those in digital formats. The Act does not specify that a moral rights waiver need be in writing, and a waiver may therefore be in writing, oral, express, or implied.[4]

Where an author waives his or her moral rights in a work in favour of an assignee or licensee of copyright, any new copyright owner or licensee may also be privy to a previous waiver of moral rights. This is true unless the author in connection with the original waiver has indicated something to the contrary in the original waiver; for instance, that the waiver did not extend any further than the owner or licensee on behalf of whom the waiver was originally made.

Testamentary Dispositions

There are specific rules in the Copyright Act dealing with moral rights upon the death of the author of a copyright-protected work. The Act states that when an author dies, his or her moral rights pass to the person to whom those rights are specifically left. Where there is no specific provision dealing with moral rights in a will and an author dies with a will that deals with copyright in the work, moral rights pass to the person to whom that copyright is left. If neither of the above two situations occur, moral rights pass to the person entitled to any other (tangible) property belonging to the author. If a person is bequeathed moral rights, he or she in turn may bequeath those same moral rights to another person.

NOTE

Since copyright can be divided in a variety of ways, be very specific about the rights set out in any agreement concerning copyright and/or waivers of moral rights. Specificity is required for many elements such as particular rights in the assignment or licence, duration of assignment or licence, territorial limitations, and royalties. As a copyright owner, make sure you only license or assign those rights that are necessary for that particular exploitation. As a licensee or assignee, make sure you obtain all the necessary rights to allow you to exploit the material in the manner you wish. Also, always keep in mind that moral rights cannot be assigned or licensed and are treated separately from copyright.

OTHER SUBJECT-MATTER

The owner of a performer's performance, sound recording, and broadcast signal may assign or license the right in whole or in part. For example, a performer may license the use of his performance for purposes of broadcasting or fixation. (However, this does not apply if the performer authorizes the use of a performance in a cinematograph.)

Moral rights in a performer's performance may not be assigned but may be waived in whole or in part, and may be bequeathed in a will.

The blank audio recording media levy may also be licensed or assigned.

THE COLLECTIVE ADMINISTRATION OF COPYRIGHT

There is nothing in the Copyright Act that states that a copyright owner must exercise copyright on an individual basis. In fact, in some circumstances, copyright holders cannot collect royalties unless they do so as a "group." There are a number of copyright-holder groups, or collectives, that administer different rights in the Act. Collectives, also known as "societies" or "licensing bodies" are specifically referred to in the Act and, in many respects, are governed by it. In certain respects, these collectives operate under their own rules. This section will discuss various aspects of collectives.

The collective exercise of copyright began in the Canadian music industry and now spreads throughout the literary and visual arts. When a copyright holder joins a collective, the copyright holder permits the collective to negotiate royalties on his or her behalf. These royalties are collectable from consumers of copyright materials, and once collected by the collective are distributed back to the appropriate copyright owners.

There are two types of licences that a collective can negotiate with users of copyright materials:

1. Blanket licences
2. Specific use licences (also called individual or transactional licences)

A blanket licence covers all the materials that a collective represents. These materials are known as the collective's repertoire. A blanket licence will allow a user to do specified things with any and all materials in the repertoire. Blanket licences are paid for in advance for a specified period of time and allow unlimited use, for example, copying or performing in public, within the terms of the licence. For instance, a licence to perform live music in a certain bar may cost $1,000, which covers a one-year period for all live music performances in that bar.

The other type of licence does not give blanket permission to use all of the copyright materials in a collective's repertoire. For example, a specific use licence requires clearance and payment each time material is used. A specific use licence requires clearance and permission for each material each time that material is used.

One of the primary reasons for the establishment of collectives under the Copyright Act is to allow them to issue blanket licences, thereby eliminating the need for a multitude of permissions to clear copyright. The collectives would collect and distribute the royalties or levies to appropriate rights holders, normally based on usage reports supplied by the licensees. Certain royalties or levies payable under the Copyright Act are *only* payable to collectives and not directly to individual rights holders. This includes the retransmission right of telecommunication signals and the blank audio recording media levy.

In addition to dealing with royalties, some collectives may take appropriate action against an infringer of copyright and may provide assistance in defending the interests of its members. Also, collectives may take an advocacy role, such as lobbying for revision of the copyright law.

Although each collective may have a different mandate and operate differently, they all share some common ground. Basically, copyright holders join the appropriate collective; that is, the collective that exercises the particular right(s) that concern their creations. The collectives then establish a royalty rate to be paid by various users of the copyright materials in their repertoire. In the case of the performing rights collective and the retransmission ones, for example, the Copyright Board, a specialized tribunal dealing only with specific copyright matters, determines this rate. In the case of other collectives like the reprography ones, the Copyright Board will set the rate and terms and conditions if so requested by either the collective or the person or user with whom the royalty rate is being negotiated. Once the rates are set, users are able to obtain blanket or specific use licences, upon paying the established fee. The collective collects all these fees, applies some of it to administration costs and distributes the remaining monies to copyright holders, based upon their set formulas.

Collectives do not deal with moral rights, and it is the responsibility of the consumer to respect the moral rights of creators or to obtain a waiver of moral rights.

Although collectives are regulated by the Copyright Act, each collective is responsible for determining its own day-to-day operations and rules; no two collectives operate in exactly the same manner. If you are interested in joining a collective, or accessing works within a collective's repertoire, you should contact the collective that deals with your type of rights and/or works. Contact information for various collectives is in Chapter 14, "Legally Using Content."

CREATIVE COMMON LICENCES

A Creative Commons (CC) licence is a licence that a creator places on his or her work that sets out the terms and conditions of use of that work. A creator can choose from the various free licences CC offers. The licences are not flexible, and a creator has to choose the one that most closely meets his or her needs. A CC licence may, for example, allow outright use of work without permissions or may allow noncommercial reproduction of a work. If you are using a work with a CC licence, read the licence to see what uses are permitted without authorization. At the time of this writing, information on CC Canada is at http://creativecommons.org/tag.ca.

SUMMARY

A copyright holder, or representative, can assign or license, on an individual basis or through a copyright collective, the economic rights in works and neighbouring rights in other subject-matter. These rights can be divided by right, time, and territory. The assignment or licence of copyrights has no effect on the transfer of ownership of moral rights. In fact, moral rights cannot be assigned or licensed, but the exercise of them may be waived. Copyrights and moral rights may be dealt with in a will.

CHAPTER 12

HOW IS COPYRIGHT INFRINGED?

All the things I really like to do are either illegal, immoral, or fattening.
—Alexander Woollcott (1887–1943), in *Wit's End* (1973)
by R.E. Drennan

WHAT IS AN INFRINGEMENT OF COPYRIGHT?

Violation of copyright means a breach of the copyright law. *Infringement* is the term used in the Copyright Act to denote this violation.

Direct infringement occurs where a right in the Act is directly infringed, and indirect infringement occurs through dealings with infringing copies. These dealings must normally be of a commercial nature.

To fully understand this chapter, you should read Chapter 9, "Rights Protected by Copyright," as well as Chapter 10, "Limitation on Rights." Chapter 13 discusses the remedies for the infringement of copyright.

TERMS USED TO DESCRIBE INFRINGEMENTS OF COPYRIGHT

Infringement or *violation* of copyright law are common terms to describe unauthorized uses of copyright-protected works. There are a number of other terms the public uses in connection with copyright infringement or related activities. These terms include *plagiarism, piracy, bootlegging,* and *counterfeiting*. These are not legal expressions found in the copyright statute, but may include activities that are referred to in the Act. These words are explained below in terms of their actual meaning and also in terms of the copyright law. Where aspects of these activities are not covered by copyright law, they may be unlawful under other areas of law.

Plagiarism

Plagiarism is a term often used in association with literary works. According to *Black's Law Dictionary*, plagiarism is "the act of appropriating the literary composition of another, or parts of passages or his writings, or the ideas or language of the same, and passing them off as the product of one's own mind." As such, plagiarism may infringe the right to reproduce a copyright-protected work and may also infringe the moral right of the author to have his or her name associated with his or her work. Plagiarism may also apply to works that are in the public domain and no longer protected by copyright. Where plagiarism is an appropriation of ideas, without the appropriation of the actual expression of those ideas, it is not an infringement of copyright since copyright does not protect ideas.

Piracy

Piracy is the illicit duplication of legitimate works or other subject-matter. For instance, reprinted books, movies, and computer software may be pirated versions. Pirated goods are usually recognized because of substandard packaging and labels, as well as quality of the copied materials. Piracy is an infringement of the right of reproduction and may also involve plagiarism. Piracy is also used to refer to "stealing" copyright materials from the Internet.

Bootlegging

Bootlegging is the unauthorized recording of a live event, such as a concert. Bootlegging (i.e., making an unauthorized audio or video recording) is an infringement of the right in a performer's performance, and if copyright-protected works are being performed, an infringement of the right in that underlying work.

Counterfeiting

Counterfeiting is making a copy of something without authority and deceiving or defrauding the public by passing that copy off as original or genuine. Where you have a counterfeit product—for instance, a tape containing music or computer software—that item as well as any affixed labels and packaging are illegally reproduced. Counterfeiting involves an infringement of the right of reproduction. Counterfeiting usually refers to trade-mark (as opposed to copyright) infringement and can also apply to products such as watches or automobile parts where there is no copyright involved.

Moral Rights Infringement

In all of the above cases, the copy may be an inferior reproduction of the original product, resulting, for example, in poor sound quality in the case of a sound recording, in poor picture quality in the case of an audiovisual recording, or containing bugs in the case of computer software—these are all arguably infringements of moral rights.

COPYRIGHT

Direct Infringement (Directly Infringing a Right)

In basic terms, copyright is infringed by doing any of the things or exercising any of the rights that only the copyright owner may do, without the consent of the copyright owner. Thus, you cannot reproduce a book, show a film to the public, post an image on a blog, or record a live performance without infringing copyright, unless you have obtained permission from the copyright holder. Also, you cannot authorize the use of any of the exclusive rights of the copyright holder.

Ignorance of the law is no excuse for the direct infringement of copyright. Further, it is irrelevant whether the work or other subject-matter is marked as being protected by copyright, whether copying is done in good faith, whether the infringer had any intention of making money, or whether the infringement was for commercial or noncommercial purposes.[1] What is relevant is that the work or other subject-matter was performed, published, recorded, and so forth without the consent of the copyright owner.

Infringement of copyright is a question of fact, and the circumstances of each alleged copyright infringement must be examined based upon its own facts. The facts of each individual case of copyright infringement must be applied to the definition of each right set out in the Act. The following section is an illustration of some of the considerations a court may take into account when hearing a copyright infringement case.

Infringement of the Right to Produce or Reproduce

An author has the right "to produce or reproduce the work or any substantial part thereof." Anyone who uses this right without the permission of the copyright holder is infringing copyright. Thus, only an author may reproduce or authorize a reproduction of his or her work, or make any "colourable imitation" of the work (i.e., a disguised reproduction). Whether something is a colourable imitation is a question of fact. "Colourable imitation" has been found in a modified Popeye character,[2] a radio broadcast of a sketch,[3] and in substantial borrowed parts of a compilation, rearranged and published in a different format.[4]

As is included in the definition of the right to reproduce a work, the reproduction right applies to a "substantial" reproduction of the original work. The infringing work, then, need not be a work copied in its entirety. It is only illegal when a substantial part of a work has been appropriated. This is a question of fact that depends upon many factors including the quality and the quantity of the portions used from the original work, the degree of competition with the original work, and the nature of the reproduction.

It is fairly straightforward that an infringement occurs when a work is copied word for word. However, where portions are added and omitted, the infringement is a question of fact, and each case must be examined on its own to see the substantiality of the reproduction or the degree of the amount taken.

Recall that there is no copyright in ideas, and therefore the use of an idea cannot be an infringement of copyright. However, when the form or expression of an idea is copied, there may be a copyright infringement. It is not an infringement where two people create similar works, based on similar ideas or facts, as long as each work is created on its own, and the creators did not have access to the other's work, thereby each used information from the original sources.

Subconscious copying may be illegal. For example, if someone hears a tune on the radio, then later "composes" a very similar tune, there may be a copyright infringement. For example, George Harrison was found to have subconsciously copied elements of the music from the Chiffons hit "He's So Fine" in his song "My Sweet Lord."[5] In a subconscious copying claim, the copyright holder must prove substantial similarity to his or her work as well as access to it, and of course, that a substantial portion was copied.

Reproducing a copy of a work may also be an infringement of this right.

In determining copyright infringement, a court will look at similarities between the two works, and not the differences. Witnesses may give evidence in their analysis of the two works in question on the similarity of the two works.

Indirect or Secondary Infringement

Indirect infringement concerns certain activities such as selling infringing copies of copyright-protected content. It also involves acts to which the copyright owner does not have exclusive rights, but that nevertheless infringe copyright. The Copyright Act states that copyright is infringed by any person who does the following activities with any work, sound recording, or fixation of a performer's performance or communication signal, that to the knowledge of that person infringes copyright (or he or she should have known that it would infringe copyright), or that it would infringe copyright if it had been made in Canada (but not under a limitation or exception in the Copyright Act):

- Sells or rents it, or by way of trade exposes or offers it for sale or rent.
- Distributes to such an extent as to affect prejudicially the owner of the copyright.
- Exhibits in public by way of trade.
- Possesses a work, sound recording, or fixation of a performer's performance or communication signal for purposes of doing any of the three above things with it.
- Imports it into Canada for sale or rent.

Unlike direct infringement, when there is indirect infringement, the infringer may plead ignorance. Where, however, copyright is marked on the protected material (e.g., the copyright symbol is placed on a work), it will be difficult for an infringer to succeed with a defence of ignorance since it is obvious that copyright probably exists in the item.

Public Performance for Profit

Further, there is indirect copyright infringement where any person who, for profit, permits a theatre or other place of entertainment to be used for the performance in public of a work or other subject-matter without the consent of the copyright holder, unless that person was not aware, and had no reasonable ground for suspecting, that the performance would be an infringement of copyright. Therefore, any owner of an entertainment establishment should be careful in contracting out the use of his or her establishment.

Secondary Infringement Related to Lesson

As discussed in Chapter 10, there are specific uses of lessons, tests, and examinations permitted by educational institutions. Subject to those permitted uses, it is an infringement of copyright for a person to do the following acts with respect to anything that the person knows or should have known is a lesson, or a fixation of a lesson: sell or rent it; distribute it to the extent that the owner of the copyright is prejudicially affected; by way of trade, distribute it, expose or offer it for sale, or rent it or exhibit in public; possess it for any of the previous acts; communicate it by telecommunication to any unauthorized person.

Infringement by Provision of Network Services

An infringement can occur by providing services through the Internet, or another digital network, that are designed primarily to enable acts of copyright infringement if infringement occurs as a result of using that service. This gives rights holders a way to enforce their rights against Internet service providers, websites, web hosts, or peer-to-peer file sharing networks who enable copyright infringement. In determining whether a service enables infringement, a court will examine the following factors:

- Whether the person expressly or implicitly marketed or promoted the service as a service that could be used to enable copyright infringement.
- Whether the person had knowledge that the service was used to enable a significant number of acts of copyright infringement.
- Whether the service has significant uses other than to enable acts of copyright infringement.
- The person's ability to limit acts of copyright infringement, and the actions taken by the person to do so.
- Any benefits the person received from enabling the acts of copyright infringement.
- The economic viability of the service if it were not used to enable copyright infringement.

Are Internet Service Providers (ISPs) and Search Engines Responsible for Their Users?

Generally, Internet service providers, search engines, and cloud computing services are not liable for copyright infringement by their users.[6] They are not liable if they merely provide passive connections for content and act solely as intermediaries for their subscribers and users.

At the time of writing this book, there is no legally required system for ISPs and others to remove allegedly infringing content hosted on their service when a copyright owner notifies the ISP. However, anyone, including Canadians, may employ the U.S. "notice and takedown" procedure if a site or search engine in the United States hosts alleged infringing content.[7] Most U.S. online hosts have designated agents and procedures for notification by content owners; when an online service provider receives a notice from a copyright owner that infringing content is available on its service, the service must quickly remove the infringing content.

There is a voluntary "notice and notice" regime currently used by Canadian ISPs. When an ISP receives a notice from a copyright owner that an ISP subscriber may be infringing copyright, the ISP forwards the notice to the subscriber. An ISP may (but is not obligated to do so) forward the notice to the subscriber who posted the allegedly infringing content; it is up to each ISP to determine its further action upon receiving a notice from a copyright owner. This is now codified in the Copyright Act but is not in effect at the time of writing this book.[8]

When the notice and notice regime in the Copyright Act comes into force, the notice of claimed infringement from the copyright owner must contain any information required by any regulations, as well as the claimant's name and address; the claimant's interest or right regarding the work or other subject-matter in question; the location date for the electronic location where the alleged infringement takes place; specifics of the alleged infringement; and specifics of the date and time of the alleged infringement. The ISP or search engine must forward the notice to the alleged infringer. The provider will have the discretion to remove allegedly infringing content. If the provider fails to share the notice with the alleged infringer or does not share it and does not explain this to the claimant/copyright owner, the claimant's only remedy is statutory damages between $5,000 and $10,000. Damages and other remedies are discussed in detail in Chapter 13.

Possession of Plates

A plate is defined in the Copyright Act as "any stereotype or other plate, stone, block, mould, matrix, transfer or negative used or intended to be used for printing or reproducing copies of any work" and "any matrix or other appliance used or intended to be used for making or reproducing sound recordings, performer's performances or communication signals. It is an infringement for any person to make or possess a plate that is specifically designed or adapted to make infringing copies of a work or other subject-matter."

MORAL RIGHTS

An infringement of moral rights occurs in a work or in a performer's performance where any act or omission is done contrary to any of the moral rights in the absence of a waiver by the author or performer. For instance, an infringement may be omitting the author's name on his or her work. Also, an infringement may be modifying a work in a manner prejudicial to the honour or reputation of an author or performer; for example, colourizing or digitally manipulating a photograph. Further, an infringement may be associating a work with a cause or product, resulting in prejudice to the honour or reputation of the author or performer.

Paintings, sculptures, and engravings are subject to lessened burdens of proof in the case of moral rights infringements. The prejudice to the honour or reputation of the creator of these works is deemed to have occurred when any painting, sculpture, or engraving is distorted, mutilated, or otherwise modified.

There is nothing in the Act that says that a single act cannot be both an infringement of copyright and moral rights. For example, an adaptation of a play without permission may be an infringement of both copyright and moral rights if the adaptation is prejudicial to the honour or reputation of the author.

Rights Management Information

It is an infringement to intentionally remove or alter any rights management information (RMI) on protected materials. RMI may identify the owner of the copyright in a work, performer's performance or sound recording, or be terms and conditions relating to the use of a work, performance, or sound recording. Examples of RMI include a copyright notice, electronic watermark, and metadata.

Technological Protection Measures

A technological protection measure (TPM) is a copyright owner authorized technology, device, or component that controls access to, or restricts a remuneration-bearing act, in a work, performer's performance fixed in a sound recording, or in a sound recording. Examples of TPMs are encryption and password protection (on content.) TPMs are sometimes referred to as digital locks. These locks can prevent unauthorized access to copyright materials and can also prevent unauthorized reproduction of copyright materials.

It is an infringement of copyright to circumvent TPMs. Infringement may occur by descrambling a scrambled work, decrypting an encrypted work, or otherwise avoiding, bypassing, removing, deactivating, or impairing a TPM. It is also an infringement to offer or provide services primarily for the purposes of circumventing a TPM, or market services for the purposes of circumventing a TPM. Further, an infringement occurs by manufacturing, importing, distributing, offering for sale or rental any technology, device, or component if aimed at circumventing a TPM.[9]

SPOTTING ILLEGAL WORKS

From time to time, you may come across what appears to be illegal reproductions of copyright-protected works or other subject-matter. For instance, you may rent a DVD that has photocopied labels, typographic errors, or incorrect credits or titles, or one that has poor picture quality and plays in mono as opposed to stereo. Or you may purchase computer software where the packaging, labeling, instruction manuals, and purchase price lead you to suspect that you have not purchased a legal copy. Also, you may come across a sound recording with a label indicating a certain artist who is, in fact, different from the artist performing on the sound recording. Films that are for sale on DVDs or available on online sites that are still in the theatres are likely unauthorized copies. Motion pictures are generally only available for purchase or rental at least two (and up to six) months after their first theatrical release. Works offered for sale from street vendors or at a flea market, or for very low prices, or only for cash, may be illegal copies.

Many associations that represent particular groups of copyright holders have antipiracy units that are equipped to make investigations on such claims. If you encounter suspicious goods, you may want to contact one of these associations. For example, Music Canada has an antipiracy unit. If you come across suspect sound recordings for sale that may infringe copyright, contact Music Canada (www.musiccanada. ca). The Motion Picture Association—Canada (MPA-C), which represents major international producers and distributors of movies, home entertainment, and TV programming in Canada (www.mpa-canada. org), investigates claims relating to the illegal production, distribution, or sale of movies, television programs, or satellite signals. More specifically, the MPA-C targets the manufacturing and distribution or sale of counterfeit DVDs; the use of the Internet for pirating motion pictures and television programs; and the illegal recording of motion pictures in theatres.

SUMMARY

Copyright may be infringed directly, by using one of the exclusive rights of the copyright holder without permission, or indirectly through certain dealings with an infringing copy of a work or other subject-matter. Moral rights can be infringed through any act or omission that is contrary to any of the moral rights.

CHAPTER 13

What Are the Remedies for the Infringement of Copyright?

I didn't want to write for pay. I wanted to be paid for what I write.

—Leonard Cohen

Remedies in General

When the rights of a copyright holder are infringed, that copyright holder is entitled to certain remedies for the infringement. These remedies could be preventing further infringement, and/or seeking compensation or redress for the infringing acts. Remedies for the infringement of copyright can be divided into three categories: border, civil, and criminal.

The infringement of copyright may involve additional violations of the law other than copyright; for instance, Criminal Code offences, trade-mark infringement, privacy rights, and contractual violations. This chapter sets out remedies specifically referring to copyright, and specifically found in the Copyright Act since these are the most prominent and most obvious remedies employed in copyright infringement cases. If you consult a lawyer, he or she will discuss whether there is an infringement of copyright and the full range of remedies in copyright law or other areas of the law. Your lawyer will also discuss the time and expense involved in copyright litigation, as well as realistic expectations with respect to your likely outcome.

The copyright owner, plaintiff, or defendant (both of these latter terms are defined below) may be a person or corporation. The exception is that the plaintiff in a moral rights infringement suit must be a natural person or the estate of a natural person.

BORDER REMEDIES

Border remedies allow allegedly infringing or pirated copyright materials being imported into Canada to be detained at the border. The rationale behind these remedies is that it is easier to stop infringing copies at the border than after they are dispersed throughout the country. Since January 1, 1994, the Canadian Copyright Act has had more comprehensive provisions dealing with the importation of infringing copyright-protected works or other subject-matter into Canada. A notable change in 1994 is that Canadian Customs officials could act on copyright materials in addition to books.

In order to get Canadian Customs officers at the border to detain suspected infringing copies of your work, you must obtain a court order. This is done by making an application to the Federal Court of Canada or to a superior court of law in any of the provinces. The person who makes the application, the "applicant," must be the copyright owner or exclusive licensee of the copyright (or a lawyer representing such people). The applicant must notify the Minister of Revenue of the court action.

The application must provide the following information:

1. That the copyright material is about to be imported into Canada or has been imported into Canada but has not yet been released, either:
   a. In the jurisdiction where the material was made and it was made without the consent of the person who then owned the copyright in that jurisdiction, or

   b. The material was made elsewhere than in a country to which the Act applies, and

2. The material, to the knowledge of the importer, would have infringed copyright if made in Canada by the importer.

If the court is satisfied that these conditions have been made, it may issue a court order. This court order will direct the Minister of National Revenue to take reasonable measures to detain the work or other subject-matter (i.e., Customs officials may detain the work at the border). The order will direct the Minister of National Revenue to notify the applicant and the importer once the works or other subject-matter have been detained and provide reasons for the detention. The court may provide for any other matters it considers appropriate.

Before making an order, the court may require some security from the applicant. The court will fix the amount of the security based on covering duties, storage, handling charges, and other amounts that may become chargeable against the works or other subject-matter. The security amount may also reflect any other reimbursement for expenses incurred by the owner, importer, or consignee of the materials.

The applicant or the importer may be given an opportunity by the Minister of Revenue to inspect the detained materials in order to substantiate or refuse, as appropriate, the applicant's claim.

The applicant must commence a court action for copyright infringement within two weeks of the goods being detained by Customs officials. Otherwise, the allegedly infringing materials will be released without notice to the applicant. This will happen if the applicant does not notify the Minister of Revenue that he or she has commenced a court action for a final determination by the court on the issues set out in the initial application.

If the court makes a final determination in favour of the applicant, the court may make any order it considers appropriate. This includes an order that the works or other subject-matter be destroyed, or be delivered to the applicant as the applicant's "property absolutely."

Whether or not the applicant is successful in his application, he is still able to pursue other remedies in the Copyright Act. The border remedies specifically included in the Copyright Act are in addition to any other rights a copyright owner may have under the Customs Act.

There are also border measures against parallel imports of books as described in Chapter 9, "Rights Protected by Copyright."

FURTHER INFORMATION ON BORDER REMEDIES CAN BE OBTAINED FROM:

Canada Border Services Agency (CBSA)

Ottawa, ON K1A 0L8

Telephone: 1.800.461.9999 (toll free within Canada)

Calls outside of Canada: 204.983.3500 or 506.636.5064

E-mail: contact@cbsa.gc.ca

Web: www.cbsa-asfc.gc.ca

Specifically, see Memorandum D19–4–3 Copyrights and Trademarks at http://www.cbsa-asfc.gc.ca/publications/dm-md/d19/d19-4-3-eng.html.

Printed Matter

In addition to, and separate from, the above border remedies are distinct remedies for the importation of "reprints" of certain copyright-protected works, "reprints of Canada copyrighted works, and reprints of British copyrighted works which have been copyrighted in Canada."[1] *Reprints* basically means reprints of books, though calendars were once stopped at the border under this provision.

If authors or publishers or other copyright owners wish to stop books from entering the country, they must state so in writing to the CBSA. Any request would require certain information such as the name and nationality of the author, publisher, title of book, and the place of publication. Once satisfied with the request, the book will be included in Tariff Item 9897.00.00 of the Customs Tariff Schedule, and all books bearing that title will be stopped at the border. No court order is required for books, although it is possible to proceed by obtaining a court order and to follow the procedures set out above for all copyright-protected works. Further information can be obtained from the CBSA at the above address.

Once a book is deemed to be in the Customs Tariff Schedule, no one, including the copyright owner, can import it (unless there is an explicit provision allowing such importation, as discussed in previous chapters).

CIVIL REMEDIES

A civil remedy allows a copyright holder to take direct action against a person (or company, etc.) who infringes his or her copyright. A copyright owner whose rights have been infringed is entitled to a number of civil remedies such as an injunction, damages, accounts of profits, delivery up and "otherwise that are or may be conferred by law for the infringement of a right." Unless copyright is registered with the Canadian Intellectual Property Office, a plaintiff is only entitled to an injunction (and no damages, etc.) if the defendant proves that, at the date of the infringement, the defendant was "not aware and had no reasonable grounds for suspecting that copyright subsisted in the work or other subject-matter." The same is true for any authors whose moral rights have been infringed. In certain circumstances, copyright owners whose rights have been infringed may join together and sue the alleged infringer as a class action. The available remedies are described below.

Although a court of law awards civil remedies, equivalent remedies may be obtained by individuals without going through lengthy and complete court proceedings. Once an alleged infringer has been notified by a copyright holder that copyright is being infringed, there are many opportunities for an out-of-court settlement. For instance, the parties might settle after a warning letter (a cease and desist letter) is issued to the alleged infringer, or after the copyright holder initiates a lawsuit with documents that have been filed with the court and that have been delivered to the alleged infringer. As well, mediation and alternative dispute resolution are increasingly popular methods of set-tling out of court. Although mediation and arbitration may allow for quicker, less expensive, and less formal ways of settling a dispute, there are advantages and disadvantages associated with each alternative dis-pute mechanism, and a lawyer could advise you on how best to pro-ceed. The copyright statute gives direction to disputing parties as to what damages and other measures are appropriate for an out-of-court settlement.

Provisions for summary proceedings are also available under the Copyright Act to help speed up the court procedures for certain infringements. As of October 1, 1999, these summary procedures are available for copyright or moral rights infringement cases, and in rela-tion to tariffs set by the Board including the private copying tariff. Unless the court determines otherwise, it will hear and determine these cases "without delay and in a summary way."

Removal or Alteration of Rights Management Information

A copyright owner is entitled to all remedies (injunction, damages, accounts, and delivery up) against anyone who removes or alters rights management information from a work, a performer's performance fixed in a sound recording, or a sound recording.

Circumvention of Technological Protection Measure

A copyright owner is entitled to all remedies (injunction, damages, accounts, and delivery up) against anyone who circumvents technologi-cal protection measures (TPMs) in a work, performer's performance fixed in a sound recording, or a sound recording. An owner may not elect statutory damages from an individual who has circumvented TPMs for his or her own private purposes.

Limitation Period on Civil Actions

A copyright holder must sue an alleged infringer within three years of the commencement of the infringement. The three-year limit may start to run from the discovery of the infringement, instead of from the commencement of the infringement, if the copyright holder can prove that he or she had no way of knowing about the infringing activity through "reasonable diligence." Also, allowing some infringement in one part of a work or other subject-matter may not bar a copyright holder from suing for infringement in the same or different work or other subject-matter after the limitation period in the infringement in that one part has expired.

This limitation period applies to infringement of copyright and moral rights.

Who May Sue?

Any person, author, or owner of copyright, or anyone having a title, right, or interest in writing in the copyright, may institute a court action for infringement of that copyright. The interest may be in the form of a written assignment or licence. Thus, a person who has mere permission (e.g., verbal permission) to use copyright material cannot sue to stop others from using the material in the same manner. Whether an interest has been granted depends on the circumstances in each case and on the wording of the licence. If a person has an interest, that interest must relate to the one for which the lawsuit is being instituted. For example, if a person is granted the exhibition right in a painting, that person may not sue for infringement of the reproduction right in the painting.

Although persons with a nonexclusive licence may not sue under the Copyright Act, they may sue for breach of contract under contract law. For instance, if Adam licenses the use of an image for his website from the copyright owner Kyle, and Kyle breaches the agreement, for example, by not providing the image to Adam in a timely fashion, then Adam may enforce his rights against Kyle for breach of contract.

For moral rights infringement only the author or performer may sue; however, if the author or performer is deceased, then his or her estate may sue. The author, performer, or estate may sue regardless of whether it owns copyright in the work or performance unless it has waived its moral rights.

The person or corporation who commences a court action is called a plaintiff.

Who Can Be Sued?

Any person who allegedly uses a copyright-protected work or other subject-matter in a manner that only the copyright owner may use it, may be sued. This includes any person who authorizes the infringing use of copyright material. It may also include persons legally responsible for the alleged infringer, such as a parent or employer. In essence, all parties involved could be sued since the Act does not specifically state who may be named as a party in a lawsuit.

The person being sued, or the person defending or denying an action commenced by the plaintiff, is called the defendant. The defendant is sometimes referred to as the alleged infringer.

Despite the wording used here, which may state, for example, that the plaintiff or defendant must prove something, it is usually the lawyer representing the plaintiff or defendant who will do these things on behalf of his or her client, the plaintiff or defendant.

Costs

In civil law matters, the costs of retaining a lawyer are the responsibility of the client, or the person who engages that lawyer. Once the matter goes to court, it is possible that the successful party may recover some of the costs, and that the unsuccessful party may be responsible for the costs of both parties. It is also possible that legal costs may be a part of a negotiated out-of-court settlement.

There are no absolute rules on the recovery of costs. The Copyright Act specifically provides that the expense or cost of a lawsuit is in the discretion of the court. Thus, it is up to a judge to decide whether costs are recoverable in a court case and in what amount. Since costs are in the discretion of the court, a court could refuse, for example, to make an order regarding costs where a plaintiff is successful in a copyright infringement suit where the infringed work or other subject-matter is considered obscene.

Where to Sue

The Copyright Act states that the Federal Court or any provincial court (including small claims court) may hear an action for copyright infringement and enforce any civil remedies. Thus, you have the option of the venue in which to commence an action.

If the amount of damages being claimed is within the limits allowed in small claims court, you may want to pursue the action on your own (but note that your claim might then be limited to damages and no injunction). The advantage of small claims court is that it is often speedier than other courts and costs can be minimized since plaintiffs often represent themselves without the aid of a lawyer. You are only eligible to sue in small claims court if the monetary compensation being claimed is within a certain limit. For example, at the time of writing this book, this amount is $25,000 in Ontario.

If you begin your action in a court other than small claims court, a choice will have to be made between commencing it in federal or provincial court. There are certain advantages and disadvantages of proceeding in either the federal or provincial court that your lawyer will outline to you. One of the main advantages of proceeding in the Federal Court as opposed to a provincial court is that the Federal Court is more specialized, having jurisdiction to deal only with specific matters, and as such is believed by some to have a greater expertise in intellectual property matters. Other advantages are that the Federal Court may give you an earlier trial date than a provincial court; there may be monetary ceilings for the claiming of damages in certain provincial courts; and the Federal Court may grant a restraining order that is valid throughout Canada whereas provincial courts have power only within their own province.

Description of Civil Remedies

Prejudgment Orders

There is always a danger that once a legal suit is commenced against an alleged infringer of copyright that that alleged infringer will quickly dispose of illegal copies of a work or other subject-matter or plates used to make it in order to eliminate any evidence of infringement. Because of this, a plaintiff may ask the court for an "Anton Pillar order," which is essentially a civil search warrant. An Anton Pillar order will order the alleged infringer to allow the plaintiff or a representative to enter and inspect the defendant's premises and seize any infringing copies or to take pictures of them prior to any court hearing. This is done without warning to the defendant.

In general, an Anton Pillar order will be granted where the harm done to the plaintiff without such an order is greater than the harm done to the defendant with the order. This remedy is quite extreme and will only be granted under certain conditions: that is, where there is strong circumstantial evidence of copyright infringement; there is very serious actual or potential damage accruing to the plaintiff; and there is very good reason to believe that the defendant has incriminating evidence and might, if warned, destroy these items before trial. The plaintiff must undertake to reimburse the defendant for any damages to the defendant caused by the granting of the order. The issuance of an order is decided on the facts of each case.

Injunctions

An injunction is an order made by a court, on behalf of a complainant, ordering someone to refrain from, or continuing, a particular activity. For example, an injunction could prevent the further showing of a film or a television program, or require certain content to be removed from a website. Injunctions are a common type of remedy for copyright infringements because they can be obtained relatively quickly and provide an immediate solution. However, they can also be costly to obtain. Injunctions can be granted either at the commencement of an action or at the end of it. There are interim, interlocutory, and permanent injunctions.

Interim Injunction

An interim injunction is granted for a short period of time, usually without notice to the alleged infringer, as part of an Anton Pillar order (as discussed above). It is granted in cases of extreme urgency where there is strong evidence that the alleged offender will abscond or destroy evidence if notified about the injunction. Generally, the interim injunction lasts for 10 days (for example, under the Rules of the Federal Court), and is continued as an interlocutory injunction, if warranted, pending the outcome of the trial.

Interlocutory Injunction

An interlocutory injunction is the continuation of an interim injunction. The alleged offender is notified about the request for an interlocutory injunction, and there is a hearing to determine whether the interlocutory should be granted. The purpose of an interlocutory injunction is to prevent irreparable harm to a plaintiff awaiting the outcome of a trial. As such, an interlocutory injunction is limited in time to the end of the trial in question or can be otherwise limited in time to a date earlier than the trial.

A plaintiff may ask a court for an interlocutory injunction at the commencement of a court action if he or she can prove that continuing the infringing activity will cause serious, irreparable harm to the plaintiff, which cannot be compensated in damages (if blatant copying, irreparable harm need not necessarily be proven, as long as there is a serious question to be tried). Whether or not an interlocutory injunction is ordered by a court depends on the facts of each case. A judge must examine the position of both parties and the possible damages to each of them. It is up to the copyright owner to satisfy the court that the interim injunction should be continued as an interlocutory injunction until the trial is completed. The alleged infringer will have an opportunity at the hearing for the interlocutory injunction to argue that the interim injunction should not be continued as an interlocutory injunction.

To obtain an interlocutory or interim injunction, there must clear and compelling evidence or irreparable harm. This means that the plaintiff will either be put out of business in short order or the application for an ex parte interim injunction is made part of an Anton Pillar application (and therefore there is strong evidence that the defendant will abscond). In most Federal Court cases, the court is prepared to award damages at the end of the trial. As a result, applications for summary judgment prior to trial have become the proceeding of choice in order to shorten an action.

Permanent Injunction

A permanent injunction is awarded by a court at the end of a trial; it orders an infringer to "permanently" stop the infringing activity. It may be ordered by a court once it has been established that copyright infringement has taken place.

Where the defendant proves that he or she was not aware of copyright and had no reasonable grounds for suspecting that copyright subsisted in the work or other subject-matter, he or she may only be subject to an injunction, and not to the other remedies listed below. If, at the date of infringement, the copyright in the work or other subject-matter was registered under the Act with the Canadian Intellectual Property Office, the defendant may be subject to all remedies (since this would be reasonable grounds for suspecting that copyright existed). Keep in mind that copyright need not be registered at the time of its creation, but may be registered, for instance, at the time when a lawsuit is being contemplated.

Injunctions with Respect to Buildings

Where a building or other structure is either built or in the process of being constructed, and it infringes or may infringe copyright when completed, an injunction cannot be obtained to stop construction or to order its demolition. The same may not be true if an injunction is obtained prior to the building or structure being built.[2] For example, an injunction may be obtained to stop a house from being built from plans where copyright has not been cleared in those plans, but once building has commenced the copyright owner will have to look at remedies other than an injunction.

Wide Injunction

Generally, an injunction will apply to specific work or other subject-matter being infringed at a specific time. However, a "wide injunction" is also possible. A wide injunction allows a court to grant an injunction not only in relation to a specific work or other subject-matter, but also with respect to preventing infringement of copyright in any of the works or other subject-matter in which the plaintiff currently has or will in the future have a copyright interest.

Damages

A copyright owner may claim monetary "damages" from an infringer of copyright, and that part of the profits made from the infringement decided by a court to be "just and proper." Damages are monetary compensation recovered in a court proceeding by a person whose copyright has been infringed. *Black's Law Dictionary* defines damages in the following manner: "A pecuniary compensation or indemnity, which may be recovered in the courts by any person who has suffered loss, detriment, or injury, whether to his person, property, or rights, through the unlawful act or omission or negligence of another."

A court may award damages to a plaintiff even if no profit was made by the infringer. In fact, it is not necessary to prove or to suffer real damages in order for an award of damages to be made: infringement is sufficient.

The amount of damages that a court may order is not set out in the Copyright Act. Thus, the court will determine this amount on a case-by-case basis. Assessing the amount of appropriate damages is a "matter of common sense."[3] Damages are determined on a "rough" basis, taking into account the amount of sales lost to the plaintiff and the amount of profit derived by the defendant.[4] Also, see the later discussion on statutory damages.

Damages should be high enough to act as a deterrent to the infringement of copyright, as opposed to a measure of damages that merely convinces a potential infringer that, from a commercial point of view, copying a work or other subject-matter is a risk worth taking. A court may base the amount of damages on the cost for the licensed use of the work or other subject-matter, or on the loss of profits in the commercial markets where the work or other subject-matter would have otherwise been exploited. Monetary losses that can be proven can also be recovered.

The discussion so far has focused on what is called compensatory or actual damages. There are, however, different kinds of damages that a court may award a plaintiff. Another type of damages is called "exemplary or punitive" damages. The purpose of these types of damages is to punish a person for flagrant misbehaviour or to set an example of the consequences of breaking the law. Such damages may be awarded where there is "blatant infringement, accompanied by total disregard for the rights of others,"[5] "fraud or malice"[6] or where there is "some form of willful or reckless disregard of the rights of the plaintiff, or a very deliberate scheme to infringe copyright."[7] Thus, the conduct and motives of the infringer will be taken into account with respect to exemplary or punitive damages.

Special Provision for Schools, Libraries, Archives, and Museums

A copyright owner whose works are not licensed by a copyright collective such as Access Copyright or Copibec (and is eligible to be) is limited in what he or she may collect for unauthorized reprographic reproduction by educational institutions, libraries, archives, and museums. The copyright owner is limited to the amount of royalties he or she would have received if he or she were a member of a collective such as Access Copyright or Copibec.

Statutory Damages

Statutory damages allow a copyright holder to collect specified damages as set out in the Copyright Act as opposed to actual damages resulting from the infringing activities. Statutory damages guarantee a minimum award once the infringement is proven without having to prove the actual loss suffered, and they also act as a deterrent to future infringements.

Under the statutory damages regime, a copyright owner may request at any time before a final judgment in a court case, in lieu of damages and profits, statutory damages of $500 to $20,000, in respect of each work or other subject-matter infringed by the defendant, as the court considers just, if the infringements are for commercial purposes. If the infringer was not aware and had no reasonable grounds to believe that he or she had infringed copyright, a court may lower the statutory damages awarded to $200.

If the infringements are for noncommercial purposes, the statutory damages are $100 to $5,000. An example of a noncommercial purpose may be an individual who downloads music from a peer-to-peer file-sharing service.

The terms *commercial* and *noncommercial* are not defined in the Act.

The court will take into account the good or bad faith of the defendant, the parties' conduct before and during the court proceedings, and the need to prevent other infringements of the copyright in question. There are specific circumstances set out in the Act to which the statutory damages provisions do not apply.

Copyright collectives, as defined in the Act, are also entitled to certain statutory damages for nonpayment of royalties. By forgoing other monetary damages, the collective may claim an award of statutory damages not less than 3, and not more than 10, times the amount of the applicable royalties, as the court considers just.

Statutory damages do not apply to parallel importation. Also, statutory damages probably do not apply to moral rights infringement.

Accounts of Profits

The notion of accounts of profits denotes the principle that an infringer has illegally made use of another's property—the copyright material—making profits therefrom and should "account" for these profits. The Act states that in addition to a court awarding damages for the infringement of copyright, it may award "such part of the profits that the infringer has made from the infringement as the court may decide to be just and proper." The account of profits would be in addition to "regular" damages.

The general rule is that an infringer must pay to the copyright owner any and all profits associated with the infringement. There is no method set out in the Act for calculating these profits. The term *profits* is not defined, but the Act states that "the plaintiff shall be required to prove only receipts or revenues derived from the infringement" and the defendant shall be required to prove "every element of cost" that he or she claims.

Returning Illegal Copies ("Delivery Up")

A copyright infringer must give the copyright owner all infringing copies of a work or other subject-matter, and all plates used to produce the infringing copies.

Matters to Prove

When a court case commences for the infringement of copyright, a number of things must be proven.[8] For instance, it must be established that copyright exists in a work or other subject-matter, that the plaintiff is the owner of the copyright in the work or other subject-matter (or is otherwise entitled to sue), that there is an infringement of copyright, and that the defendant is responsible for that infringement.

There are two presumptions set out in the Copyright Act to help a plaintiff prove a case of copyright infringement. First, there is a presumption that copyright subsists in a work or other subject-matter. This presumption means that a work or other subject-matter in which infringement is claimed is automatically presumed to be protected by copyright, or in other words, a plaintiff need not prove this point. Thus, a defendant who wishes to prove otherwise—that is, that copyright does not exist in the work or other subject-matter—has the burden of proof of doing so.

A burden of proof simply means that one of the parties, that is, the defendant, must prove a fact or prove a fact in dispute. In order for a defendant to prove that copyright does not exist in the work, he or she would present evidence to the contrary, for example, that proves that the work is not original (in the copyright sense of the word) or is in the public domain.

Second, there is a presumption of ownership. The author of a work, or performer, maker, or broadcaster of other subject-matter, is presumed to be the owner of the copyright in that work or other subject-matter. The defendant may prove the contrary of this presumption. For example, the defendant may produce a written assignment or other evidence that a written assignment exists and that the author, performer, maker, or broadcaster is not the owner of the copyright.

There are two further subsections relating to the presumption of ownership. The first presumption relates to the situation where an author's name appears on a work, or the name of a performer, maker, or broadcaster is indicated on the other subject-matter. This provision provides that if a name is on a work or other subject-matter in such a manner as to indicate that he or she is the author of the work, or performer, maker, or broadcaster of other subject-matter, then that person is presumed to be the author, performer, maker, or broadcaster, unless the contrary is proven. Notice that there is no requirement that the copyright symbol appear on the work or other subject-matter, or that there be a statement expressing that copyright belongs to the author, performer, maker, or broadcaster indicated on the work or other subject-matter. The second presumption relates to the situation where a name other than the author's name appears on a work, or the performer's, maker's, or broadcaster's name appears on other subject-matter. This section provides that where no name is indicated on a work, or other subject-matter, as its author, performer, maker, or broadcaster, or the name is not the real name of the author, performer, maker, or broadcaster, or one by which he or she is commonly known, and a name purporting to be that of the publisher or proprietor of the work or other subject-matter is listed, their name will be presumed to be the owner of the copyright for infringement proceedings unless the contrary is proven.

Once the existence of copyright and proper ownership of the work or other subject-matter are established, the plaintiff must prove that an infringement took place: for example, that the defendant reproduced a substantial part of the work or other subject-matter in question (and did not go to a common source in doing so). The plaintiff must prove the infringement. In order to do so, the court may look at direct and indirect (circumstantial) evidence, can hear parties' testimony and the testimony of other witnesses including experts, can compare the two works or other subject-matter, looking for similarities and dissimilarities, examine the repetition of errors (unless it can be proven that errors existed in a common source consulted by the parties), and consider if it was possible for the defendant to complete the work within the given time frame. Note that infringement of copyright is not measured by assessing the harm to a copyright owner—either the infringement occurs or it does not occur.

Once the plaintiff has presented the case, it is up to the defendant to prove that he or she has not infringed copyright. For example, if two works are very similar but not exact, the defendant may bring evidence that his or her work was created independently, using common sources. Alternatively, the defendant may bring evidence showing that any similarity is coincidental and that, in fact, the defendant had no access to the allegedly infringed work. Also, the defendant may prove that his or her use of the work or other subject-matter was within one of the exceptions in the Copyright Act and therefore does not constitute an infringement of copyright. Although innocence is not generally a defence with relation to copyright infringement, it may be claimed with respect to indirect infringement (or commercial uses of copyright materials). If the defendant is successful in the defence, he or she will not be found liable for copyright infringement.

If the defendant is unsuccessful in defending a copyright infringement case, the plaintiff is entitled to a number of remedies. These remedies will be included in the claim against the defendant when the lawsuit commences and are discussed earlier under the heading "Description of Civil Remedies."

CRIMINAL REMEDIES

The criminal sanctions that relate to copyright infringements are found in the Copyright Act and not in the Criminal Code. These sanctions are available in specific circumstances set out in the Act. Criminal sanctions may be more appropriate than civil remedies where the extent of the infringement makes it too costly for an individual to sue, or where the nature of the illegal conduct should be set as an example in order to deter others from engaging in the same or similar activities. However, with criminal sanctions, the complainant has no absolute right to proceed, as the ultimate decision whether to charge an individual rests with the police, and the ultimate decision whether to proceed rests with the Crown (i.e., the government). The police and Crown must make their decisions independent of factors that may be of interest to a complainant and may not be influenced by private interests. All a victim can do is file a complaint with the police. It is then up to the police to investigate the alleged crime. There are Royal Canadian Mounted Police (RCMP) across Canada seeking out copyright offenders.

The complainant receives no direct monetary compensation where criminal charges are laid.

A criminal proceeding is not a bar to a civil proceeding.

Historically, the police have sought to charge large-scale operators under the criminal provisions, for commercial dealings of copyright goods, for example, video or software piracy on a large scale. The law does not, however, limit the criminal remedies to such cases.

By calling the RCMP, provincial police, or city police, an investigation may be undertaken to substantiate a claim of a criminal offence.

The RCMP has "A Guide for Victims of Copyright and Trademark Infringement." See http://205.193.86.86/fep-pelf/ipr-dpi/guide-eng .htm. The Guide states, "The RCMP will record all complaints and allegations of copyright or trademark infringement and will criminally deal with each complaint or allegation on a case by case basis." Commercial infringement at the manufacturing, importation, and commercial wholesale distribution levels, and dismantling an entire criminal organization involved in illicit activities, is the investigational priority of the RCMP. A checklist for reporting copyright and trademark offences is in that Guide. If there is a viable complaint within the priorities of the RCMP, after a due investigation, the Department of Justice will prosecute the copyright offence and the Provincial Crown will prosecute any Criminal Code offence. According to the Guide, the role of the rights holder is to enforce private rights; assist law enforcement; and increase public awareness.

ACTIVITIES THAT CONSTITUTE A CRIMINAL OFFENCE

Infringing Copies

The following activities knowingly done with illegal copies (copies of copyright-protected works or other subject-matter made without the permission of the copyright owner) may come within the criminal sanctions of the Copyright Act:

- Making for sale or rent.[9]
- Selling or renting, or by way of trade exposing or offering for sale or hire.

- Distributing for the purpose of trade, or to such an extent as to affect prejudicially the owner of the copyright.
- Exhibiting in public, by way of trade.
- Importing for sale or rent into Canada.

Whether one of these activities is done with knowledge is a matter of fact for the courts to decide upon examination of all the facts of the case.

Where any of the above activities takes place, the infringer may be subject to a maximum fine and to a maximum prison term. Both the fine and imprisonment may be simultaneously imposed. There are two sets of maximum fines and imprisonment terms set out in the Act depending on how the Crown decides to proceed in the particular case. The Crown has the choice to proceed by summary conviction or by indictment. Generally, offences punishable on summary conviction are less serious crimes and are subject to a lesser penalty than those tried by indictment. A first offence of copyright infringement may, for example, proceed by way of summary conviction. In the case of a summary conviction, the infringer may be subject to a maximum fine of $25,000 or to imprisonment for a term up to six months, or to both. In the case of a conviction on indictment, the infringer may be subject to a fine of up to $1 million or to imprisonment for a term of up to five years, or to both. Note that the fine and imprisonment periods are maximum amounts. The court may choose appropriate fines and/or imprisonment periods within these limitations, depending upon the facts of the particular cases. The different procedures for proceeding, summary conviction procedure, and the procedure on indictment, are set out in the Criminal Code. On summary conviction proceedings, there is a limitation period. For example, in Ontario, the charge must be laid within two years of the discovery of the offence. There is no limitation period for matters the Crown elects to proceed on by way of indictment.

INFRINGING PLATES AND PERFORMANCES

Further, it is an offence to knowingly make or possess any plate for making infringing copies, or to cause a work or other subject-matter to be performed in public for private profit, without authorization. The fines and imprisonment terms are the same as stated above.

Even before criminal remedy proceedings begin (i.e., a trial) with respect to infringing plates, the court may order that all apparently infringing copies of the work or other subject-matter or all plates in the possession of the alleged infringer that may be used to make illegal copies be destroyed or delivered to the copyright owner, or otherwise dealt with as the court may think fit.

Additionally, a person who, without written consent, knowingly performs or causes to be performed in public for private profit an infringing work or other subject-matter that is part or whole of any dramatic or operatic work or music composition, may be subject to a fine on summary conviction not exceeding $250, and in a second or subsequent offence, to a $250 fine or imprisonment for two months, or both.

Finally, any person "who makes or causes to be made any change in or suppression of the title, or the name of the author, of any dramatic or operatic work or musical composition . . . or who makes or causes to be made any change in the work or composition in public for private profit, may be subject on summary conviction to a maximum fine of $500, or in a second or subsequent offence, to the $500 fine and imprisonment up to four months, or both."

RECORDING A FILM IN A THEATRE

Under the Copyright Act, it is illegal to camcord a movie for commercial redistribution or make a copy of it for sale or rental. In addition, a relatively recent amendment[10] to the Criminal Code creates two new offences in the Criminal Code: the recording of a movie in a movie theatre without the consent of the theatre manager; and the recording of a movie in a movie theatre without the consent of the theatre manager for the purpose of selling, renting, or other commercial distribution of a copy of the recorded movie. In such cases, the court has the authority to order the forfeiture of anything used in the commission of these offences. This is an offence for all movies and not just for copyright-protected movies; the offence also applies to a movie in the public domain.

SUMMARY

A copyright holder whose creations have been used without permission is entitled to certain remedies including border, civil, and criminal ones.

CHAPTER 14

LEGALLY USING CONTENT

I don't necessarily agree with everything I say.

—Marshall McLuhan (1911–1980)

THE "USE" OF COPYRIGHT MATERIALS

People who want to use copyright materials (or content) often think that because a certain work is protected by copyright, that work cannot be used. This is a false assumption. When a work is protected by copyright, that work may be used in a variety of ways; however, any use (at least those covered by the Copyright Act) must be authorized by the copyright owner, or by a representative of the copyright owner (unless that right is subject to an exception as discussed in Chapter 10). This chapter deals with obtaining authorization or permission to use materials protected by copyright. When the term *use* is seen in this book, it refers to the use of copyright material in the copyright sense of the word. For instance, use may refer to a reproduction of a work or public performance of a sound recording. It does not refer to, for example, lending a copy of a print book to a friend.

WHEN IS PERMISSION REQUIRED?

General Rule

Every time you use copyright material in a manner that only the copyright owner has the right to do, you must obtain permission from the copyright owner. As you now know, owning the tangible aspect of a work protected by copyright does not exempt you from obtaining permission, since ownership of the tangible work does not necessarily mean that you own copyright in that work. For example, owning a painting does not necessarily mean that you own copyright in that painting. If you own the "physical property"—that is, the painting—you cannot reproduce it or exhibit it in public without permission from the copyright holder. The same is true with other subject-matter.

The copyright law does not usually distinguish between commercial and noncommercial uses of a copyright-protected work when it comes to permissions (one exception is for commercial rentals of sound recordings and computer software).[1] Generally, if copyright exists in a work, and if there is no specific exception for that particular use, then permission of the copyright owner must be obtained in order to use the work. Even amateurs who are dealing with a copyright-protected work, such as a theatre group performing a play, must get permission to perform a copyright-protected work. This general rule applies to works found on the Internet.

Using copyright-protected works in Canada—even foreign works, provided they are protected in Canada—is always according to the provisions in the Canadian copyright law. The use of Canadian copyright-protected works in other countries would be under the copyright laws of that country (provided that country and Canada have copyright relations). This chapter deals with the use of copyright materials in Canada.

Misconceptions about Permissions

To understand permissions, it is helpful to clear up misinformation about how permissions work in Canada. Below are some misconceptions with explanations on their validity.

Misinformation: If you put forward great efforts to obtain permission, but you are unsuccessful in your efforts, you may use the work.

Truth: You may only use the copyright-protected work if you have permission or have an unlocatable copyright owner licence from the Copyright Board of Canada. Any documented efforts may be useful in applying for an unlocatable copyright owner licence from the Copyright Board of Canada.

Misinformation: Everything on the Internet is in the public domain and can be freely used without permission.

Truth: Unless the content specifically says it can be used without permission in all manners or in the specific manner in which you hope to use the content, you need to obtain permission.

Misinformation: Publishers own the rights in the work of their authors.

Truth: Publishers often license the works from their authors for publication and other uses. Ownership of the copyright is subject to the publishing agreement between the author and publisher. Contacting a publisher is a first good step for copyright clearance in a book. The publisher will be in a position to tell you whether they own copyright and who may give you rights to reproduce portions of the book, the whole book, or adapt or otherwise use the book in a copyright sense.

Misinformation: A Creative Commons licence means you can freely use a work.

Truth: Each Creative Commons licence allows different uses without obtaining permission. Read the licence and see what is permitted.

Misinformation: Only registered works are protected by copyright.

Truth: Copyright protection is automatic in Canada; you do not need to register a work in order to be protected by copyright.

Misinformation: The Canadian Copyright Act says that you can copy 3 percent of a work without obtaining permission.

Truth: You do not need permission to use an insubstantial part of a work; however, *insubstantial* is not defined. The Act does not state any specific amount that you can copy without obtaining permission.

Misinformation: If a work does not have a copyright symbol, ©, then you may freely use the work without obtaining permission.

Truth: Copyright has always been automatic in Canada. Using a copyright symbol is a good way to educate people that there is copyright in your work, but whether or not you use the symbol and notice, you automatically have copyright protection upon the creation of the work.

Misinformation: All Canadian government works are in the public domain.

Truth: Works created by employees of the federal government, and works created for the federal government by independent contractors, are protected by copyright.

Misinformation: Fair dealing never applies when a work is used in a for-profit situation.

Truth: Fair dealing is decided on a case-by-case basis taking into account several factors. The fact that a work is used for a for-profit purpose is one of the factors a court will take into account when making a determination of fair dealing.

Misinformation: Quoting a few sentences from an article or book always requires permission.

Truth: In more circumstances than not, it will not be necessary to obtain permission to use a small quote from a work. However, there is no definitive answer to this; it is a matter to be decided on a case-by-case basis.

Misinformation: You need permission to summarize the ideas in a newspaper article.

Truth: Ideas, facts, and history are not protected by copyright and may be freely used and summarized in one's own words.

Misinformation: All permissions to use a copyright-protected work must be in writing.

Truth: Only transfers of ownership need be in writing. Mere permissions to use content can be given orally.

All of these topics are discussed in relevant portions in this book.

Clearing Rights in Digital Works

Clearing rights for the use of online and off-line or stand-alone digital products is similar to clearing rights for the use of nondigital works. However, getting the appropriate clearances for multimedia products can be a massive undertaking. A single compact disc (CD-ROM) can store over 650 megabytes of information, roughly equivalent to 250,000 pages of text. A single-sided, double layer DVD can store 7.96 GB or four hours of movie time. Multimedia products by their nature consist of content capable of being digitized such as text, sound, images and full-motion video, and underlying software.

In addition, the new media developer/producer/publisher must clear rights to use copyright-protected works in the multimedia work as well as rights to allow end users to do certain things with the multimedia work such as streaming, downloading, making print copies, interactive use, and more.

QUESTIONS TO ASK WHEN OBTAINING PERMISSIONS

If you plan to use a work, these are some of the questions you should ask yourself:

Are you using a work or other subject-matter protected by the Canadian Copyright Act?

Is the duration of copyright still running, or is the work in the public domain?

Are you adapting or translating a public domain piece? If so, are you certain that you are using the actual public domain work and not an adaptation of it (as that adaptation may still be protected by copyright)?

Are you using a substantial portion of that work or other subject-matter?

Are you using it in the copyright sense by reproducing it, performing it in public, adapting it, making it available to the public, broadcasting it, and so forth?

Is there an exception in the law that permits you to use that work or other subject-matter without obtaining permission?

Are you modifying the work in a manner that may be prejudicial to the honour or reputation of the creator?

Does the author's name appear in association with your use of the work?

Do you already have permission or a licence to use the work? For example, do you have previous permission that covers this use as well? Is the work in a database you already license? Is the use covered by an agreement you have with a copyright collective? Is there implied consent to use the work?

OBTAINING PERMISSION

Once you have established that the use of a work or other subject-matter requires permission from its copyright owner (see above questions), you must obtain the necessary permission prior to using the work. There is no one-stop clearance centre for copyright in Canada. Tracking down a copyright owner may depend upon common sense, ingenuity, resourcefulness, and contacts. Obtaining permission can be as simple and quick as sending and receiving an e-mail, or it can take hours, days, or even months of difficult and creative work, and even then there is no guarantee that you will locate a copyright holder or obtain permission from him or her. So it is best to start as early as you can to obtain permission to use copyright materials. This chapter lists some of the numerous sources where you can go to obtain permission for specific types of copyright-protected works or specific rights.

Only a copyright owner (or his or her representative) can give you permission to use copyright materials. Chapter 7, "Who Owns Copyright?," will help you determine ownership in copyright materials.

Keep in mind that the ownership of copyright can be transferred in whole or in part. If you have direct access to a copyright holder, you may want to contact that person for copyright clearance. However, you should be aware that in many instances it is a representative or heir of the copyright owner who may give you permission or guide you to the person who can give permission. Representatives of the author may include lawyers and agents. A representative may also be a copyright collective, whose primary job is to clear copyright and who acts on behalf of many copyright holders. Copyright collectives are discussed in Chapter 11, "How Can Rights Be Exploited?"; and specific copyright collectives are discussed further on.

If you are clearing rights in online content, you should initially review the website (or other online space) for its terms and conditions of use. The terms may address how you may use content found on the site. In addition, there may be a permissions tab or rights and reproduction tab that guides you directly to the appropriate rights clearance person. Also, the site may be working with a company that licenses its content on its behalf, and this may be indicated on the site. Look for buttons on the site (for example, on newspaper sites) that say such things as PRINT, E-MAIL, SAVE, SHARE, REPUBLISH that guide you online to the required permissions. Note that not all content on a site is owned by the site and in some situations you may be directed to the content owner, or a representative of that owner.

In some circumstances you may be able to infer permission from the circumstances. For example, you can infer from certain conduct that permission is granted in those circumstances. For example, due to the nature of Twitter social media, you can imply that you have permission to retweet or copy the original tweet.[2] However, you should not infer that you have permission to repost a tweeted image on your blog or in a print article.

Locating a Copyright Owner

Finding the owner of a copyright-protected work or other subject-matter is not always straightforward. In the case of a published work, you may wish to contact the publisher or producer to help you establish the whereabouts of the owner of copyright. You should contact one of the copyright collectives if it administers particular rights in particular works or other subject-matter. You may also want to contact any associations or organizations who might have some contact with, or knowledge of, the copyright owner. The Internet may also be helpful in locating a copyright owner. A lawyer may be able to assist you in locating a copyright holder. Also, there are specialized companies whose job it is to search for copyright owners in Canada and abroad, and to clear rights and permissions, and to negotiate licences to use copyright-protected works.[3]

Further, you should search through the Register of Copyrights at the Client Service Centre of the Canadian Intellectual Property Office (CIPO), or hire someone to undertake a search on your behalf. You can search online or in person.

Since copyright registration is not mandatory in Canada, not all copyright owners will be listed in the Register of Copyrights. One should not assume that because a work is not registered, that is it not protected by copyright. Nevertheless, the Register does contain information about many copyright holders and authors. If you do not check the Copyright Office Register, you may be subject to more serious remedies (damages and not just an injunction) in a copyright infringement court case.

Online searches: For all copyrights registered as of October 1, 1991, you can search the Canadian Copyrights Database on the CIPO website. The Database is updated every 24 hours during office hours. Before you undertake a search, read the search tips at www.cipo.ic.gc.ca/eic/site/cipointernet-internetopic.nsf/eng/wr00462.html.

In-person searches: Generally, a manual search must be undertaken for any works registered before October 1, 1991, and any assignments made prior to this date. These searches can only be done at the Client Service Centre in Gatineau, Quebec. Complete pre-1991 registration information is available in microfiche, index card, and microfilm. You can hire someone to undertake a search on your behalf if you are unable to visit the Client Service Centre in person. The records of the Copyright Office are open to the public and are free of charge. Assistance is

available to use the search facilities, and copies of, or extracts from, the
Register, or copies of certificates, licences, or other documents can be
obtained for a fee. The Client Service Centre is located at:

Canadian Intellectual Property Office
Place du Portage I
Room C-229, 2nd Floor
50 Victoria St.
Gatineau, Quebec K1A 0C9
Business hours: 8:30–17:00
Telephone:1.866.997.1936 (toll free from anywhere in Canada and
   the U.S.)
Fax: 819.953.CIPO (2476)
E-mail: cipo.contact@ic.gc.ca
Web: www.cipo.ic.gc.ca

Depending on the circumstances, you may wish to check foreign
copyright offices, such as the one in the United States. Online searches
in the U.S. Copyright Office Catalog are available for U.S. registrations
made after January 1, 1978. For works registered prior to that date, you
must consult the Catalog of Copyright Records, which are all in the
process of being digitized. Further information on researching copyrights in the U.S. Copyright Office is at:

U.S. Copyright Office
101 Independence Avenue SE
Washington, DC 20559–6000
Telephone: 202.707.3000 or 1.877.476.0778 (toll free from Canada
   and the United States)
Web: www.copyright.gov/records/

COPYRIGHT COLLECTIVES

One representative of a copyright owner may be a copyright collective.
Where a copyright owner is a member of a collective, the collective

may be contacted in order to obtain permission to use his or her works. Even if the creator is not represented by the collective you contact, the collective may be able to provide you with information to help you locate a copyright owner.

OBTAINING PERMISSION FOR SPECIFIC WORKS

Below is a list of organizations and collectives that operate in certain areas. Since new organizations and collectives are formed from time to time and the mandate of existing ones may change, the information here should not be taken as being conclusive. The collectives and organizations listed below may not necessarily be "collective societies" as defined in the Copyright Act and therefore may not be under the jurisdiction of the Copyright Board. The organizations and collectives listed below, however, are places that creators and users should be aware of with respect to giving or obtaining permission to use copyright materials. In addition, a list of copyright-related organizations and copyright collectives can be found on the site of the Copyright Board at www .cb-cda.gc.ca/societies-societes/index-e.html.

Many of the copyright organizations and collectives have agreements with similar organizations and collectives in different countries and can provide permission to use foreign works in Canada. For example, if you want to perform a song by a British composer, contact the Canadian collective that represents British composers' performing rights in Canada (SOCAN).

Depending on the nature of the copyright collective or organization, you may be able to obtain an individual or transactional licence for a specific work for use one time only, or a blanket licence that provides access to a large repertoire of works for multiple copying over a specific period of time. Some collectives and organizations allow requests for permissions to be made online from their websites.

Where the information is available at the time of writing this book, the list below includes information on clearing rights for electronic or digital uses. However, you will see that clearing electronic rights through an organization or collective is still a growing area and may require permission directly from the copyright owner.

Literary Works

The Canadian Copyright Licensing Agency, known as Access Copyright (and formerly CANCOPY), administers the rights for text and visual works in published print materials such as books, magazines, journals, and newspapers. Access Copyright licenses users throughout Canada, excluding Quebec. Authors, visual artists, and publishers can directly join Access Copyright or may have membership in Access Copyright through membership in their national and regional organizations.

Access Copyright provides individuals and organizations with permission to use content in their repertoire for print and digital copying. Access Copyright provides two kinds of licences. A comprehensive or blanket licence provides permissions in advance (e.g., for a period of a year) for copying according to specific terms and conditions, such as a chapter from a book. Blanket licence fees are generally based on the number of users. Individual or transactional licences are also available for copyright permission requests to reproduce specific or individual works when a blanket licence is not available; fees are based on the number of pages copied multiplied by the number of copies made. Typically, those who obtain blanket licences are educational institutions; businesses; schools; municipal, provincial, and federal governments; not-for-profit organizations; and copy shops. In addition to licensing, Access Copyright enforces the copyright interests of the rights holders it represents.

Access Copyright has bilateral agreements with 31 other similar organizations (called reproduction rights organizations or RROs) and has bilateral agreements with 29 other jurisdictions around the world. Access Copyright collects from foreign RROs for Canadian works copied outside of Canada and distributes them to Canadian authors, visual artists, and publishers. If you need to reproduce content from outside of Canada, Access Copyright may be able to provide you with the necessary rights through its reciprocal arrangements.

FOR FURTHER INFORMATION, CONTACT:

Access Copyright
The Canadian Copyright Licensing Agency
One Yonge Street, Suite 800
Toronto, Ontario M5E 1E5
Telephone: 416.868.1620 or 1.800.893.5777 (toll free)
Fax: 416.868.1621
E-mail: info@accesscopyright.ca
Web: www.accesscopyright.ca

If you have a blanket licence with Access Copyright, you have access
to literary works throughout Canada, through the arrangement Access
Copyright has with Copibec (la société québécoise de gestion collective
des droits de reproduction.) In addition, Copibec's repertoire includes
the various publications of the different ministries of Quebec through
its agreement with Les Publications du Quebec, which enables it to
manage their reproduction rights. If you are based in Quebec, contact
Copibec to enquire about the literary materials in its repertoire and
how to obtain a licence to use them.

FOR FURTHER INFORMATION, CONTACT:

Copibec
Société québécoise de gestion collective des droits de reproduction
606, rue Cathcart, bureau 810
Montréal, Québec H3B 1K0
Telephone: 514.288.1664 or 1.800.717.2022 (toll free)
Fax: 514.288.1669
E-mail: info@copibec.qc.ca
Web: www.copibec.qc.ca

Dramatic Works

Playwrights Guild of Canada (PGC) clears copyright with respect to the
public performance of English-language plays for schools, community
groups, or amateur theatre groups. This includes the public performance
or public reading of a play. At the time of writing, it may take up to two

weeks to process a rights request. Rights for professional performances are obtained from the author or the author's agent. PGC has up-to-date agent information. At the time of writing, the standard rates to perform an amateur production of a full-length play are $100 for the first performance and $85 for each subsequent performance; and for a one-act play, $85 for the first performance and $70 for each subsequent performance. As an example, if your community is performing a full-length play on a Thursday, Friday, and Saturday night, the public performance fee is $270.

PGC has a publishing imprint, Playwrights Canada Press (www .playwrightscanada.com) for the reproduction and sale of its members' scripts. Regarding the reproduction of scripts, PGC is a member of Access Copyright as are many of PGC's individual members. Thus, Access Copyright should be contacted with respect to the reproduction of plays.

FOR FURTHER INFORMATION, CONTACT:
Playwrights Guild of Canada
215 Spadina Avenue, Suite #210
Toronto, Ontario M5T 2C7
Telephone: 416.703.0201
Fax: 416.703.0059
E-mail: info@playwrightsguild.ca
Web: www.playwrightsguild.ca

La Société des auteurs et compositeurs dramatiques (SACD) clears copyright with respect to the public performance, both amateur and professional, of French-language scripts for plays, television programs, and movies.

FOR FURTHER INFORMATION, CONTACT:
Société des auteurs et compositeurs dramatiques
4446, boulevard Saint-Laurent, bureau 202
Montréal, Québec H2W 1Z5
Telephone: 514.738.8877
Fax: 514.342.4615
E-mail: schlittler@sacd.ca
Web: www.sacd.ca

Musical Works

As you know, the copyright in a musical work is separate and distinct from the copyright in a sound recording embodying that musical work.

Like most copyright holders, copyright holders of musical works enjoy a bundle of rights in these works. The most commonly used rights with respect to musical works are the rights of public performance and reproduction.

PUBLIC PERFORMANCE RIGHT

Performing rights societies have been in existence in Canada since 1925. The Society of Composers, Authors and Music Publishers of Canada (SOCAN) is the name of the copyright collective for performing rights in musical works. SOCAN collects and distributes performing royalties for public performances in Canada of Canadian and international musical works. Performing rights exist around the world, and SOCAN has reciprocal agreements with foreign performing rights organizations that collect fees abroad on behalf of Canadians, and that give access to Canadian licensees to international music.

SOCAN administers nondramatic performing rights or *small rights*. If you need to clear rights for performances to the public of live or recorded music at bars, school dances, offices, stores, or over television and radio, SOCAN can assist you. Dramatic performing rights or *grand rights* for complete performances of operas, ballets, musicals, and other dramatic works must be obtained directly from the copyright owner. SOCAN only administers the public performance and communication by telecommunication to the public rights; it does not administer reproduction rights in sound recordings and musical works. Mechanical rights, synchronization rights, print rights, translation rights, moral rights, and neighbouring rights are separately discussed below.

The cost of a SOCAN licence depends on various factors, which may include where the music is being publicly performed, the seating capacity of the venue, and/or the nature of the event where the music is played.

There are more than 20 tariffs set by the Copyright Board of Canada for the various different uses of music. In some circumstances, you may require more than one licence from SOCAN. SOCAN will help you determine the licence(s) you need and provide those licences to you.

The list of situations and venues where performing rights for musical works must be cleared is quite extensive. Tariffs are set for many such categories, including:

MUSIC AT AN EVENT
- Receptions, conventions, assemblies, fashion shows.
- Sporting events.
- Strolling musicians and buskers; or recorded music in parks, streets, and public areas.
- Marching bands; floats with music.
- Circuses, ice shows, fireworks, displays, sound light shows, and similar events.
- Comedy shows and magic shows.
- Recreational facilities operated by a municipality, school, college, university, agricultural society, or similar community organizations.

LIVE MUSIC
- Popular or classical concerts.
- Live music in bars, restaurants, or similar venues.

MUSIC ON NEW MEDIA (INTERNET AND MOBILE)
- Audio websites.
- On demand streaming.
- Internet television and radio.
- Ring tones and ring backs.
- Hotel and motel in-room services.
- Game sites.
- Satellite radio.

MUSIC IN A BUSINESS OR ORGANIZATION
- Live music in a restaurant, store, school, or library.
- Recorded music for dancing.

- Skating rink.
- Telephone music on hold.
- Fitness and dance instruction.
- Karaoke and similar establishments.
- Recreational facilities operated by a municipality, school, college, university, or similar community organization.

MUSIC IN BROADCASTS

- Commercial and noncommercial radio, television, and cable.

If your use of music falls into any of the above categories or a related category, or any public performance for which permission is required, visit the SOCAN website. The site has extensive information for each kind of use of live or recorded music that is performed in public. There is a summary information sheet, fee calculator, and licence form for each kind of use.

If you are a composer, songwriter, or lyricist, you may be entitled to royalties when your songs are played on radio or television or performed in public, or in any of the above-mentioned venues and situations, in Canada or around the world. Eligible music composers, songwriters, or lyricists must have created a musical work or part of a musical work that has been published by a music publisher or recorded or performed (or will be) in a public forum that is subject to licensing by SOCAN. Music creators may apply online to join SOCAN. Check the SOCAN website for eligibility requirements for music publishers' membership in SOCAN.

FOR FURTHER INFORMATION, CONTACT:

SOCAN
41 Valleybrook Drive
Toronto, Ontario M3B 2S6
Telephone: 416.445.8700 or 1.800.55SOCAN (76226)
Fax: 416.445.7108
E-mail: licence@socan.ca
Web: www.socan.ca

REPRODUCTION RIGHT

A musical work can be reproduced in a number of ways: by audio reproduction, by audiovisual reproduction, and by reprographic reproduction. These reproductions are called mechanical licencing.

You have to clear the reproduction right whether you are a record producer cutting a new CD, or a choir recording a song still protected by copyright, or if you are using music on a television program or film, or on the Internet.

Copyright in a musical work, including the reproduction right, is usually assigned to a music publisher. The music publisher will try to maximize the copyright royalties for the song composer and lyricist. It is not unusual for a songwriter to act as his or her own publisher. A publisher and songwriter usually make an arrangement to share equally in the proceeds from the exploitation of a song. If you want to reproduce a song, you deal with the music publisher, as the music publisher is contractually bound to give the songwriter his or her share.

There are tens of thousands of music publishers, from large conglomerates to individual songwriters, with varying sized repertoires. The Canadian Musical Reproduction Rights Agency Limited (CMRRA) is an organization that represents a large number of Canadian and multinational publishers.[4] CMRRA is a nonexclusive agent. Thus, music publishers represented by CMRRA can enter into licencing arrangements through CMRRA, or directly with users.

FOR FURTHER INFORMATION, CONTACT:
Canadian Musical Reproduction Rights Agency Limited
56 Wellesley Street West, Suite 320
Toronto, Ontario M5S 2S3
Telephone: 416.926.1966
Fax: 416.926.7521
E-mail: inquiries@cmrra.ca
Web: www.cmrra.ca

The Society for Reproduction Rights of Authors, Composers and Publishers in Canada (SODRAC) represents a large number of authors, composers, and music publishers in Quebec. It also represents music publishers from over 100 countries.

FOR FURTHER INFORMATION, CONTACT:
Society for Reproduction Rights of Authors, Composers and
Publishers in Canada
Tower B, Suite 1010
1470 Peel
Montreal, Quebec H3A 1T1
Telephone: 514.845.3268 or 1.888.876.3722 (toll free)
Fax: 514.845.3401
E-mail: sodrac@sodrac.ca
Web: www.sodrac.ca

Audio Reproduction

Rates for the reproduction right in a musical work are settled by negotiation between the record industry and the music publisher, and, as a result, there is an industry standard rate. If you need to clear rights in order to make an audio recording of a musical work, contact the music publisher, CMRRA, or SODRAC.

Audiovisual Reproduction

Each time you include a musical work in a film, television program, commercial, or online, you must negotiate a royalty rate with the music publisher, CMRRA, or SODRAC. There are no "industry standard" rates as they depend on the nature, extent, medium, duration, and term of use. The rights are referred to as synchronization (or "synch") rights. You also need a synch licence for the use of a musical work in an audio-only production such as radio commercial.

Sheet Music

To obtain rights to reproduce sheet music from books, contact the music publisher.

Sound Recordings

Reproduction Right

Since copyright clearance to use a musical work does not include the use of a recording of that work, separate copyright permission must be obtained to "reproduce" the sound recording embodying the musical work.

For the reproduction of a sound recording within a film, television program, or commercial (radio or television), you will normally need to obtain the permission of the record company that owns the recording.

Audio-Video Licensing Agency Inc. (AVLA) is a nonexclusive agency that administers some sound recording reproduction rights for some uses, for example, music videos (see below) and the reproductions made by disk jockeys. The available licences are found on the AVLA website.

FOR FURTHER INFORMATION, CONTACT:

Audio-Video Licensing Agency Inc.
85 Mowat Avenue
Toronto, Ontario M6K 3E3
Telephone: 416.922.8727 or 1.800.668.8820 (toll free)
Fax: 416.967.9415
E-mail: info@avla.ca
Web: www.avla.ca

Neighbouring Rights

Sound recording performers and producers receive royalty payments from those who use their sound recordings for public performance, broadcast, and new media. Re:Sound collects royalties for recorded music from various types of users, including radio stations, pay audio services, satellite radio companies, gyms, nightclubs, and background music users in restaurants, stores, and hotels. Collected royalties are distributed equally between artists (recording artists, background performers, and session musicians) and record companies through two "subcollectives" representing record companies and three collectives representing performers.

FOR FURTHER INFORMATION, CONTACT:

Re:Sound
1235 Bay Street, Suite 900
Toronto, ON M5R 3K4
Telephone: 416.968.8870
Fax: 416.962.7797
E-mail: info@resound.ca
Web: www.resound.ca

Levy on Blank Audio Recording Media

Music rights holders including songwriters, composers, music publishers, recording artists, musicians, and record companies are entitled to a private copying levy (i.e., royalty) for copies made of music for personal use. The Canadian Private Copying Collective (CPCC)/ Société canadienne de perception de la copie privée (SCPCP) collects a small levy on the blank audio recording media that is usually used for private copying of music. Consumers do not directly pay the levy; manufacturers and importers of blank audio recording media are responsible for the payment. The type of media included in the levy can change, and updated information is on the website of the CPCC. Eligible beneficiaries are paid their share of the levy through the CPCC's member copyright collectives: CMRRA, SODRAC, SOCAN, and Re:Sound.

FOR FURTHER INFORMATION, CONTACT:

CPCC/SCPCP
150 Eglinton Avenue East, Suite 403
Toronto, Ontario M4P 1E8
Telephone: 416.486.6832 or 1.800.892.7235 (toll free)
Fax: 416.486.3064
E-mail: inquiries@cpcc.ca
Web: www.cpcc.ca

Music Videos

AVLA also licenses the rights in music videos. If you are reproducing a music video or showing it in public or on television, AVLA can help you obtain copyright permission.

Artistic Works

There are two copyright collectives that represent artistic works in Canada, the Canadian Artists Representation Copyright Collective (CARCC), and SODRAC. These collectives' websites list their members. Their members are visual artists, designers, craftspeople, cartoonists, illustrators, printmakers, illustration artists, sculptors, video artists, and architects. CARCC and SODRAC administer rights in artistic works such as exhibition, reproduction, and telecommunication.

If you want to exhibit an artistic work of a Canadian artist, or reproduce the work, for example, on the cover of a book or in a calendar, photocopy it, use it in a television program, or include it in a DVD, website, or social media site, you should contact CARCC or SODRAC.

CARCC and SODRAC represent their members abroad through bilateral agreements with similar organizations. SODRAC also represents foreign creators for the use of their works in Canada.

FOR FURTHER INFORMATION, CONTACT:

Canadian Artists Representation Copyright Collective Inc.
214 Barclay Road
Ottawa, ON K1K 3C2
Telephone: 613.232.3813 or 1.866.502.2722 (toll free)
Fax: 613.232.8384
E-mail: carcc@carcc.ca
Web: www.carcc.ca

Contact information for SODRAC is set out above.

USING GOVERNMENT OF CANADA WORKS

Federal Government of Canada Materials

Department of Justice Statutes, Decisions, and So Forth

According to a Reproduction of Federal Law Order as included in Appendix VII, anyone may, without charge or requesting permission, reproduce enactments and consolidations of enactments of the Government of Canada, and decisions and reasons for decisions of federally constituted courts and administrative tribunals. This is provided that due diligence is exercised in ensuring the accuracy of the materials reproduced and that the reproduction is not represented as an official version.

Other Federal Government of Canada Works

Other than statutes, decisions, and so on, as mentioned above, all other federal government material, may be reproduced, in part or in whole, by any means, without permission if for personal or public noncommercial purposes or for cost-recovery purposes. This is true unless otherwise specified in the material being reproduced. The reproduction must be exact, and the original work must not be modified. Personal and public noncommercial purposes means a distribution of the material for one's own purposes or for a distribution at large where no fees whatsoever will be charged. Cost-recovery means charging a fee for the purpose of recovering printing costs and other costs associated with the production of the reproduction.

If your reproduction without permission qualifies, then you must exercise due diligence in ensuring accuracy when reproducing the materials. You must include the complete title of the work reproduced, as well as the author organization. You must state that the reproduction is a copy of an official work that is published by the Government of Canada and that the reproduction is not in affiliation with, or with the endorsement of the Government of Canada.

Permission to reproduce Government of Canada works is always required if the work is being revised, adapted, or translated. This is true even if the purpose of the reproduction is for personal or public noncommercial distribution, or for cost-recovery purposes. Adaptation includes reproducing Government of Canada works in a different format. For example, reproducing a print publication in a CD-ROM. Revision means to alter or modify a Government of Canada work by amending the original content, possibly resulting in changes to the essence of the original work or the intended message of the original work.

Permission is always required when the reproduced work will be distributed for commercial purposes.

When providing permission, the Government of Canada will usually provide a nonexclusive licence. This means that the Government of Canada reserves the copyright and grants rights to the licensee for a specific purpose, duration, and territory.

Applying for Crown Copyright Clearance

There is an online crown copyright questionnaire to help you determine if written permission is required to use Government of Canada works. There are three questions:

1. For what purpose(s) do you intend to use the Government of Canada work(s)? The choices to select from are Adaptation, Reproduction, Revision, and Translation.
2. What is the end use of the work? The choices to select from are Commercial, Cost Recovery, Noncommercial, and Promotional.
3. Does the Government of Canada work(s) you wish to use require that you obtain written permission? The choices to select from are Yes, No, or I Don't Know.

By completing the online questionnaire, you will then be taken to another screen, which tells you whether permission is required or not to use the Government of Canada works. If you need permission, you will need to submit an Application for Copyright Clearance of Government of Canada Work(s). You may complete and submit this application online or mail it or fax it to Public Works and Government Services Canada. A copy of the Application for Copyright Clearance of Government of Canada Works is available online and is included in Appendix VIII in this book.

FOR FURTHER INFORMATION, CONTACT:
  Crown Copyright Officer
  Crown Copyright and Licensing
  Publishing and Depository Services
  Public Works and Government Services Canada
  Ottawa, Ontario K1A 0S5
  Telephone: 613.996.6886
  Fax: 613.998.1450
  E-mail: publications@tpsgc-pwgsc.gc.ca
  Web: http://publications.gc.ca

Copyright materials of Crown corporations must be cleared through the specific Crown Corporation. For instance, the Canadian Broadcasting Corporation (CBC) and the National Film Board (NFB) can give permission to use works in which they own the copyright. Also, the House of Commons, the Senate, Statistics Canada, and the National Research Council can clear the copyright in copyright materials owned by them.

Provincial and Territorial Government Materials

Provincial and territorial government materials must be cleared through the particular provincial department responsible for the administration of copyright. The exception is the province of Quebec; Copibec's repertoire includes the various publications of the different ministries of Quebec. It is up to each province and territory to set its own rules governing what content (e.g., publications, legislation) requires permission and under what circumstances.

Municipal Government Materials

Municipal government materials must be cleared through the particular municipal department responsible for the administration of copyright.

UNLOCATABLE COPYRIGHT OWNERS

If you have used all your resources to identify or locate a copyright owner and have been unsuccessful, you may be allowed to use the copyright material in question without directly obtaining permission from the copyright holder.[5] The Canadian Copyright Act has a provision (since 1988) that allows the Copyright Board to provide licences for the use, including digital use (e.g., digitization, use in an e-book) and online use, of published works where the copyright holder cannot be located.

In order to use works of unlocatable copyright holders, you must apply to the Copyright Board and satisfy it that the copyright owner cannot be located. In order to satisfy the Copyright Board, you must convince it that every effort has been made to locate the copyright holder. Proof may include evidence of correspondence and phone calls you have sent to possible rights holders or representatives, including any copyright collectives or estate executors, as well as associations or organizations relevant to the work or copyright holder, contacting publishing houses, libraries, universities, museums, and extensive online searches. If the Board is not satisfied that sufficient research has been undertaken to locate the copyright holder, it may advise you to continue your efforts, and may even suggest how to go about locating a copyright holder.

If the Board is satisfied by your efforts, it may, at its discretion, give permission (i.e., issue a licence) to use the work. This permission is nonexclusive; that is, others may be given the same permission for the same work. The permission is valid only in Canada; it does not protect you from infringement proceedings for uses outside the country, even if the author is Canadian. For example, if you post the work on the Internet, you will be responsible for uses outside of Canada if the work is accessed outside of Canada. You could limit access outside of Canada through technological measures, or you could investigate the laws in other countries to see if permission is required for use of the same work in other countries. The licence issued by the Board is subject to any terms and conditions, including royalty payments, that the Board may establish.

The copyright owner may, within five years after expiration of the licence, collect the royalties that are set out in the licence. If the royalties cannot be collected, the copyright owner may start a court action to recover them. In many cases, reasonable royalties are set by the Board and ordered to be paid to the appropriate copyright collective, who may then put the royalties towards the general benefit of its members. However, the copyright collective is obligated during the five-year period to pay these royalties to a copyright owner who establishes ownership of the work. A copyright owner cannot terminate a licence granted by the Copyright Board unless this is part of the terms and conditions of the licence granted by the Board.

The unlocatable copyright owner provision is open to any individual or organization trying to access a particular copyright work, including librarians, teachers, students, researchers, curators, archivists, publishers, sound and filmmakers, and business people. The unlocatable copyright owner provision only applies to published works. There is no equivalent provision for unpublished works.

To apply for a licence, you must submit an application in writing (i.e., not by telephone) to the Copyright Board. There is no form provided by the Board for making this application. The application may be in French or English; the decision by the Board is usually rendered in the same language as the application. The application may be submitted by e-mail. The application should contain the following information:

- The description of the work (type, title, year of publication, and any other related information).
- The names and nationalities of the author, copyright owner, and publisher/producer, etc.
- If the author is dead, the date of death.
- Your intended use of the work. Be specific and provide as much detail as possible. For example, if you want to reproduce written material to include in a book, indicate the length of the written material, a description of the book, including its length, the

purpose of the book, whether it is for free distribution or for sale (if for sale, include the suggested sale price).

- It is also helpful if you include with your application:
- The material you want to reproduce.
- The period of time in which you want to use the work.
- A full description of your efforts to locate the copyright holder. Include copies of any relevant material such as letters, faxes, and copies of e-mail correspondence.
- The name, title, address, telephone, fax number, and e-mail address of the licence applicant. If the applicant is different from the person/organization intending to use the work, provide information on that person/organization.

Based on the above information, the Board will issue you a licence if it considers that you have done everything possible to locate the copyright owner. If you provide sufficient information, the Board can respond as quickly as 30 days from the date of your application, but it will not guarantee such a quick response. Because each application has to be carefully examined, it is best to make your application to the Board as soon as you can and not to wait until the last minute.

If the Board issues a licence, the licence will indicate the authorized use (e.g., how many reproductions are permitted for what distribution and for what purpose), the length of the licence, the licence fee (which the copyright owner can claim within five years of the licence's expiry date), appropriate permissions wording/credit to be presented with the work, and any other terms and conditions the Board considers appropriate. You may only use the work in the manner prescribed by the licence; you need to obtain permission for all other uses, as well as for uses outside of Canada.

At the time of writing this book, only eight applications have been denied by the Board (see www.cb-cda.gc.ca/unlocatable-introuvables/denied-refusees-e.html). To date, 264 licences have been granted by the Board (see www.cb-cda.gc.ca/unlocatable-introuvables/licences-e.html). Following are summaries of three recent licences granted by the Board.

On September 30, 2011, Catherine Taddo in Ontario was issued a nonexclusive licence authorizing the mechanical reproduction and communication to the public by telecommunication of the musical work "Men Are Like Street Cars" by Louis Jordan or Charley Jordan. The licence allows the making of 600 CDs, as well as reproducing and sharing online the work for digital sales via iTunes and in MP3 format. When the licence expires on December 31, 2016, the authorized reproduction must be completed. Catherine Taddo must pay $49.80 to the CMRRA for mechanical rights. The CMRRA must reimburse any person who establishes before December 31, 2021, ownership of the copyright in the works in the licence. Regarding digital sales, Catherine Taddo must pay to any person who establishes before December 31, 2021, ownership of the copyright in the works covered in the licence, royalties amounting to the total, per download, that will be payable to the SOCAN 22.A (1996–2006) and CMRRA-SODRAC Inc. (2005–2007), Online Music Services Tariffs on the date of the sale. The following credit must be prominently displayed: "Used with permission under a nonexclusive licence issued by the Copyright Board of Canada in co-operation with the Canadian Musical Reproduction Rights Agency (CMRRA)."

On September 23, 2010, McGraw-Hill Ryerson Limited was issued a nonexclusive licence for the reproduction and communication to the public by telecommunication of a drawing by Sidney Clark Ells. The licence allows the reproduction in print and in any electronic format of the particular drawing identified as *Hudson Bay Company's Transport, near La Loche Portage (Manitoba)*, published in 1956 in Northland Trails by S.C. Ells, Burns & MacEachern. The drawing will be published in a grade 11 textbook entitled *MB History 11*. Up to 20,000 copies of the textbook may be reproduced with the drawing. The licence expires on December 31, 2020. All textbooks must be manufactured by that date. All protected digital uses of the work must also cease by that date. McGraw-Hill Ryerson must pay $331 to the Canadian Artists Representation Copyright Collective (CARCC). CARCC is required to pay this amount to any person who can establish ownership of the work before December 31, 2025. The following credit must be prominently displayed with the work and in all versions of the book: "Drawing by S.C. Ells known as *Hudson Bay Company's Transport, near La Loche Portage (Manitoba)*." Used with permission under a nonexclusive licence issued by the Copyright Board of Canada in co-operation with The Canadian Artists Representation Copyright Collective."

On July 24, 2012, the Canadian Institute of Natural and Integrative Medicine (CINIM) was issued a nonexclusive licence for the digital reproduction and the communication to the public by telecommunication of two jokes. The licence expires on December 31, 2015. The CINIM must pay $15 to Access Copyright. The following credit must be prominently presented next to each joke: "This version of the short story '[Enter name of Jokes]' is used with permission under a nonexclusive licence issued by the Copyright Board of Canada in cooperation with Access Copyright, the Canadian Copyright Licensing Agency, as its author remains unknown."

If you are applying for an unlocatable owner licence, review several of the issued licences, especially the terms and conditions of the licence. In your application, explain to the Board your intended uses. If you are publishing an e-book, for how long do you need permission? Or if you are posting the work on a website, is it reasonable for you to remove the work at the expiration of a short licence or do you want to request a licence for an extended period of time? The Board has some flexibility in the terms and conditions in the licences it issues, and for some online uses you may want to request a licence for the life of copyright subject to a right of retraction should the copyright owner show up and wish to end the licence. Be reasonable in your requests.

FOR FURTHER INFORMATION, CONTACT:
Copyright Board of Canada
56 Sparks Street, Suite 800
Ottawa, Ontario K1A 0C9

Telephone: 613.952.8621
Fax: 613.952.8630
E-mail: secretariat@cb-cda.gc.ca
Web: www.cb-cda.gc.ca

MORAL RIGHTS

Obtaining permission to use a copyright-protected work provides you permission for the "economic" right; however, it does not provide you any permission regarding moral rights. In other words, clearing copyright does not mean that you have cleared the moral rights in a work or in a performer's performance. By obtaining permission to use a work, you may use that work "as is." You may not modify or adapt or "morph" the work. According to the Copyright Act, you cannot distort, mutilate, or otherwise modify a copyright-protected work if that would be prejudicial to the honour or reputation of the author. If the work is a painting, sculpture, or engraving, you cannot change the work whatsoever, that is, prejudice to honour or reputation of the author is not a condition. Keep in mind that a change in the location of a work, the physical means by which a work is exposed, or the physical structure containing a work, and steps taken in good faith to restore or preserve a work do not by themselves constitute a distortion, mutilation, or other modification of a copyright-protected work.

Further, even if you have permission to use a copyright-protected work, the author has the right to have his or her name appear in association with the work, to use a pseudonym, or to remain anonymous. Lastly, someone who has permission to use a copyright-protected work does not have the right to use the work in association with a product, service, cause, or institution if that use is prejudicial to the honour or reputation of the author.

As discussed earlier, moral rights belong to the author of a work. This is true even if the owner of a work is someone other than the author of a work. For example, an employer may own copyright in a staff-written script; however, the writer of that script owns the moral rights in it.

Unlike copyright, moral rights cannot be licensed or assigned. Moral rights, however, may be waived and may be passed on upon death. This is discussed in Chapter 11, "How Can Rights Be Exploited?"

SUMMARY

If you are planning to use a work or other subject-matter protected by copyright, you must obtain permission and/or pay a royalty, prior to that use. There are number of sources to clear copyright permission, including the copyright owner and various copyright-related organizations and copyright collectives.

CHAPTER 15

An Overview of American Copyright Law

I always try to write on the principle of the iceberg. There is seven-eighths of it underwater for every part that shows.

—Ernest Hemingway

The Relevance of American Copyright Law to Canadians

If your work is being distributed or reproduced in the United States, this chapter is pertinent since you are protected in the United States under American copyright law.[1] Also, if you are employed by a U.S. company and (physically in Canada) or are entering into an agreement with a U.S. organization, you need to know the differences between Canadian and U.S. copyright law. Even where your work is not being distributed or reproduced in the United States and/or you are not working with or for a U.S. organization, the U.S. Copyright Office may be of assistance to Canadians with respect to registering and depositing their works and searching for owners of copyright materials. In addition, much of what we read about copyright law is U.S.-based; it is important for Canadians to be able to distinguish the U.S. copyright law from Canadian copyright law.

U.S. Copyright Act

Article I, Section 8 of the United States Constitution empowers the U.S. Congress to deal with copyright matters. It states: "The Congress shall have Power. . . . To promote the Progress of Science and useful Arts, by securing for limited Times to Authors and Inventors the exclusive Right to their respective Writings and Discoveries." As such, copyright law is a federal matter governed by a federal copyright statute. (See, however, the section below on Moral Rights in which state law also deals with copyright matters.) The Copyright Law of the United States is found in title 17 of the United States Code at www.copyright.gov/title17/.

WORKS PROTECTED IN THE UNITED STATES

In the United States, copyright exists "in original works of authorship fixed in any tangible medium of expression, now known or later developed, from which they can be perceived, reproduced, or otherwise communicated, either directly or with the aid of a machine or device." Works explicitly protected under the American copyright legislation include the following categories:

- Literary works (including computer software).
- Musical works (including any accompanying words).
- Dramatic works (including any accompanying music).
- Pantomimes and choreographic works.
- Pictorial, graphic, and sculptural works.
- Motion pictures and other audiovisual works.
- Sound recordings.
- Architectural works.

Ideas, facts, history, and the like are not protected by copyright in the U.S. The U.S. Copyright Act explicitly states that copyright protection does not "extend to any idea, procedure, process, system, method of operation, concept, principle, or discovery . . ."

Government Works

U.S. government works do not have copyright protection. U.S. government works are in the public domain and may be freely used without permission. This applies to any work prepared by an employee of the United States or federal government, created as part of that person's official duties.

Not all government works are freely available for use by the public. In some situations, the U.S. government does own copyright in works. The U.S. government may be a copyright owner and may obtain copyrights through an assignment, bequest, or other transfer. For example, a work created by an independent contractor such as a consultant, free-lance writer, or artist, may be assigned to the U.S. government. When a copyright is transferred or assigned to the U.S. government, the government then is a copyright owner.

The U.S. government may also have a licence to include copyright material in a work created by or for the government. In this situation, the copyright owner continues to own the copyright in its material, regardless of the fact that the material is being included in a government work that, as a whole, is not protected by copyright. To reproduce that government work incorporating third-party licensed content, you will need permission from that third-party copyright owner. Third-party content is content owned by someone other than the government.

Outside the United States, the protection of U.S. government works is dependent upon the laws of that country. Thus, if a U.S. government document is being photocopied in Canada, you apply the copyright laws of Canada. This means that in some situations, an unprotected work in the United States will be protected in Canada. It also means that you may be in the odd situation of seeking permission to use a U.S. government work in Canada although that work is available for free in the United States.

RIGHTS GRANTED IN THE UNITED STATES

The bundle of exclusive rights granted to copyright holders under the U.S. Copyright Act include the following:

- To reproduce a copyrighted work in copies or phonorecords.
- To prepare derivative works based upon the copyrighted work.
- To distribute copies or phonorecords of the work to the public by sale or other transfer of ownership, or by rental, lease, or lending.
- To publicly perform literary, musical, dramatic, and choreographic works, pantomimes, and motion pictures and other audiovisual work.
- To publicly display literary, musical, dramatic and choreographic works, pantomimes, and pictorial, graphic, or sculptural works, including the individual images of a motion picture or other audiovisual work.
- To perform a sound recording by digital audio transmission.

In addition, copyright holders may authorize others to use any of the rights listed above.

MORAL RIGHTS

The explicit moral rights protection that exists in the American Copyright Act (through an amendment made to it by the Visual Artists Rights Act of 1990 [VARA]) applies to only one group of creators—visual artists, or more accurately, those who create "works of visual art." The moral rights provision provides the author of a work of visual art the right to claim authorship of that work (i.e., have his or her name on the work), and to prevent the use of his or her name as the author of any visual artwork that he or she did not create. In addition, the author of a work of visual art has the right to prevent the use of his or her name where the work is distorted, mutilated, or otherwise modified in a manner that would be prejudicial to his or her honor or reputation, and to prevent any destruction of a work of "recognized stature" and any intentional or grossly negligent destruction of that work. The author has the above rights, may not transfer such rights, and maintains these rights even if he or she is no longer the copyright owner of the work. The author may waive these moral rights by signing a written document to that effect. In general, these moral rights last until December 31 of the year in which the author dies.

LIMITATIONS ON EXCLUSIVE RIGHTS

Fair Use

The U.S. principle of fair use was first codified in the U.S. Copyright Act of 1976. The purposes set out in the statute for fair use are as follows: criticism, comment, news reporting, teaching (including multiple copies for classroom use), scholarship, and research. These purposes are illustrative, and other uses such as parody and pastiche may also be fair uses.

The purpose of the use is only one factor to be considered in deciding whether a use is fair. The law requires that the following factors be considered to determine whether fair use applies in any particular circumstance:

1. The purpose and character of the use, including whether such use is of a commercial nature or is for nonprofit educational purposes.
2. The nature of the copyrighted work.
3. The amount and substantiality of the portion used in relation to the copyrighted work as a whole.
4. The effect of the use upon the potential market for or value of the copyrighted work.

Fair use as found in section 107 of the U.S. Copyright Act is a defence to a claim of copyright infringement. Fair use is intentionally flexible to allow a court to consider any particular case before it.

Under fair use, acknowledgement of the source is not necessary.[2]

Exceptions for Libraries, Archives, and Educational Institutions

Fair use may be a defence to anyone using copyright materials in the United States. In addition, there are exceptions in the United States, or limitations on exclusive rights, for specific uses or user groups such as libraries and archives. Section 108 of the U.S. Copyright Act allows certain libraries to make copies of copyright materials for preservation, private study, and interlibrary loan.

In addition to fair use applying to education, the U.S. Copyright Act has incorporated the TEACH Act in section 110(2) to allow certain institutions to use copyright material in distance learning and online education in prescribed circumstances.

U.S. Limitations in Canada

You should not assume that an act constituting a copyright infringement under Canadian law is an infringement in the United States. According to national treatment under the Berne Convention (discussed in Chapter 5), when a work is used in the United States, it is subject to the fair use defence and the exceptions set out in the U.S. Copyright Act. Likewise, when U.S. content is used in Canada, it is subject to the fair dealing defence and the exceptions in the Canadian Copyright Act.

LENGTH OF PROTECTION

The general rule of copyright protection in the U.S. is life-plus-70. Until October 1998, the general duration of copyright protection in the U.S. was life-plus-50. In 1998, the Sonny Bono Copyright Term Extension Act extended the term of copyright an additional 20 years, making the term for most works the life of the author plus 70 years. Therefore, under current U.S. copyright law, works created on or after January 1, 1978, enjoy the general term of copyright protection of life-plus-70.

Copyright expires at the end of the calendar year of the 70th year; that is, December 31 of that year. As such, Canadian works are protected in the United States for life-plus-70 years where U.S. works are protected in Canada for life-plus-50 (since you apply the copyright law where the work is being used).

The duration of protection for works created, but not published or registered, before January 1, 1978 is life-plus-70, but in all cases the copyright in these works lasted at least until December 31, 2002. If the work was created before January 1, 1978, and published between January 1, 1978, and December 31, 2002, the copyright will not expire before December 31, 2047. The duration of copyright for pre-1978 works that are in their original or renewal term of copyright is 95 years from the date the copyright was originally secured.[3] With various changes to the U.S. Copyright Act, it is often difficult to determine duration of copyright protection for works created before 1978 in the United States. Two tables are helpful in making this determination; When U.S. Works Pass Into the Public Domain by Lolly Gasaway at www.unc.edu/~unclng/public-d.htm; and Copyright Term and the Public Domain in the United States by Peter Hirtle at http://copyright.cornell.edu/resources/publicdomain.cfm.

There are specific provisions in the U.S. law for the duration of copyright in specific circumstances. For example, where there is a "work made for hire," that is, a work was prepared by an employee within the scope of his or her employment, or where a certain work is specially ordered or commissioned for use in particular works (for example, a contribution to a motion picture or other audiovisual work), the term of copyright protection is 95 years from the date of publication or 120 years from the date of creation of the work, whichever expires first. Further, where there is an anonymous or pseudonymous work, the duration of copyright is 95 years from first publication or 120 years from creation, whichever is shorter. This provision applies if the author's identity is not revealed in the U.S. Copyright Office records.

OWNERSHIP OF WORKS

Employment Situations and Assignments of Copyright

If you are working in the United States or for or with an American individual or company, be aware that the United States has different laws and industry standards from Canada for works created in the course of employment as well as for commissioned works.

In the United States, copyright generally and initially belongs to the author. However, in employment or what is referred to as "work made for hire" situations, the employer or other person for whom the work was prepared is considered the author and owner of the copyright. This is true unless the employer and "employee" have expressly agreed otherwise in writing. Examples of works made for hire include a video game created by a staff game creator for Video Game Corporation, a newspaper article written by a staff journalist for publication in the *Los Angeles Times*, and a musical arrangement written for ZZZ Music Company by a salaried staff arranger. It also includes a script commissioned for a film even where no salaried employment relationship exists, if the scriptwriter and film producer sign an agreement to the effect that it is a work made for hire.

The U.S. Copyright Act defines a work made for hire as:

1. a work prepared by an employee within the scope of his or her employment; or
2. a work specially ordered or commissioned for use as a contribution to a collective work, as a part of a motion picture or other audiovisual work, as a translation, as a supplementary work, as a compilation, as an instructional text, as a test, as answer material for a test, or as an atlas, if the parties expressly agree in a written instrument signed by them that the work shall be considered a work made for hire. For the purpose of the foregoing sentence, a "supplementary work" is a work prepared for publication as a secondary adjunct to a work by another author for the purpose

of introducing, concluding, illustrating, explaining, revising, commenting upon, or assisting in the use of the other work, such as forewords, afterwords, pictorial illustrations, maps, charts, tables, editorial notes, musical arrangements, answer material for tests, bibliographies, appendixes, and indexes, and an "instructional text" is a literary, pictorial, or graphic work prepared for publication and with the purpose of use in systematic instructional activities.

The copyright in works that are specifically commissioned, other than the types of works discussed in (2) above, belong to the person who creates the work, not the person who commissions and often pays for the work. Therefore, if you hire someone to create a work for you, other than the works listed in paragraph (2), you need to have a written assignment transferring the copyright if you are going to own the copyright. It is almost always easier to obtain an assignment before work on the project begins. For that reason, assignment provisions often are included in the contract retaining the contractor and describing the scope of the work. This type of agreement is frequently used when software programmers are hired to write a specific program.

Also, in certain industries in the United States, you may automatically be asked to assign, as oppose to license, certain copyrights as a precondition of being hired to work on a specific project. For instance, American movie and television producers may require an assignment of the publishing rights to a musical score. Similarly, if you write a spec script for a film, you will initially own the copyright in the script; however, if you sell the script to an American production company or studio, they will require an assignment of the copyright. Many U.S. book publishers also request an assignment of copyright from their authors in their standard agreements offered to authors (especially newer authors). Even if the assignment of rights is not obvious, be on guard for American contracts that automatically vet copyright ownership in the party specially ordering or commissioning certain types of works, such as collections and audiovisual works, including motion pictures and certain computer software and multimedia projects. Keep in mind that contractual arrangements can override the statutory law; also, you may be able to negotiate better terms in a contract than those initially offered to you.

Joint Ownership

The U.S. Copyright Act defines a joint work as "a work prepared by two or more authors with the intention that their contributions be merged into inseparable or interdependent parts of a unitary whole." Copyright in a joint work is held jointly by all of its creators and authors. This means that each collaborator co-owns the copyright, shares equally in royalties, and can license the work on a nonexclusive basis to a third party as long as the profits are fairly accounted for to each of the other copyright owners.

There is a fine line between contributing to a work and coauthoring a work. In the case of a written book, for example, the editor is not a joint author, whereas each person who contributes discrete sections of a book may be a joint author and hold joint copyright in the book. If different people each contribute different chapters to a book, each person may be a joint author; or, if the chapters are separable and each chapter can stand on its own, the author of each chapter may own a copyright in his or her own chapter rather than a joint copyright applying to the book as a whole. Whether or not there is joint ownership of the copyright will depend on the specific facts. (Under a different scenario, each author who contributes a chapter to a book may assign the copyright in his or her chapter to the editor or publisher rather than be a joint owner.)

In the United States, if the collaborators want to define their relationship differently from what is set out above, it must be stated in a written agreement. If you are a Canadian (where the law differs in this area), and are jointly creating a work with an American, it is best to have your agreement set out in writing prior to the start of the project.

REGISTRATION AND COPYRIGHT NOTICE REQUIREMENTS

Copyright protection is automatic in the United States when the work is created and in some fixed form. Automatic protection is relatively new in the United States where publication, registration, and using a proper copyright notice were once necessary for copyright protection. This all changed when the United States joined the Berne Convention in 1989. Under the current law, for works first published on or after March 1, 1989, registration or inclusion of any form of copyright notice is not required to preserve the life-plus-70 protection. Before March 1, 1989, the use of the copyright notice was necessary on all published works, and omitting it could result in loss of copyright protection. However, there are corrective steps that may be followed under certain circumstances to ensure that copyright was not lost for this reason.

Despite the absence of formal requirements, including registration, to obtain copyright protection under the current law, the law provides many incentives for registering a copyright with the United States Copyright Office, even for non–U.S.-originated works. For instance, registering before or within five years of a work's first publication provides *prima facie* evidence of copyright validity and of the truth of the statements contained in the registration certificate. Also, registering published works before or within three months of publication, or before infringement, permits successful plaintiffs in infringement suits to seek special statutory damages and lawyers' fees (otherwise, only an order of actual damages and profits is available to the copyright owner of a published work). Furthermore, registration establishes a public record of the copyright claim. Thus, an infringer cannot claim that he or she had no way of knowing a copyright existed and therefore is less likely to be found to be an innocent infringer, which could lead to a reduction in damages payable to the copyright owner. Registration may be made at any time. Both published and unpublished works may be registered.

For copyright owners of works of U.S. origin, registering the work is a prerequisite to being entitled to file an infringement suit in a U.S.

court. As a general rule, under U.S. law, the prelitigation registration requirement does not apply to foreign (i.e., non-U.S.) authors including persons or companies who initially acquired copyright protection under the Canadian Copyright Act, and by virtue of the international copyright conventions, acquired copyright protection in the United States (unless publication occurred simultaneously in Canada and the United States).[4] But a non-U.S. citizen or resident who acquires a copyright in a work created in the United States must comply with the registration requirement before bringing suit for copyright in the United States. You should check into the details of this if you think your work may be of U.S. origin.

If you do register in the United States, you might want to take advantage of other U.S. Copyright Office benefits, for instance, voluntary recording of transfers of copyright ownership and grants of exclusive rights under a licence. Also, a copyright registration may be recorded with the U.S. Customs Service, who will prevent unauthorized copies of the copyright-protected work from entering the United States. Specifics on registering a work with the U.S. Copyright Office are in Chapter 4.

U.S. Digital Copyright Legislation

On October 28, 1998, the Digital Millennium Copyright Act (DMCA) updated the U.S. Copyright Act. Among other things, the DMCA helps copyright owners protect their digital content through its provisions on anticircumvention and copyright management information.

Regarding anticircumvention, the DMCA protects against the tampering with copyright protection technologies and rights management systems. The DMCA prohibits unauthorized circumvention of technological measures controlling access to or restricting use of a copyright-protected work, as well as certain devices and services used for such unauthorized circumvention. The types of technological measures protected include scramblers, encryption, and other technologies that copyright owners use to control or restrict access to their works. For example, the law might be violated by tampering with digital rights management software to make unauthorized copies of a sound recording or video or descrambling a cable television signal.

In addition, the DMCA prohibits deliberate tampering with copyright management information, including knowingly providing false copyright management information, or distributing false copyright management information, "with the intent to induce, enable, facilitate or conceal infringement." Copyright management information includes the title of a work, the name of its author and the copyright owner, other identifying information, and terms and conditions for use of the work, provided they are "conveyed in connection with" copies, phonorecords, performances, or displays of the work. It also prohibits intentionally removing or altering copyright management information, or knowingly distributing or publicly performing works from which the copyright management information has been removed or altered.

Further, the DMCA provides a limitation on the potential liability of Internet service providers (ISPs) for certain copyright infringements by their customers and others (e.g., employees and agents). Under specified circumstances, ISPs with infringing materials placed on their systems by third-party users will not be liable for monetary relief such as "damages, costs, attorneys' fees, and any other form of monetary payment," or for certain injunctions or other equitable relief for infringement of copyright. This is commonly referred to as the *safe harbor* provision. In order to qualify, ISPs in the United States must provide a notification system and a procedure for dealing with DMCA-Compliant notifications. This is why you see DMCA notice and take-down policies on U.S. sites relating to claims of copyright infringement by customers, subscribers, or users. Generally, there is a notice of claimed infringement, which advises the alleged copyright owner or their agent to provide the Designated Copyright Agent as identified with an electronic or physical signature of the person authorized to act on behalf of the copyright owner, a description of the alleged infringing work, address, telephone number, and e-mail address, and a statement that the alleged claim of infringement is made in good faith and is accurate. Upon receipt of such a notice, the ISP must provide a take-down procedure and a DMCA counternotification procedure. Note that although the DMCA Notice and Takedown Policy is not valid in Canada or in other countries, ISPs outside the United States often voluntarily follow a similar procedure.

The DMCA expressly permits authorized institutions to make up to three digital preservation copies of an eligible copyright-protected work, electronically loan those copies to other qualifying institutions; and permits preservation, including by digital means, when the existing format in which the work has been stored becomes obsolete.

HOW TO OBTAIN FURTHER INFORMATION ON U.S. COPYRIGHT LAW

The U.S. Copyright Office has extensive information on many aspects of its law. One of the roles of the U.S. Copyright Office is to provide general information (not legal advice or opinions) on U.S. copyright law. The best place to begin your research is at the Office's website at www.copyright.gov. You can also email the Office a question at www.copyright.gov/help/general-form.html. You can call the Office at 202.707.5959. There is no toll free number from Canada.

SUMMARY

Copyright holders who are protected under the Canadian Copyright Act are protected when their works are distributed or reproduced in the United States where they enjoy the rights and remedies set out in the U.S. Copyright Act. Using U.S. content in Canada is subject to Canadian copyright law. Although there are many similarities between the copyright laws in the two countries, there are differences with respect to the registration system, ownership of copyright in works created by employees, maintaining and enforcing copyright protection, and exceptions from the law—all of which should be taken into account when exploiting copyright-protected works in the United States.

APPENDIX I

COPYRIGHT ACT

The Canadian Copyright Act, consolidated with amendments made to it since its enactment in 1942, related information and related regulations are at http://laws.justice.gc.ca/eng/acts/C-42/index.html. You can search any words within this html version of the Act. The Act is also available in PDF. Previous versions of the Act are also available on this Government of Canada Justice Laws website.

COPYRIGHT MODERNIZATION ACT

Order Fixing Various Dates as the Dates on Which Certain Provisions of the Act Come into Force

http://www.gazette.gc.ca/rp-pr/p2/2012/2012-11-07/html/si-tr85-eng.html

COPYRIGHT MODERNIZATION ACT

Order Fixing Various Dates as the Dates on which Certain Provisions of the Act Come into Force

P.C. 2012-1392 October 25, 2012

His Excellency the Governor General in Council, on the recommendation of the Minister of Industry, pursuant to section 63 of the *Copyright Modernization Act* ("the Act"), chapter 20 of the Statutes of Canada, 2012, fixes

- (*a*) the day on which this Order is published in the *Canada Gazette*, Part II, as the day on which section 1, subsection 2(2), sections 3, 4 and 6 to 8, subsections 9(1) and (2), section 10, subsections 11(1) and (3) and 12(1) and (3), section 13, subsections 15(1), (3) and (5) and sections 17 to 46, 47 (other than sections 41.25 and 41.26 and subsection 41.27(3) of the *Copyright Act*, as enacted by that section), 48, 49 and 51 to 62 of the Act come into force;

- (*b*) the later of the day on which this Order is published in the *Canada Gazette*, Part II, and the day on which the WIPO Copyright Treaty, adopted in Geneva on December 20, 1996, comes into force for Canada as the day on which subsection 2(1) and section 5 of the Act come into force; and

- (*c*) the later of the day on which this Order is published in the *Canada Gazette*, Part II, and the day on which the WIPO Performances and Phonograms Treaty, adopted in Geneva on December 20, 1996, comes into force for Canada as the day on which subsections 9(3) and (4), 11(2), (4) and (5) and 12(2), section 14, subsections 15(2) and (4) and sections 16 and 50 of the Act come into force.

APPENDIX III

APPLICATION FOR REGISTRATION OF A COPYRIGHT IN A WORK

www.cipo.ic.gc.ca/eic/site/cipointernet-internetopic.nsf/vwapj/
DA-CR-form1-eng.pdf/$file/DA-CR-form1-eng.pdf

Canadian Intellectual Property Office
An Agency of Industry Canada

Office de la propriété intellectuelle du Canada
Un organisme d'Industrie Canada

APPLICATION FOR REGISTRATION OF A COPYRIGHT IN A WORK

Please print. For assistance in completing the form, please refer to the "Assistance" page.

NOTICE: INFORMATION ENTERED IN THIS APPLICATION WILL BE PUBLISHED ON THE COPYRIGHT ONLINE DATABASE THAT IS AVAILABLE FOR PUBLIC INSPECTION ON CIPO'S WEBSITE.

Note: It is the applicant's responsibility to ensure the accuracy of the included information.

Privacy Notice
All personal information created, held or collected by the Canadian Intellectual Property Office is protected under the *Privacy Act*. This means that you will be informed of the purpose for which it is being collected and how to exercise your right of access to that information. You will be asked for your consent where appropriate. Read the full notice: cipo.ic.gc.ca/notice

1. **Title of the work:**
   Enter the title of a single work. Descriptive matter that does not form part of the title should not be included.

2. **Category of the work:**
   Select the category that best describes the work.

   ☐ Literary (works consisting of text, i.e., books, pamphlets, computer programs, etc.);
   ☐ Musical (musical compositions, with or without words);
   ☐ Artistic (paintings, drawings, maps, sculptures, plans, photographs, etc.);
   ☐ Dramatic (screenplays, scripts, plays, films, etc.).

3. **Publication:**
   Select whether the work is published or unpublished. If the work is published, enter the full date (year, month and day) and the place of first publication.

   ☐ The work is unpublished

   OR

   ☐ The work is published

   Date of first publication (yyyy/mm/dd): _____

   Place of publication:

   City/Town   Province/State

   Country

 Canada

 CIPO   OPIC

4. Owner:
Enter the name and address of the owner of the copyright. To add additional owners, please attach a separate sheet.

Family name

First name

OR Name of other legal entity

Address

City/Town

Province/State

Country

Postal/Zip Code

························ **OPTIONAL INFORMATION** ························

Telephone

Fax

Email Address

---

5. Author:
Enter the name of the author of the work. **Note:** The individual who created the work should be named as the author except in the case of a photograph, where some other legal entity can be named. To add additional authors, please attach a separate sheet.

☐ **Same as owner** - Select if the author information is identical to the owner information, and proceed to Section 6.

Note: A corporation should not be named as an author, except in the case of a photograph.

Family name

First name

OR Name of other legal entity

If deceased, date of author's death (yyyy/mm/dd):

························ **OPTIONAL INFORMATION** ························

Address

City/Town

Province/State

Country

Postal/Zip Code

(continued)

(continued)

6. Declaration:

I/We hereby declare that the applicant is:

- ☐ the author of the work;
- ☐ the owner of the copyright in the work;
- ☐ an assignee of the copyright;
- ☐ a licensee of the copyright.

7. Agent (if applicable):
This section is to be completed only if the application is being submitted by an agent acting on behalf of the applicant.

Family name

First name

AND/OR Name of firm

Address

City/Town

Province/State

Country

Postal/Zip Code

⋯⋯⋯⋯⋯⋯⋯⋯ **OPTIONAL INFORMATION** ⋯⋯⋯⋯⋯⋯⋯⋯

Telephone

Fax

Email Address

8. Fee:

In accordance with Item 1 of the Tariff of Fees, the prescribed fee is required for each application for registration of a copyright. Payment should be submitted at the same time as the application using CIPO's Fee Payment Form. Please see the "Assistance" page for further details.

All correspondence should be addressed to:

Copyright Office
Canadian Intellectual Property Office
Industry Canada
Place du Portage I
50 Victoria Street
Gatineau, QC K1A 0C9

Telephone: 1-866-997-1936
Facsimile: 819-953-2476
Internet address: **cipo.gc.ca/copyrights**
Email: **cipo.contact@ic.gc.ca**

Please do not send copies of your work.

APPENDIX IV

APPLICATION FOR REGISTRATION OF A COPYRIGHT IN A PERFORMER'S PERFORMANCE, SOUND RECORDING, OR COMMUNICATION SIGNAL

www.cipo.ic.gc.ca/eic/site/cipointernet-internetopic.nsf/vwapj/
DA–CR–form2–eng.pdf/$file/DA–CR–form2–eng.pdf

Canadian Intellectual Property Office

An Agency of Industry Canada

Office de la propriété intellectuelle du Canada

Un organisme d'Industrie Canada

APPLICATION FOR REGISTRATION OF A COPYRIGHT IN A PERFORMER'S PERFORMANCE, SOUND RECORDING OR COMMUNICATION SIGNAL

Please print. For assistance in completing the form, please refer to the "Assistance" page.

NOTICE: INFORMATION ENTERED IN THIS APPLICATION WILL BE PUBLISHED ON THE COPYRIGHT ONLINE DATABASE THAT IS AVAILABLE FOR PUBLIC INSPECTION ON CIPO'S WEBSITE.

<u>Note</u>: It is the applicant's responsibility to ensure the accuracy of the included information.

Privacy Notice

All personal information created, held or collected by the Canadian Intellectual Property Office is protected under the *Privacy Act*. This means that you will be informed of the purpose for which it is being collected and how to exercise your right of access to that information. You will be asked for your consent where appropriate. Read the full notice: cipo.ic.gc.ca/notice

---

1. Title of the subject-matter:
Enter the title of the subject-matter. **Note:** *The application must relate to the registration of only one performer's performance, sound recording or communication signal.*

---

2. Subject-matter:
Select the type of subject-matter. For a performer's performance, enter the date of its first fixation in a sound recording or of its first performance if it is not fixed. Enter the date of first fixation for a sound recording, or the date of broadcast in the case of a communication signal.

Type

☐ Performer's performance

    ☐ 1st Fixation

    OR

    ☐ 1st Performance

    Date _____ (yyyy/mm/dd)

☐ Sound recording – 1st Fixation

    Date _____ (yyyy/mm/dd)

☐ Communication signal – Broadcast

    Date _____ (yyyy/mm/dd)

3. Owner:

Enter the name and address of the owner of the copyright. To add additional owners, please attach a separate sheet.

Family name

First name

OR Name of other legal entity

Address

City/Town

Province/State

Country

Postal/Zip Code

························· **OPTIONAL INFORMATION** ·························

Telephone

Fax

Email Address

4. Declaration:

I/We hereby declare that the applicant is:

☐ the owner of the copyright in the subject-matter;

☐ an assignee of the copyright;

☐ a licensee of the copyright.

5. Agent (if applicable):

This section is to be completed only if the application is being submitted by an agent acting on behalf of the applicant.

Family name

First name

AND/OR Name of firm

Address

City/Town

Province/State

Country

Postal/Zip Code

························· **OPTIONAL INFORMATION** ·························

Telephone

Fax

Email Address

(continued)

(continued)

6. Fee:

In accordance with Item 1 of the Tariff of Fees, the prescribed fee is required for each application for registration of a copyright. Payment should be submitted at the same time as the application using CIPO's Fee Payment Form. Please see the "Assistance" page for further details.

All correspondence should be addressed to:

Copyright Office
Canadian Intellectual Property Office
Industry Canada
Place du Portage I
50 Victoria Street
Gatineau, QC K1A 0C9

Telephone: 1-866-997-1936
Facsimile: 819-953-2476

Internet address: **cipo.gc.ca/copyrights**
Email: **cipo.contact@ic.gc.ca**

Please do not send copies of your work

APPENDIX V

EDUCATIONAL PROGRAM, WORK, AND OTHER SUBJECT-MATTER RECORD-KEEPING REGULATIONS

http://laws-lois.justice.gc.ca/eng/regulations/SOR-2001-296/index.html

CANADA

CONSOLIDATION

Educational Program, Work and Other Subject-matter Record-keeping Regulations

SOR/2001-296

Current to July 10, 2013

Published by the Minister of Justice at the following address:
http://laws-lois.justice.gc.ca

OFFICIAL STATUS
OF CONSOLIDATIONS

Subsections 31(1) and (3) of the *Legislation Revision and Consolidation Act*, in force on June 1, 2009, provide as follows:

Published consolidation is evidence

31. (1) Every copy of a consolidated statute or consolidated regulation published by the Minister under this Act in either print or electronic form is evidence of that statute or regulation and of its contents and every copy purporting to be published by the Minister is deemed to be so published, unless the contrary is shown.

...

Inconsistencies in regulations

(3) In the event of an inconsistency between a consolidated regulation published by the Minister under this Act and the original regulation or a subsequent amendment as registered by the Clerk of the Privy Council under the *Statutory Instruments Act*, the original regulation or amendment prevails to the extent of the inconsistency.

NOTE

This consolidation is current to July 10, 2013. Any amendments that were not in force as of July 10, 2013 are set out at the end of this document under the heading "Amendments Not in Force".

Registration
SOR/2001-296   August 1, 2001

COPYRIGHT ACT

Educational Program, Work and Other Subject-matter Record-keeping Regulations

P.C. 2001-1404   August 1, 2001

The Copyright Board, pursuant to subsection 29.9(2)ᵃ of the *Copyright Act*, hereby makes the annexed *Educational Program, Work and Other Subject-matter Record-keeping Regulations*.

Ottawa, July 18, 2001

Her Excellency the Governor General in Council, on the recommendation of the Minister of Industry, pursuant to subsection 29.9(2)ᵃ of the *Copyright Act*, hereby approves the making by the Copyright Board of the annexed *Educational Program, Work and Other Subject-matter Record-keeping Regulations*.

INTERPRETATION

1. The definitions in this section apply in these Regulations.

"Act" means the *Copyright Act*. (*Loi*)

"collective society" means a collective society that carries on the business of collecting the royalties referred to in subsection 29.6(2) or 29.7(2) or (3) of the Act under a tariff that has been certified as an approved tariff pursuant to paragraph 73(1)(*d*) of the Act. (*société de gestion*)

"copy identifier" means the number or other reference code assigned to the copy of a program, work or subject-matter in accordance with section 3. (*code d'identification de l'exemplaire*)

"educational institution identifier" means the number or other reference code assigned to an educational institution in accordance with section 4. (*code d'identification de l'établissement d'enseignement*)

"institution" means an educational institution or a person acting under its authority. (*établissement*)

APPLICATION

2. These Regulations apply in respect of

(*a*) copies of news programs and news commentary programs that are made pursuant to paragraph 29.6(1)(*a*) of the Act; and

(*b*) copies of works and other subject-matter that are made pursuant to paragraph 29.7(1)(*a*) of the Act.

GENERAL PROVISIONS

3. An institution shall assign a number or other reference code to every copy of a program, work or subject-matter that it makes.

4. A collective society may assign a number or other reference code to an educational institution.

MARKING OF COPY

5. An institution that makes a copy of a program, work or subject-matter shall mark on the copy, or on its container, the copy identifier and, if applicable, the educational institution identifier.

RECORDING OF INFORMATION

6. (1) Subject to subsection (2), an institution that makes a copy of a program, work or subject-matter shall complete, in a legible manner, an information record in the form set out in the schedule regarding

(*a*) the copying of the program, work or subject-matter;

(*b*) all performances in public of the copy for which royalties are payable under subsection 29.6(2) or 29.7(2) or (3) of the Act; and

(*c*) the destruction of the copy.

(2) Subsection (1) does not apply to the copy of a program made pursuant to paragraph 29.6(1)(*a*) of the Act if the copy is destroyed, in a manner that complies with section 7, within 72 hours after the making of the copy.

DESTRUCTION OF COPY

7. Destruction of a copy of a program, work or subject-matter shall be accomplished by

(*a*) destroying the medium onto which the program, work or subject-matter was copied; or

(*b*) erasing the copy of the program, work or subject-matter from the medium.

SENDING OF INFORMATION RECORD

8. (1) Subject to subsection (2), an institution shall send to each collective society

(*a*) within 30 days after the date on which the Board first certifies a tariff as an approved tariff pursuant to paragraph 73(1)(*d*) of the Act, a copy of every information record on which entries have been made during the period between the date on which these Regulations come into force and the date on which the tariff was certified; and

(*b*) after that, on or before January 31, May 31 and September 30 in each year, a copy of every information record on which entries have been made during the four months preceding the month in which the record is sent.

(2) Once a copy of a program, work or subject-matter has been destroyed, the institution may send the original information record in respect of the copy to a collective society.

RETENTION OF INFORMATION RECORD

9. An institution shall retain the original information record in respect of a copy of a program, work or subject-matter until two years after the copy is destroyed unless, during that time, the institution sends the original information record to a collective society.

COMING INTO FORCE

10. These Regulations come into force on the 30th day after the day on which they are registered.

SCHEDULE
(Subsection 6(1))

INFORMATION RECORD

Educational Institution identifier (if assigned): _____

Name and address of institution: _____

_____

_____

_____

Contact name: _____

Telephone: _____ Facsimile: _____ E-mail: _____

Details of Program, Work or Subject-matter

Copy identifier: _____

Title of program, work or subject-matter: _____

Other identifying information: _____
[e.g. episode title, subject, segment description, song title(s)]

Duration of segment copied: _____ minutes

Date of broadcast (yy/mm/dd): _____ Time of broadcast: _____

Name, network, call sign or other identifier of the broadcaster: _____

Record of Public Performances

(List only performances for which royalties are payable)

yy/mm/dd   yy/mm/dd

_____   _____

_____   _____

_____   _____

_____   _____

(Use separate sheet to list additional performances)

Record of Destruction

I certify that the copy of the program, work or subject-matter identified above has been destroyed.

Name: _____ Title: _____

Signature: _____ Date of Destruction (yy/mm/dd): _____

EXCEPTIONS FOR EDUCATIONAL INSTITUTIONS, LIBRARIES, ARCHIVES, AND MUSEUMS REGULATIONS

http://laws-lois.justice.gc.ca/eng/regulations/SOR-99-325/index
.html

CANADA

CONSOLIDATION

Exceptions for Educational Institutions, Libraries, Archives and Museums Regulations

SOR/99-325

Current to July 10, 2013

Last amended on May 15, 2008

Published by the Minister of Justice at the following address:
http://laws-lois.justice.gc.ca

OFFICIAL STATUS
OF CONSOLIDATIONS

Subsections 31(1) and (3) of the *Legislation Revision and Consolidation Act*, in force on June 1, 2009, provide as follows:

Published consolidation is evidence

31. (1) Every copy of a consolidated statute or consolidated regulation published by the Minister under this Act in either print or electronic form is evidence of that statute or regulation and of its contents and every copy purporting to be published by the Minister is deemed to be so published, unless the contrary is shown.

...

Inconsistencies in regulations

(3) In the event of an inconsistency between a consolidated regulation published by the Minister under this Act and the original regulation or a subsequent amendment as registered by the Clerk of the Privy Council under the *Statutory Instruments Act*, the original regulation or amendment prevails to the extent of the inconsistency.

NOTE

This consolidation is current to July 10, 2013. The last amendments came into force on May 15, 2008. Any amendments that were not in force as of July 10, 2013 are set out at the end of this document under the heading "Amendments Not in Force".

Registration
SOR/99-325   July 28, 1999

COPYRIGHT ACT

**Exceptions for Educational Institutions, Libraries,
Archives and Museums Regulations**

P.C. 1999-1351   July 28, 1999

His Excellency the Governor General in Council, on
the recommendation of the Minister of Industry, pursuant to subsections 30.2(6)[a], 30.21(4)[a] and 6[a] and
30.3(5)[a] of the *Copyright Act*, hereby makes the annexed
*Exceptions for Educational Institutions, Libraries,
Archives and Museums Regulations*.

INTERPRETATION

1. (1) In these Regulations, "Act" means the *Copyright Act*.

(2) In these Regulations, a reference to a copy of a work is a reference to a copy of all or any substantial part of a work.

NEWSPAPER OR PERIODICAL

2. For the purpose of subsection 30.2(6) of the Act, "newspaper or periodical" means a newspaper or a periodical, other than a scholarly, scientific or technical periodical, that was published more than one year before the copy is made.

RECORDS KEPT UNDER SECTION 30.2 OF THE ACT

3. In respect of activities undertaken by a library, an archive or a museum under subsection 30.2(1) of the Act, section 4 applies only to the reproduction of works.

4. (1) Subject to subsection (2), a library, an archive or a museum, or a person acting under the authority of one, shall record the following information with respect to a copy of a work that is made under section 30.2 of the Act:

(*a*) the name of the library, archive or museum making the copy;

(*b*) if the request for a copy is made by a library, archive or museum on behalf of a person who is a patron of the library, archive or museum, the name of the library, archive or museum making the request;

(*c*) the date of the request; and

(*d*) information that is sufficient to identify the work, such as

(i) the title,

(ii) the International Standard Book Number,

(iii) the International Standard Serial Number,

(iv) the name of the newspaper, the periodical or the scholarly, scientific or technical periodical in which the work is found, if the work was published in a newspaper, a periodical or a scholarly, scientific or technical periodical,

(v) the date or volume and number of the newspaper or periodical, if the work was published in a newspaper or periodical,

(vi) the date or volume and number of the scholarly, scientific or technical periodical, if the work was published in a scholarly, scientific or technical periodical, and

(vii) the numbers of the copied pages.

(2) A library, an archive or a museum, or a person acting under the authority of one, does not have to record the information referred to in subsection (1) if the copy of the work is made under subsection 30.2(1) of the Act after December 31, 2003.

(3) A library, an archive or a museum, or a person acting under the authority of one, shall keep the information referred to in subsection (1)

(*a*) by retaining the copy request form; or

(*b*) in any other manner that is capable of reproducing the information in intelligible written form within a reasonable time.

(4) A library, an archive or a museum, or a person acting under the authority of one, shall keep the information referred to in subsection (1) with respect to copies made of a work for at least three years.

(5) A library, an archive or a museum, or a person acting under the authority of one, shall make the information referred to in subsection (1), with respect to copies made of a work, available once a year to one of the following persons, on request made by the person in accordance with subsection (7):

(*a*) the owner of copyright in the work;

(*b*) the representative of the owner of copyright in the work; or

(*c*) a collective society that is authorized by the owner of copyright in the work to grant licences on their behalf.

(6) A library, an archive or a museum, or a person acting under the authority of one, shall make the information referred to in subsection (1) available to the person making the request, within 28 days after the receipt of the request or any longer period that may be agreed to by both of them.

(7) A request referred to in subsection (5) must be made in writing, indicate the name of the author of the work and the title of the work, and be signed by the person making the request and include a statement by that person indicating that the request is made under paragraph (5)(*a*), (*b*) or (*c*).

5. [Repealed, SOR/2008-169, s. 5]

PATRONS OF ARCHIVES

6. (1) If a person registers as a patron of an archive, the archive shall inform the patron in writing at the time of registration that

(*a*) any copy of a work under section 30.21 of the Act is to be used solely for the purpose of research or private study; and

(*b*) any use of that copy for any other purpose may require the authorization of the copyright owner of the work.

(2) If a person requests a copy of a work from an archive under section 30.21 of the Act and the person has not registered as a patron of the archive, the archive shall inform the person in writing at the time of the request

(*a*) that any copy is to be used solely for the purpose of research or private study; and

(*b*) that any use of a copy for a purpose other than research or private study may require the authorization of the copyright owner of the work in question.

SOR/2008-169, s. 6.

STAMPING OF COPIED WORKS

7. A library, archive or museum, or a person acting under the authority of one, that makes a copy of a work under section 30.2 or 30.21 of the Act shall inform the person requesting the copy, by means of text printed on the copy or a stamp applied to the copy, if the copy is in printed format, or by other appropriate means, if the copy is made in another format,

(*a*) that the copy is to be used solely for the purpose of research or private study; and

(*b*) that any use of the copy for a purpose other than research or private study may require the authorization of the copyright owner of the work in question.

NOTICE

8. An educational institution, a library, an archive or a museum in respect of which subsection 30.3(2), (3) or (4) of the Act applies shall ensure that a notice that contains at least the following information is affixed to, or within the immediate vicinity of, every photocopier in a place and manner that is readily visible and legible to persons using the photocopier:

"WARNING!

Works protected by copyright may be copied on this photocopier only if authorized by

(*a*) the *Copyright Act* for the purpose of fair dealing or under specific exceptions set out in that Act;

(*b*) the copyright owner; or

(*c*) a licence agreement between this institution and a collective society or a tariff, if any.

For details of authorized copying, please consult the licence agreement or the applicable tariff, if any, and other relevant information available from a staff member.

The Copyright Act provides for civil and criminal remedies for infringement of copyright."

COMING INTO FORCE

9. These Regulations come into force on September 1, 1999.

APPENDIX VII

REPRODUCTION OF FEDERAL LAW ORDER

http://laws-lois.justice.gc.ca/eng/regulations/SI-97-5/page-1
.html

CANADA

CONSOLIDATION

Reproduction of Federal Law Order

SI/97-5

Current to July 10, 2013

Published by the Minister of Justice at the following address:
http://laws-lois.justice.gc.ca

OFFICIAL STATUS
OF CONSOLIDATIONS

Subsections 31(1) and (3) of the *Legislation Revision and Consolidation Act*, in force on June 1, 2009, provide as follows:

Published consolidation is evidence

31. (1) Every copy of a consolidated statute or consolidated regulation published by the Minister under this Act in either print or electronic form is evidence of that statute or regulation and of its contents and every copy purporting to be published by the Minister is deemed to be so published, unless the contrary is shown.

...

Inconsistencies in regulations

(3) In the event of an inconsistency between a consolidated regulation published by the Minister under this Act and the original regulation or a subsequent amendment as registered by the Clerk of the Privy Council under the *Statutory Instruments Act*, the original regulation or amendment prevails to the extent of the inconsistency.

NOTE

This consolidation is current to July 10, 2013. Any amendments that were not in force as of July 10, 2013 are set out at the end of this document under the heading "Amendments Not in Force".

Registration
SI/97-5   January 8, 1997
OTHER THAN STATUTORY AUTHORITY

Reproduction of Federal Law Order

Registration
SI/97-5   January 8, 1997
OTHER THAN STATUTORY AUTHORITY

Reproduction of Federal Law Order

P.C. 1996-1995   December 19, 1996

Whereas it is of fundamental importance to a democratic society that its law be widely known and that its citizens have unimpeded access to that law;

And whereas the Government of Canada wishes to facilitate access to its law by licensing the reproduction of federal law without charge or permission;

Therefore His Excellency the Governor General in Council, on the recommendation of the Minister of Canadian Heritage, the Minister of Industry, the Minister of Public Works and Government Services, the Minister of Justice and the Treasury Board, hereby makes the annexed *Reproduction of Federal Law Order*.

P.C. 1996-1995   December 19, 1996

Anyone may, without charge or request for permission, reproduce enactments and consolidations of enactments of the Government of Canada, and decisions and reasons for decisions of federally-constituted courts and administrative tribunals, provided due diligence is exercised in ensuring the accuracy of the materials reproduced and the reproduction is not represented as an official version.

SI/98-113(F).

APPENDIX VIII

APPLICATION FOR COPYRIGHT CLEARANCE OF GOVERNMENT OF CANADA WORKS

http://publications.gc.ca/site/eng/ccl/copyrightClearance/application.pdf

Government of Canada   Gouvernement du Canada

Canadä

Crown Copyright File No.: _____

Application for Copyright Clearance of Government of Canada Works

Privacy Statement
Provision of the information requested on this form is voluntary. The personal information collected is to be used to respond to your request for copyright clearance on Government of Canada works. We may share this information with other government departments if your inquiry relates to these departments. An incomplete form may result in the rejection of your request or a time delay in processing your request. The personal information will be maintained in the Personal Information Bank of Public Works and Government Services Canada, number PWGSC PPU 150 and it will be protected, used and disclosed in accordance with the Privacy Act. Under this Act, you have the right to access your personal information and request changes to incorrect information. The information will be retained by the Department indefinitely until the retention and disposal schedule is determined and then disposed accordingly.

For assistance in completing this form, please contact us at the coordinates shown on the last page of this form. Please note that this form applies to **Government of Canada works only**, and that **all fields marked by an asterisk (*) must be completed**.

---

1. APPLICANT INFORMATION

(*) **Complete Name:** Title (Mr., Mrs., Ms.), First Name and Last Name

Organization

(*) **Type of Organization**

(*) **Postal Address**

(*) **City/Town**   (*) **Province/State**   (*) **Postal/Zip Code**   (*) **Country**

(*) **Telephone Number**   **Facsimile Number**   **E-Mail Address**

Web Site Address

(*) **If permission is granted, person/organization in whose name permission is to be issued**

☐ Individual named above   ☐ Organization named above   ☐ Other (Specify below)

Government Gouvernement
of Canada du Canada

Canada

Crown Copyright File No.: _____

---

2. INFORMATION ON THE APPLICANT'S WORK

(*) Purpose

☐ Reproduction   ☐ Adaptation   ☐ Revision

☐ Translation (Specify languages of your work below)

[ ]

N.B. If the Government of Canada material has been adapted or revised, copies of your adapted/revised work <u>and</u> the Government of Canada material must be included with your request.

(*) Title of your work

[ ]

(*) Format(s) in which your work will be produced

☐ Audio CD   ☐ Audiocassette   ☐ Braille   ☐ CD-ROM

☐ Diskette   ☐ DVD   ☐ Electronic / Internet ☐ Large Print

☐ Map   ☐ Microfiche   ☐ Paper   ☐ Videocassette

(*) End Use

☐ Commercial   ☐ Non-commercial ☐ Cost-recovery ☐ Promotional

(*) Sale or Cost-recovery Price

[ ]

(*) Number of Copies to be printed/produced

[ ]

<u>OR</u>

(*) URL(s) for Web page(s) where the work will be published

[ ]

(continued)

(continued)

▮◆▮ Government   Gouvernement
      of Canada   du Canada

Canadä

Crown Copyright File No.: _____

---

3. INFORMATION ON THE GOVERNMENT OF CANADA WORK

(*)Title of Crown Work

Year / Date of Publication

YYYY

(*) Format of Source Material

☐ Audio CD   ☐ Audiocassette   ☐ Braille   ☐ CD-ROM

☐ Diskette   ☐ DVD   ☐ Electronic / Internet   ☐ Large Print

☐ Map   ☐ Microfiche   ☐ Paper   ☐ Videocassette

(*) **Reference Numbers** (ISBN, ISSN, Catalogue / Publication Number)

<u>OR</u>

(*) **Exact URL where source material is published**

(*) Precise description of material to be used

☐ Database   ☐ Figure   ☐ Footage   ☐ Illustration

☐ Logo   ☐ Map   ☐ Photo   ☐ Table

☐ Text   ☐ Whole Work   ☐ Other (Specify additional information below)

Volume / Issue   **Page No(s)**

Table / Figure No.   **Image / Photo No. / Description**

Additional Information (If you require more space, please attach a separate sheet)

Government Gouvernement
of Canada du Canada

Canada

Crown Copyright File No.: _____

4. ADDITIONAL INFORMATION

Applicant Reference Number (If you wish to assign one)

I would appreciate a response by

yyyy/mm/dd

Have you previously received approval to use the same material(s)?

☐ Yes ☐ No

If yes, previous Crown Copyright File No.

Please address all correspondence to:

Crown Copyright Officer
Crown Copyright and Licensing Section
Publishing and Depository Services
Public Works and Government Services Canada
350 Albert Street, 5th Floor
Ottawa, ON Canada, K1A 0S5
Telephone: (613) 996-6886 | **Facsimile:** (613) 998-1450 | **Email:** droitdauteur.copyright@tpsgc-pwgsc.gc.ca

NOTES

CHAPTER 1 UNDERSTANDING INTELLECTUAL PROPERTY

1. *A Guide to Patents*, Canadian Intellectual Property Office, www.cipo.ic.gc.ca/eic/ site/cipointernet-internetopic.nsf/eng/wr01090.html, accessed May 15, 2013.
2. See Canadian Intellectual Property Office Practice Notice dated March 28, 2012, www.cipo.ic.gc.ca/eic/site/cipointernet-internetopic.nsf/eng/wr03439.html, accessed May 15, 2013.
3. Briefly, common law evolves through decisions in court cases (sometimes called case law); statutes are written laws approved and enacted by Parliament.

CHAPTER 2 COPYRIGHT LAW IN CANADA

1. R.S.C, 1985, c. C-42, as amended.
2. The Copyright Modernization Act is at http://www.parl.gc.ca/HousePublications /Publication.aspx?Language=E&Mode=1&DocID=5697419. The Order Fixing Various Dates as the Dates on which Certain Provisions of the Act Come into Force is in Appendix II to this book. Also, check www.copyrightlaws.com for any updates on the remaining provisions coming into effect.
3. See www.cb-cda.gc.ca/about-apropos/mandate-mandat-e.html, accessed May 15, 2013.

CHAPTER 3 IS YOUR CREATION ELIGIBLE FOR COPYRIGHT PROTECTION?

1. The Supreme Court of Canada provides a good summary of originality in CCH Canadian Ltd. v. Law Society of Upper Canada, [204] 1 S.C.R. 339, paragraphs 14–25.

2. Canadian Admiral Corporation Ltd. v. Rediffusion Inc. (1954), Ex. C.R. 382, 20 C.P.R. 75.

3. Apple Computer, Inc., v. MacKintosh Computers Ltd., [1988] 1 F.C. 673 (C.A.), aff'd (1990), 30 C.P.R. 257 (S.C.C.).

4. Prior to January 1, 1996, the term *treaty country* would have been restricted to a Berne Convention country. If a work is subject to copyright as of January 1, 1996, in any treaty country and is not in the public domain, it will be eligible for protection in Canada. In other words, the work need not be created or published after January 1, 1996.

5. At the time of writing this book, Canada is not yet a member of the WCT but will likely be a member shortly. If this is an issue to you, check to see if Canada has yet joined the WCT at www.wipo.int.

6. At the time of writing this book, Canada is not yet a member of the WPPT but will likely be a member shortly. If this is an issue to you, check to see if Canada has yet joined the WPPT at www.wipo.int.

CHAPTER 4 ARE FORMALITIES REQUIRED TO OBTAIN COPYRIGHT PROTECTION?

1. This is set out in the Preamble to the Library and Archives of Canada Act at http://laws.justice.gc.ca/eng/acts/L-7.7/page-1.html#h-1, accessed May 20, 2013.

2. Chapter 7, "Who Owns Copyright?," discusses authorship and ownership of works and other subject-matter.

3. The concepts of licence and assignment, and licensee and assignee, are discussed in Chapter 11.

4. Poor man's copyright is downplayed by the U.S. Copyright Office, which points out in its FAQs www.copyright.gov/help/faq/faq-general.html, accessed May 20, 2013, that "There is no provision in the copyright law regarding any such type of protection, and it is not a substitute for registration." In one New York state case, Smith v. Berlin, 141 N.Y.S. 2d 110 (1955), the court dismissed evidence of a work mailed to oneself because of the ease of possible tampering with the envelope and replacing its contents. The court held that the evidence did not prove anything. Poor man's copyright may have a different perspective in Canada due to the nature of its registration system and the lack of a government depository for works protected by copyright. In fact, poor man's copyright may be looked upon as providing further proof where registration for a work has been made with the Canadian Copyright Office.

CHAPTER 5 CANADA AND INTERNATIONAL COPYRIGHT LAW

1. However, Berne Convention Article 7(8) states: "In any case, the term shall be governed by the legislation of the country where protection is claimed; however, unless the legislation of that country otherwise provides, the term shall not exceed the term fixed in the country of origin of the work." See previous discussion under National Treatment.
2. See Study on Copyright Limitations and Exceptions for Librarians and Archives, prepared by Kenneth Crews on behalf of WIPO at www.wipo.int/meetings/en/doc_details.jsp?doc_id=109192, accessed May 20, 2013.
3. Check www.wipo.int to see if and when Canada joins these treaties, accessed May 20, 2013.
4. As per Chapter 5, note 3, at the time of writing Canada is not a member of the WCT, and treaty country means a Berne or UCC country or WTO member. However, the Copyright Act has been amended to include WCT country as part of the definition of a treaty country but this particular amendment is not in force at the time of writing.
5. Note that the WPPT is not included here because the WPPT protects neighbouring rights. See Chapter 9, "Rights Protected by Copyright."

CHAPTER 6 WHAT IS PROTECTED BY COPYRIGHT?

1. University of London Press Ltd. v. University Tutorial Press Ltd., [1916] 2 Ch. 601.
2. Robertson v. Thomson Corp., [2006] 2 S.C.R. 363, 2006 SCC 43.
3. University of London Press Ltd. v. University Tutorial Press Ltd.
4. Flamand v. Société Radio-Canada (1967), 53 C.P.R. 217 (Que S.C.).
5. It may be possible for a "nonfixed" lecture to be protected as a performer's performance.
6. Keatley Surveying Ltd. v. Teranet Inc., 2012 ONSC 7120.
7. Kantel v. Frank E. Grant, Nisbet and Auld Ltd., [1933] Ex. C.R. 84.
8. Ludlow Music Inc. v. Canint Music Corp. Ltd. (1967), 35 Fox. Pat. C. 114 (Ex. Ct.).
9. A logo on a chocolate bar wrapper can receive concurrent trade-mark and copyright protection: Euro-Excellence Inc. v. Kraft Canada Inc., [2007] 3 S.C.R. 20, 2007 SCC 37.
10. For an explanation of "absolute" right of integrity, see Chapter 9, "Rights Protected by Copyright," specifically the section "Special Treatment of Artistic Works."

11. King Features Syndicate, Inc. v. O. & M. Kleeman Ltd., [1941] A.C. 417 (H.L.).

12. Wood v. Boosey (1868), L.R. 3 Q.B. 223.

13. Neudorf v. Nettwerk Productions Ltd., [1999] B.C.J. No. 2831 (B.C.S.C.).

14. CCH Canadian Ltd. v. Law Society of Upper Canada, [2004] 1 S.C.R. 339, 2004 SCC 13.

15. See "Are Tweets Copyright-Protected?" in *WIPO Magazine* at www.wipo.int/wipo_magazine/en/2009/04/article_0005.html, accessed May 21, 2013.

CHAPTER 7 WHO OWNS COPYRIGHT?

1. Performers arguably enjoy the "attributes" of author of their performances to the extent that they have moral rights. They are also first owners of their performances, in the same manner that most authors are first owners of their works.

2. In most European countries, the director of a film is normally its author, but elsewhere in the world, the debate continues.

3. Robertson v. Thomson Corp., 2006 SCC 43.

CHAPTER 8 THE DURATION OF COPYRIGHT

1. This is in fact an extension of copyright for some corporate authored photographs. See blog post, "Canada's New Photography Copyright Regime: Clearance Challenges," by Bob Tarantino at www.entertainmentmedialawsignal.com/canadas-new-photography-copyright-regime-clearance-challenges/, accessed May 31, 2013.

CHAPTER 9 RIGHTS PROTECTED BY COPYRIGHT

1. National Breweries, Ltd. v. A. Paradis, [1925] S.C.R. 666.

2. See discussion in Warman v. Fournier, 2012 FC 803.

3. Hawkes & Son (London), Ltd. v. Paramount Film Service, Ltd., [1934] Ch. 593 (C.A.).

4. Entertainment Software Association v. Society of Composers, Authors and Music Publishers of Canada, 2012 SCC 34, [2012] 2 S.C.R. 231.

5. Also, a legitimate copy of a work may be kept out of Canada if it is made in a country to which the Act does not apply. For example, if a computer program CD is manufactured in Taiwan with the consent of the copyright owner, the Canadian exclusive licensee of that copyright owner could keep the work out of Canada. If

someone wanted their exclusive licensee to be able to keep a parallel import out of Canada, it would be better to manufacture it in a nontreaty rather than in a treaty county.

6. Prior to 1988 and the exhibition right being added to the Copyright Act, most major public art galleries and museums voluntarily followed an exhibition fee schedule for loaned and donated works, which was established by Canadian Artists' Representation/Le front des artistes canadiens (CARFAC, www.carfac.ca).

7. For further reading on the exhibition right, see Wanda Noel, *The Right of Public Presentation: A Guide to the Exhibition Right* (Ottawa: Canadian Conference of the Arts, 1990).

8. Millar v. Taylor (1769), 4 Burr. 2303, 98 E.R. 201 (C.A.).

9. Morang v. Lusueur (1911), 45 S.C.R. 95.

10. However, since the right of paternity applies only in relation to uses covered by the economic rights, if author "A" used a pseudonym on an article, nothing prevents Author "B" from stating the real name of A in a subsequent article where there is no reproduction or other copyright use of A's work.

11. Snow v. The Eaton Centre Ltd. (1982), 70 C.P.R. (2d) 105 (Ont. H.C.). See photograph at http://en.wikipedia.org/wiki/File:TorontoEatonCentre.jpg, accessed June 18, 2013, and imagine red ribbons wrapped around the necks of the geese!

CHAPTER 10 LIMITATIONS ON RIGHTS

1. The concept of fair dealing is often compared, or used interchangeably, with the American concept of "fair use." Caution should be taken when talking about "fair dealing" and "fair use" as they are not exactly the same; for further discussion, see Chapter 15, "An Overview of American Copyright Law."

2. Prior to the addition of parody to fair dealing, in 2012, certain parodies were allowed. In one court case, a parody of various graphical representations of the St. Hubert stylized head of a rooster was held to violate copyright. In another case, where an advertising agency prepared a parody of the words of the musical *Downtown* and used it for radio advertising purposes in Ottawa, it was held to violate copyright.

3. At the time of writing this book, Access Copyright commenced a lawsuit against York University for its policy on interpreting fair dealing. See Federal Court File No. T-578–13, The Canadian Copyright Licensing Agency ("Access Copyright") and York University, filed April 8, 2013.

4. In a Backgrounder to the Copyright Modernization Act, the Government of Canada states: "The bill includes a change to the provisions for fair dealing that will

enable the use of copyrighted materials for the purpose of education in a structured context, in a manner that takes into consideration the legitimate interests of the copyright owner." See www.ic.gc.ca/eic/site/crp-prda.nsf/eng/h_rp01237.html, accessed June 18, 2013.

5. To get a deeper understanding of fair dealing in Canada, read CCH Canadian Ltd. v. Law Society of Upper Canada [2004] 1 S.C.R. 339, http://scc.lexum .org/decisia-scc-csc/scc-csc/scc-csc/en/item/2125/index.do, accessed June 18, 2013.

6. Hubbard v.Vosper, [1972] 2 Q.B. 95 (Eng. C.A.).

7. This is unlike fair use in the U.S. Copyright Act, which explicitly includes "teaching (including multiple copies for classroom use)."

8. Zamacois v. Douville and Marchand, [1943] 2 D.L.R. 257 (Ex. Ct).

9. Allen v. Toronto Star Newspaper Ltd. (1995), 63 C.P.R. (3d) 517 (Ont. Ct. (Gen. Div.)).

10. In this case, the defendant, the Law Society of Upper Canada, maintained one of the largest collections of legal materials in Canada. It was open to lawyers, the judiciary, law students, and other authorized researchers. The library had a "custom photocopy service" in which legal materials are reproduced by the library staff and delivered in person, by mail, or by fax to requesters. In 1993, CCH and other publishers ("the respondents") sought a declaration that the Law Society had infringed copyright when the law library reproduced a legal case or article. The Supreme Court held that the Law Society did not infringe copyright when a single copy of a reported decision, case summary, statute, regulation, or limited selection of text from a treatise was made by the library in accordance with its access policy. It should be noted that the library had an Access Policy, which the Supreme Court took into account in interpreting fair dealing. The Court held that this Policy "places appropriate limits on the type of copying that the Law Society will do. It states that not all requests will be honoured. If a request does not appear to be for the purpose of research, criticism, review or private study, the copy will not be made."

11. Alberta (Education) v. Canadian Copyright Licensing Agency (Access Copyright) 2012 SCC 37, [2012] 2 S.C.R. 345, http://scc.lexum.org/decisia-scc-csc/scc-csc/ scc-csc/en/item/9997/index.do, accessed June 18, 2013.

12. Society of Composers, Authors and Music Publishers of Canada v. Bell Canada, 2012 SCC 36, [2012] 2 S.C.R. 326, http://scc.lexum.org/decisia-scc-csc/scc-csc/ scc-csc/en/item/9996/index.do, accessed June 18, 2013.

13. See Government of Canada publication: What the *Copyright Modernization Act* Means for Consumers, www.ic.gc.ca/eic/site/crp-prda.nsf/eng/rp01186.html, accessed June 18, 2013.

14. This is an amendment from the Copyright Modernization Act.
15. Composers, Authors & Publishers Assn. of Canada Ltd. v. Kiwanis Club of West Toronto, [1953] 2 S.C.R. 111.

CHAPTER 11 HOW CAN RIGHTS BE EXPLOITED?

1. Fly by Nite Music Co. v. Record Warehouse Ltd. (1975), 20 C.P.R. (2d) 263 (Fed.T.D.).
2. Wards, Lock & Co. v. Long, [1906] 2 Ch. 550.
3. See Lesley Ellen Harris, *Licensing Digital Content: A Practical Guide for Librarians* (Chicago: ALA Editions, 2009).
4. See David Vaver, *Copyright Law* (Toronto: Irwin Law, 2000), 165, 231.

CHAPTER 12 HOW IS COPYRIGHT INFRINGED?

1. The exception to this rule is the "commercial" rental right in sound recordings and computer programs, as discussed in Chapter 9, "Rights Protected by Copyright."
2. King Features Syndicate Inc. v. Benjamin H. Lechter, [1950] Ex. C.R. 297.
3. Kantel v. Frank E. Grant, Nisbet & Auds Ltd., [1933] C.R. 84.
4. British Columbia Jockey Club v. Standen (1985), 8 C.P.R. (3d) 283 (B.C.C.A.).
5. Bright Tunes Music Corp. v. Harrisongs Music Ltd., 420 F. Supp. 177 (1976) (U.S. District Court, S.D.N.Y.). In the Canadian case of Gondos v. Hardy (1982), 64 C.P.R. (2d) 145 (Ont. H.C.), the plaintiff claimed that "The Homecoming" by Hagood Hardy and "Moment of Love" by Rudy and Jerry Toth, infringed his composition "Variations on a Theme in A Minor."
6. Society of Composers, Authors and Music Publishers of Canada v. Canadian Assn. of Internet Providers, 2004 SCC 45, [2004] 2 SCR 427, at http://scc .lexum.org/decisia-scc-csc/scc-csc/scc-csc/en/item/2159/index.do, accessed 31 May 2013.
7. The United States has a "notice and takedown" procedure which is highly publicized. It is explained at www.plagiarismtoday.com/2008/05/15/takedown-faq/, accessed May 31, 2013.
8. See "Copyright Modernization Act: Order Fixing Various Dates as the Dates on Which Certain Provisions of the Act Come into Force" in Appendix II for all sections of the Copyright Act that are not yet in effect at the time of writing this book.
9. The technological protection measures are set out in section 41 of the Copyright Act over nine pages; for a complete understanding of TPM in Canada, read this section.

CHAPTER 13 WHAT ARE THE REMEDIES FOR THE INFRINGEMENT OF COPYRIGHT?

1. See Code 9959 of Schedule VII to the Customs Tariff. Also, "copyrighted in Canada" means a work with a Canadian Copyright Office certificate, but the remedy is not limited to works with a Canadian author or publisher. The words "Canadian copyrighted works" are interpreted to mean any printed material protected by copyright in Canada, which would include works protected from all Berne countries and not just those works of Canadian citizens.
2. Randall Homes Ltd. v. Hardwood Homes Ltd. (1987), 17 C.P.R. (3d) 372 (Man. Q.B.).
3. Kaffka v. Mountain Side Developments Ltd. (1982), 62 C.P.R. (2d) 157 (B.C.S.C.).
4. Slumber-Magic Co. Ltd. v. Sleep-King Adjustable Bed Co. (1984), 3 C/P.R. (3d) 81 (B.C.S.C.).
5. M.C.A. v. Gillberry & Hawke Advertising Agency Ltd. (1976), 28 C.P.R. (2d) 52 (Fed. T.D.).
6. Zamacois v. Douville, [1943] 2 D.L.R. 257.
7. Bishop v. Stevens (1990), 72 D.L.R. (4td) 97 (S.C.C.).
8. This relates to infringement of copyright rather than infringement of moral rights.
9. This would include camcording a movie for commercial purposes, that is, for the purpose of making a copy of it for sale or rent.
10. Bill C-59, an Act to Amend the Criminal Code (unauthorized recording of a movie) was passed in the House of Commons on June 13, 2007. Of interest, "First Canadian convicted of movie piracy for taping Sweeney Todd" by Canwest News Service, www.canada.com/edmontonjournal/news/story.html?id=314377ba-c1da-413e-baf2-33c0c99717b0, accessed 18 June 2013. In addition to $1,495 CDN in fines and probation for year, the convicted man "is also prohibited from entering any movie, or from purchasing, owning or taking any video recording equipment—including one on a cellphone—outside his home during this probation period."

CHAPTER 14 LEGALLY USING CONTENT

1. There is a distinction between commercial and noncommercial purposes of infringement in relation to the amount of damages a copyright owner can collect. This is discussed in Chapter 13.
2. This example assumes that tweets are in fact protected by copyright.
3. For example, many professional freelancers who do permissions and research across a variety of genres including text, music, as well as visual, and for books, new media, films and more, belong to the Visual Researchers Society of Canada, www.visualre search.ca/, accessed June 18, 2013.

4. It was announced in 2012 that SOCAN, CMRRA, and SODRAC are exploring opportunities to create a more integrated approach to the management of performing and reproduction rights of music creators and publishers in Canada. See www.socan.ca/news/cmrra-socan-sodrac-exploring-integrated-approach-music-rights-management, accessed June 18, 2013.

5. The term *orphan works* is often used to describe copyright-protected works whose owners cannot be located. The U.S. Government defines an orphan work as "an original work of authorship for which a good faith, prospective user cannot readily identify and/or locate the copyright owner(s) in a situation where permission from the copyright owner(s) is necessary as a matter of law." See www.copyright.gov/orphan/, accessed June 18, 2013.

CHAPTER 15 AN OVERVIEW OF AMERICAN COPYRIGHT LAW

1. Chapter 5 explains international copyright law. In brief, national treatment in the international copyright treaties results in applying the law where a work is used.

2. However, you may want to acknowledge the source for different reasons such as ethics and plagiarism.

3. Unlike Canada, renewal of copyright used to be permitted in the United States.

4. Even though a Canadian author may file an infringement suit in the United States without a registration certificate issued by the U.S. Copyright Office, a U.S. court may not award statutory damages and attorneys' fees, and actual damages (such as lost revenue, licences, out-of-pocket expenses) might be more difficult to prove.

About the Author

Lesley Ellen Harris is an author, educator, and lawyer. She earned her J.D. from Osgoode Hall Law School in 1985 and was called to the Ontario Bar in 1987. From 1987 through 1991, she worked as Senior Copyright Officer, Heritage Canada, revising Canada's copyright laws. Since 1991, Ms. Harris has written screenplays (and even had one optioned!), books, articles, blog posts, and tweets; taught thousands of nonlawyer students about copyright; and consulted on Canadian, American, and international copyright issues with a variety of organizations.

Ms. Harris develops and teaches in-person and online courses at the university level, as professional development in conjunction with several professional associations, and through Copyrightlaws.com. At the professional development level, Ms. Harris's goal is to provide practical courses that help nonlawyers manage their copyright and licensing issues.

Ms. Harris works with for-profit and nonprofit organizations, publishers, libraries, archives, museums, educational institutions, corporations, associations, and government departments to create educational materials on copyright, copyright compliance policies, permissions guidelines and procedures, ensuring copyright compliance in digital projects, measures to protect content and monitor unauthorized uses of content, and much more. Her approach is pragmatic, business-oriented, and strategic.

Ms. Harris has spoken on copyright law at conferences in the United States, Canada, Mexico, and Europe.

Ms. Harris's articles have been published internationally in *Billboard*, *Copyright* (Review of the World Intellectual Property Organization), *Journal of the Copyright Society of the U.S.A.*, *Written By* (Writers Guild of America, West), and *Osgoode Hall Law Journal*. She is the author of *Digital Property: Currency of the 21st Century*; *Licensing Digital Content: A Practical Guide for Librarians*, 2nd edition; and *A Canadian Museum's Guide to Developing a Digital Licensing Agreement Strategy*, 2nd edition. Ms. Harris is editor of *The Copyright & New Media Law Newsletter*.

Visit Ms. Harris's blog at www.copyrightlaws.com.

INDEX